Epistemology

Epistemology

A Guide

John Turri

WILEY Blackwell

This edition first published 2014
© 2014 John Wiley & Sons, Ltd

Registered Office
John Wiley & Sons, Ltd, The Atrium, Southern Gate, Chichester, West Sussex, PO19 8SQ, UK

Editorial Offices
350 Main Street, Malden, MA 02148-5020, USA
9600 Garsington Road, Oxford, OX4 2DQ, UK
The Atrium, Southern Gate, Chichester, West Sussex, PO19 8SQ, UK

For details of our global editorial offices, for customer services, and for information about how to apply for permission to reuse the copyright material in this book please see our website at www.wiley.com/wiley-blackwell.

The right of John Turri to be identified as the author of this work has been asserted in accordance with the UK Copyright, Designs and Patents Act 1988.

Library of Congress Cataloging-in-Publication Data

Turri, John.
  Epistemology : a guide / John Turri.
    pages   cm
  Includes bibliographical references and index.
  ISBN 978-1-4443-3369-5 (cloth) – ISBN 978-1-4443-3370-1 (pbk.)   1. Knowledge,
Theory of.   I. Title.
  BD143.T87 2014
  121–dc23
                                                        2013016118
A catalogue record for this book is available from the British Library.

Cover image: Cornelis Norbertus Gysbrechts (fl. 1659-72), *Vanitas still life seen through a trompe l'oeil window.* © Private Collection / The Bridgeman Art Library.
Cover design by Nicki Averill Design.

Set in 10.5/13.5pt Palatino by SPi Publisher Services, Pondicherry, India
Printed in Malaysia by Ho Printing (M) Sdn Bhd

1   2014

For Angelo

Contents

Contents

Contents

Preface

Epistemology is the philosophical discipline that studies the evaluative dimensions of cognition, their metaphysical bases, and the language we use to ascribe cognitive states. This book introduces you to a wide range of topics in epistemology, including skepticism, knowledge, justification, understanding, evidence, epistemic value, virtue epistemology, contextualism, invariantism, naturalism, testimony, perception, memory, and the a priori. It is designed and written especially to accompany the second edition of *Epistemology: An Anthology* (Blackwell Publishing, 2008), edited by Ernest Sosa, Jaegwon Kim, Jeremy Fantl, and Matthew McGrath. You can profit from this book even if you don't read it alongside the anthology, but you'll profit from it more if you do.

This book's design is modular. It consists of 60 sections corresponding to the anthology's selections. Each is intended to be brief, accessible even to the beginner, and, to the extent possible, independently intelligible. You can glean the main aim and argument of any selection in the anthology by studying the relevant section in this book. I have focused especially on providing examples and clarifying key concepts and methodological points that are essential to the main arguments, but which the beginner couldn't reasonably be expected to be familiar with.

This book's sections can't be entirely independent, however, because the topics discussed across the selections aren't entirely independent. Indeed, many selections were chosen precisely because they complement one another. So while understanding this or that selection may be your only goal – and for some purposes this would be eminently reasonable – you'd then be missing out on some interesting and important connections running through multiple selections, both within and across the anthology's divisions. Of course, this book can't cover all the ideas, arguments, and connections in the anthology, because that would defeat the goal of brevity. It would also make it much more difficult to help you distinguish the central from the peripheral, which is crucial to achieving proficiency in any field.

Since brevity and accessibility demand selectivity, I should be clear about the general principle I've employed in trying to meet that demand. I have focused on the main theses and arguments found in the selections and sought to emphasize areas where the authors are – or, with a little imagination, easily could be – in conversation with one another. The hope is that this promotes not only brevity and accessibility but also integrity within and continuity across the various sections.

Acknowledgments

I would like to thank Ernest Sosa, Jeremy Fantl, and Matt McGrath for supporting this project. I thank Jeff Dean and Jen Bray for their support and for helping to guide the project to completion. Thanks also to Wesley Buckwalter, Trystan Goetze, and many students in epistemology courses at Huron University College and the University of Waterloo for evaluating parts of the manuscript. Thanks to Peter Blouw for work on the index. I owe my family an enormous debt of gratitude for supporting (and tolerating!) me while I worked (too) many long hours on this project, with all the sacrifice that entails: thank you Vivian, Sarah, Geno, Mom, Dad, Rich, Doug, Kelly, Mallory, and Julia. Finally, my greatest debt is to my older son, Angelo, who between the ages of 9 and 12 read every section of this book multiple times and offered valuable comments and suggestions at every stage. He is not only my son but also my greatest student and a true friend. I dedicate this book to him.

§ 1

The best case for skepticism about the external world? (Stroud, "The Problem of the External World")

We're all intimately familiar with what goes on in our own minds. We make plans, form opinions, experience pleasure and pain, and so on. It's also natural to suppose that we know a lot about what goes on *outside* our own minds too, about the world around us, based on the information we get through our senses of sight, hearing, smell, taste, and touch. Natural as that idea may be, it's surprisingly easy to get yourself into a skeptical frame of mind about the possibility of such knowledge. Can we really know anything about the world outside our own minds?

Barry Stroud aims to understand the attraction of skepticism about the external world, why knowledge of the external world based on sense experience poses a philosophical problem. To accomplish this, he focuses intensely on the argument presented at the

Stroud, Barry, "The Problem of the External World," Chapter 1 in *The Significance of Philosophical Skepticism* (Oxford: Clarendon Press, 1984). © 1984 by Barry Stroud.

Epistemology: A Guide, First Edition. John Turri.
© 2014 John Wiley & Sons, Ltd. Published 2014 by John Wiley & Sons, Ltd.

beginning of Rene Descartes's *Meditations on First Philosophy* (published originally in 1641), the most influential work of one of the most influential philosophers of all time.

Let's note a couple important points before we proceed. First, people who reflect on knowledge nearly unanimously agree that knowledge requires truth, or as it's sometimes put, that knowledge is factive.[1] This means that we can know something only if it is true or a fact. We cannot know a falsehood. (We can of course *believe* a falsehood, but that's a different matter.) Now if you think that knowledge is not factive, I recommend a simple solution: everywhere we here speak of "knowledge," understand it to mean "knowledge *of the truth*," and every time we claim or ask whether someone "knows that so-and-so," understand it to mean "*knows it's true* that such-and-such." Second, something can be possible without being real or actual. Indeed lots of things are possible that aren't actual. For instance, it's possible for winged horses to exist, even though none actually do. Likewise for wizards, dragons, phlogiston, the luminiferous ether, etc. With those points in mind, let's proceed.

Imagine Descartes at work in his study on a cold night, sitting a few feet from a comforting fire. Unsure for the moment how his narrative should best proceed, he takes a break and turns his attention to the fire. He sees its colorful flames flitting and flickering; he hears it crackling and popping; he feels its heat emanating; he smells the fragrant wood burning. In light of all this, Descartes of course believes he's near a fire. But do these sense experiences enable him to know he's near a fire?

It's hard to imagine Descartes's senses putting him in a better position to gain knowledge of the external world. He is as well-positioned as any of us could ever hope to be. So if the answer to our question at the end of the previous paragraph is "No," then it seems very likely that we never know anything about the external world, at least by way of our senses.

---

[1] For some recent controversy over the "truth requirement" on knowledge, see Allan Hazlett, "Factive Presupposition and the Truth Condition on Knowledge," *Acta Analytica* 27.4 (2012): 461–478, and John Turri, "Mythology of the Factive," *Logos & Episteme* 2.1 (2011): 143–152.

The way things look, sound, smell, and feel make it appear to Descartes as though he's near a fire, and it's this appearance that he trusts when judging that he's near a fire. But of course things might appear *exactly* the same in a perfectly realistic dream. And a perfectly realistic dream is a genuine possibility. It's certainly possible for him to have all those sensations despite merely dreaming that he's near a fire. Indeed, any sensory experience might be a mere component of a perfectly realistic dream. Thus sense experience, being equally compatible with dreaming or waking, could never enable him to know that he is awake rather than merely dreaming.

As Descartes recognizes, if he's merely dreaming that he's near a fire, then he certainly doesn't know that he's near a fire. And he also recognizes it is at least possible that he's merely dreaming. So he knows that a certain genuine possibility, the *dream-possibility* (as Stroud calls it), is incompatible with his knowing that he's near a fire. So in order to know that he's near a fire, he must know that the dream-possibility is false.

Notice that, on this way of thinking, in order for the dream-possibility to potentially threaten Descartes's knowledge of the fire, he doesn't need to know, or even so much as believe, that it is actually true. No, the dream-possibility threatens simply because Descartes recognizes that it is possibly true, and that if it were actually true, he wouldn't know that he's near a fire.

Could Descartes ever come to know that the dream-possibility is false? Sense experience itself won't enable such knowledge because, as we've already said, any sense experience is perfectly compatible with the dream-possibility. But isn't there some test he could perform to determine whether he is merely dreaming? Unfortunately not, because in order for him to learn from the test, he'd need to know that he wasn't merely dreaming that he was performing the test!

If you're wondering why he couldn't then just perform a second test to determine whether he's merely dreaming that he performed the first test, consider: he could equally well be dreaming that he's performing the second test. The same is true for a third test he might perform to determine whether he's merely dreaming that he performed the second test. And so on. No matter how many tests he performs, the same problem recurs. And since it's not possible to perform an infinite series of tests, we find no relief in this direction.

Let's encapsulate the preceding line of thought in the following argument, broken up into two parts to enhance clarity. The main argument goes like this:

1. If Descartes doesn't know that he's near a fire, then we never know anything about the external world. (Premise)
2. Descartes doesn't know that he's near a fire. (Premise)
3. So we never know anything about the external world. (From 1 and 2)

The argument is logically valid: if its premises are true, then its conclusion must be true too. That leaves us to ask whether its premises are true. 1 is at least very plausible, and Stroud is willing to grant it. That leaves only 2 to seriously question. The following supplementary argument supports 2:

a. Descartes knows that the dream-possibility is incompatible with his knowing that he's near a fire. (Premise)
b. If Descartes knows that a possibility is incompatible with his knowing some specific claim, then in order for him to know the specific claim, he must know that the possibility in question is false. (Premise)
c. So in order for Descartes to know that he's near a fire, he must know that the dream-possibility is false. (From a and b)
d. But Descartes couldn't know that the dream-possibility is false. (Premise)
e. So Descartes doesn't know that he's near a fire. (From c and d)

Notice that (e) is exactly the same as 2.

Should we accept this argument? Stroud wonders whether we can seriously entertain the skeptical conclusion expressed by 3, because it's allegedly either absurd or even unintelligible. But merely rejecting it as absurd or unintelligible deprives us of the opportunity to learn something potentially important about knowledge (or at least about our concept of knowledge). Accordingly, he challenges those of us inclined to reject the conclusion to *locate the argument's flaw*. Whatever it is, it isn't obvious.

Stroud suggests that (c) is false. Yet (c) follows from (a) and (b), so rejecting (c) requires us to reject at least one of (a) and (b). (a) is obviously true, which leaves (b).

The problem is that (b) is arguably "embodied" in our ordinary procedures for "making and assessing knowledge-claims." Consider for instance a bird watcher who judges a certain bird to be a goldfinch. We ask her why she thinks it's a goldfinch. "Because it's yellow," she says. "But for all you've said," we respond, "it's possible that it's a canary – canaries are yellow too." We don't think she knows it's a goldfinch, because she knows very well that canaries aren't goldfinches, and yet she doesn't know it's not a canary. She must rule out this relevant possibility, *the canary-possibility*, in order to know it's a goldfinch.

The question then becomes whether the dream-possibility is in all relevant respects similar to the canary-possibility, so that when we insist that the bird watcher must rule out the canary-possibility, we thereby commit ourselves to insisting that Descartes must rule out the dream-possibility. Does Descartes have to rule out the dream-possibility in order to know there's a fire nearby, as the bird watcher must rule out the canary-possibility in order to know that she's looking at a goldfinch? If not, why not? Each subject knows the possibility in question is incompatible with his or her knowing the claim in question. So what *could* be the difference?

A plausible explanation of the difference, should there be any, would go a long way toward resolving "the problem of the external world." Therein lies the challenge, and potential reward, of confronting philosophical skepticism.

References

Allan Hazlett, "Factive Presupposition and the Truth Condition on Knowledge," *Acta Analytica* 27.4 (2012): 461–478.

John Turri, "Mythology of the Factive," *Logos & Episteme* 2.1 (2011): 143–152.

§ 2

Proving the external world exists (Or: Let's all give Moore a hand!) (Moore, "Proof of an External World")

Suppose we disagree about the number of books on the desk. You say there are at least two. I disagree. And it's no mere verbal disagreement – we're referring to the same desk, and mean the same thing by "book" and "at least two," etc. How might you prove your point?

Here's one way. You walk over, point to one book sitting on the desk, and then point to another, all while saying, "Here's one book on the desk, and here's another. So there are at least two books on the desk." I couldn't rightly criticize the proof. I'd have to concede the point. What else could I possibly be looking for in a proof? Your premises ("here's one book the desk, and here's another") are different from your conclusion ("there are at least two books on the

Moore, G. E., "Proof of an External World," extracted from pp. 147–70 in Thomas Baldwin (ed.), *G. E. Moore: Selected Writings* (London & New York: Routledge, 1993). © 1993 by Thomas Baldwin.

Epistemology: A Guide, First Edition. John Turri.

desk"), in which case you didn't simply *beg the question.* Your conclusion follows straightforwardly from your premises, and you know that it does. And you obviously know the premises – after all, you aren't blind, you're looking right at the books, and you've correctly verbally identified them. Without question, your proof perfectly settles the matter in your favor.

Immanuel Kant, perhaps the most influential of all modern philosophers, once said it was "a scandal to philosophy" that the existence of real, mind-independent external objects "must be accepted merely on *faith*" rather than a "satisfactory proof."[1] Kant thought he had rescued philosophy from scandal by giving such a proof, indeed, the *only* possible such proof. Setting aside the merits of Kant's own proof, G.E. Moore denied that Kant's was the only possible such proof. A much simpler and fully convincing proof is readily available.

Moore offers his proof by saying, "Here's one hand, and here's another. So external objects exist," as he gestures and holds his hands up before us. This proof, Moore says, is "perfectly rigorous." It meets the three criteria we noted earlier when discussing your proof about the number of books on the desk. Its premises are different from its conclusion; its conclusion follows, as Moore knows, straightforwardly from its premises; and finally, Moore obviously knows the premises.

Might a satisfactory proof require more than meeting those three criteria? Not if our ordinary practice is any indication. As with your earlier proof about the books, we "constantly take proofs of this sort as absolutely conclusive."

Note an interesting connection with Stroud's discussion from §1. We wondered whether Descartes was right to claim that he must know the dream-possibility is false in order to know that he's near a fire. And Stroud worried that Descartes was indeed right about that, because such a requirement might be "nothing more than an instance of a general procedure we recognize and insist on in making and assessing knowledge-claims in everyday" life, which procedure helps to define

---

[1]   Quoted by G.E. Moore at the beginning of his "Proof of an External World." The quote is alluded to but does not explicitly appear in the excerpt included in the anthology.

out concept of knowledge. Here Moore appeals to our everyday procedures for offering and evaluating *proofs*.

Moore anticipates that some will say his so-called proof fails. One type of critic insists that in order for Moore's proof to really succeed, he must also prove his premises – prove that *here is one hand* and that *here is another*. If this critic is right, then the three criteria we earlier identified aren't sufficient for a conclusive proof after all. At least sometimes, a conclusive proof requires more. Moore rejects this, and explicitly disavows any intention to prove his premises. He doubts it could be done, because proving them requires proving that he's not merely dreaming that he has hands. And even though he has "conclusive reasons" (or "conclusive evidence") that he's not merely dreaming, he cannot articulate that evidence to us, which he of course must do in order to offer a proof.

One is reminded of a scene in Robert Louis Stevenson's *The Strange Case of Dr. Jekyll and Mr. Hyde*. A shaken and ill Jekyll tells his friend Utterson that Mr. Hyde "will never more be heard of." When Utterson suggests – rightly, it turns out, as the story subsequently unfolds – that Jekyll's assertion might not be entirely warranted, Jekyll replies, "I have grounds for certainty that I cannot share with anyone."[2] What does Jekyll mean by "cannot" here? He might mean that he cannot prudently share it with anyone. Revealing his relation to Hyde would be disastrous to Jekyll personally, so prudence forbids it. And, indeed, this is likely the first interpretation to occur to the reader. But great writers imbue their work with many layers of meaning, and in light of Moore's discussion, one wonders whether there's more to Jekyll's last claim than first meets the eye. Perhaps Jekyll (also) meant that he is simply incapable of sharing at least some of his reasons. This is made all the more plausible later when Jekyll writes that his transformational experiences were marked by "indescribably new" sensations.[3] But this shouldn't be

---

[2] In the Section "Incident of the Letter."
[3] In the section "Henry Jekyll's Full Statement of the Case."

all that surprising; at times all of us have experiences that are "beyond words."

Another type of critic claims that Moore fails to meet one of the everyday criteria for successful proofs: Moore doesn't know that his premises are true. But why think that? Is it not, as Moore says, simply absurd to suggest that he didn't know he was gesturing toward his hands as he performed his proof? The critic thinks not. To know something, she claims, requires that you be able to prove it – no knowledge without proof, as it were. And as Moore himself admits, the critic continues, Moore cannot prove his premises, so he doesn't know them. But Moore rejects this as well, claiming, "I can know things, which I cannot prove."

Have you ever known something that you wanted to convince someone of, but found yourself saying, "If only I could prove it," or more despairingly, "But I just can't prove it!"? In the episode "Identity Crisis" of the television show *CSI*, Gil Grissom and Catherine Willows are confounded by a computer fingerprint analysis which fails to confirm that Judge Douglas Mason is in fact Grissom's nemesis Paul Millander, the long-sought serial killer. Grissom says to Catherine, "I don't care what the computer says – that guy is Paul Millander." Catherine replies, "Yeah, we know that. How do we prove it?" They of course go on to prove it. But that's not the important point. You can imagine them finding out that they simply cannot prove it. Indeed for a moment viewers are left to think as much when they learn that a repository storing relevant vital records burned down long ago. Yet this doesn't lead us to think, as we watch the episode, that Grissom and Catherine don't really know that Mason is Millander. Through a combination of memory and visual recognition, Grissom knew Mason was Millander the moment he set eyes on him in Mason's courtroom. Catherine learned it based on Grissom's testimony. But at that point in the story they weren't able to prove it. At least, that's how the screenwriters portrayed it, and viewers didn't detect any incoherence in the plot or dialog. This suggests that Moore is right when he says that knowledge does not require proof.

§ 3

Some ways of resisting skepticism (Moore, "Four Forms of Scepticism")

Recall the *dream-possibility* from §1: it is genuinely possible for all your sense experiences to be part of a perfectly realistic dream, rather than accurate portrayals of the world around you. The dream-possibility featured centrally in Stroud's understanding of Descartes's skeptical reasoning. Descartes also discussed another skeptical possibility: the *demon-possibility*. You think your sensations are caused by ordinary objects in the world around you. But the demon-possibility says it's genuinely possible for all your sensations to be part of an elaborate deception created by a supremely powerful evil demon.

The demon-possibility impressed Bertrand Russell, one of G.E. Moore's friends and perhaps the most famous Anglo-American philosopher of the twentieth century. This section focuses on Moore's response to Russell's discussion of the demon-possibility.

Moore, G. E., "Four Forms of Scepticism," pp. 220–2 in *Philosophical Papers* (New York: Collier Books, 1962). © 1962 by G. E. Moore.

Epistemology: A Guide, First Edition. John Turri.
© 2014 John Wiley & Sons, Ltd. Published 2014 by John Wiley & Sons, Ltd.

Russell worried that we can't know that the demon-possibility is false. Moore says we can and do know it's false.

Russell and Moore framed the demon-possibility differently from how I did just a moment ago. They speak of a "malicious demon" producing "percepts" in me, in which case these percepts are not produced by the sort of external objects we think normally surround us. But this is a mere verbal difference. We may understand *percepts* to be nothing other than the *sense experiences* or *sensations* we've discussed so far, such as the visual experience of a flame flickering, the sound of a fire crackling, the feeling of heat emanating from the fire, the smell of wood burning, and so on.

After some preliminary work to decide how best to understand what Russell means by "logical possibility," Moore ultimately settles on the following as the most charitable interpretation of Russell's argument. (The numbering used here does not correspond to Moore's numbering.)

1. If the truth of the demon-possibility is compatible with everything we know immediately, then we can't know for certain that the demon-possibility is false. (Premise)
2. The truth of the demon-possibility is compatible with everything we know immediately. (Premise)
3. So we cannot know for certain that the demon-possibility is false. (From 1 and 2)

Notice the qualifier "for certain" after "know." Sometimes Moore drops the qualification. But usually he doesn't. Up till now we've talked about *knowledge*, not *certain knowledge*. I leave it up to you to consider carefully whether there are relevant differences between *knows* and *knows for certain*, and how it might affect the debate.

Before evaluating the argument, let's clarify what we mean by "knowing *immediately*." Some of our beliefs are based on reasoning. Some aren't. Of those that aren't, perhaps some have no basis at all: we *just believe* them. But not all our beliefs are like that. Some that aren't based on reasoning are still based on *something*. For example, your belief that there's a text in front of you is based *on sight*.

11

Compare that to my belief that my son must be home. I don't see him. But I see his jacket hanging in the closet. And I know that he wouldn't leave home without his jacket in this weather. From this I infer that he's home. Call a belief based on reasoning *inferential*. Call a belief based on nothing *baseless*. Call a belief that is neither baseless nor inferential *immediate*. Likewise, call knowledge based on nothing (if such a thing is possible) *baseless*. Call knowledge based on reasoning *inferential*. And call knowledge that is neither baseless nor inferential *immediate*.

Now we can evaluate the argument. The first thing to note is that it's logically valid: if its premises are true, then its conclusion must be true too. So if Moore rejects the conclusion, which he does, he should reject at least one of the premises.

Moore accepts 2. He thinks we know immediately things about our own minds, but *not* things about the external world. I might know that this is a pencil, or that I have hands, or that Michael Jackson died in June 2009, or that the evil demon is not deceiving me. But I don't know any of these things immediately. So assuming that our earlier threefold distinction among baseless, inferential, and immediate knowledge exhausts the different ways we could know things, it follows that our knowledge of the external world must be either baseless or inferential. And Moore indeed agrees that it's inferential. (He doesn't seem to have seriously considered in this context whether it might be baseless; see §20 for a view that advocates baselessness for some knowledge.)

We find many different types of inference or argument. (I won't distinguish between inferences and arguments.) But for our purposes we can divide good arguments into two main types: deductive and nondeductive. Presumably, only good inferences produce knowledge. A good deductive argument is *logically valid*. We've seen this term used already several times in this book. A logically valid argument has the following important property: if its premises are true, then its conclusion must be true too. Put otherwise, the truth of its premises absolutely guarantees the truth of its conclusion. A good nondeductive argument is *logically strong*. We've not yet seen this term used. A logically strong argument is such that if its premises are true, then its conclusion is at least probably true. Put otherwise, the truth of its premises makes its conclusion at least likely. A good deductive argument is not the least bit risky. But a good nondeductive argument is still risky.

Does Moore think our inferential knowledge of the external world is deductive or nondeductive? Nondeductive. He says that such knowledge is based on "analogical or inductive arguments." Analogical and inductive arguments are nondeductive.

How do these arguments about the external world go? Their premises are things that we know immediately about our own mind, for example, premises about what sort of sensory experiences we seem to be having. Their conclusions are the things we know about the external world. The truth of the premises doesn't absolutely guarantee the truth of the conclusion, or else we would have a good *deductive* argument, not merely a good nondeductive argument. (Think carefully about why that's so.)

This brings us to the heart of the disagreement between Russell and Moore. Russell thought that only good deductive inferences could enable inferential knowledge that is also certain. Moore thought that at least some nondeductive inferences could do so as well. That's one main reason why Russell accepted 1, whereas Moore rejected it.

Moore had at least one thing to say in his defense on this point. Moore and Russell both might agree, for example, that

4. We know for certain that this is a pencil *only if* nondeductive inference enables certain knowledge.

With that in mind, we must ask ourselves: what's more plausible, that we *do* know for certain that this is a pencil, or that nondeductive inference *doesn't* enable certain knowledge? Moore chooses the former. He says it's much more plausible that we do know for certain that this is a pencil. So, he reasons, it's rational to conclude that nondeductive inference enables certain knowledge.

Moore indicates that he's willing to reason similarly about other things too. For instance, if you convinced him that nondeductive inference couldn't enable certain knowledge after all, then he'd reject 4. He'd conclude that either (i) we do after all have a good *deductive* argument from what we know immediately about our minds to conclusions about the external world, or (ii) we can after all know things about the external world *immediately*.

More generally, suppose we give Moore a choice between two things:

A. The claim that we do have certain knowledge about the external world.

B. Any theoretical claim about what knowledge requires, which implies we that *don't* have certain knowledge of the external world.

He'll always say A is more plausible and reasonable. We'll see more of this general argumentative strategy from Moore in the next section.

§4

Plausibility and possibilities (Moore, "Certainty")

There are at least three different responses to the sort of skeptical argument Stroud presented in §1. We might

A. deny that the dream-"possibility" is a genuine possibility after all, in which case it does not threaten our knowledge of the external world, or
B. deny that in order to know things about the external world, we must know that the dream-possibility is false, or
C. insist that we do know that the dream-possibility is in fact false.

Other responses are surely conceivable, but here we'll focus on these. There's no restriction on combining two or more of them.

Stroud suggested that he favors option B, but he didn't positively endorse it or develop this response at length. He was more concerned

Moore, G. E., "Certainty," extracted from pp. 171–96 in Thomas Baldwin (ed.), *G. E. Moore: Selected Writings*, (London & New York: Routledge, 1993). © 1993 by Thomas Baldwin.

Epistemology: A Guide, First Edition. John Turri.
© 2014 John Wiley & Sons, Ltd. Published 2014 by John Wiley & Sons, Ltd.

to convince us that endorsing C while rejecting B must result in "total failure." He also saw "little hope" for option A. At one point or another in "Certainty," Moore embraces the strategy Stroud judges a total failure and a strategy very similar to the one Stroud judges nearly hopeless!

As Moore stands before his audience lecturing, both he and the skeptic agree that if he doesn't know the dream-possibility is false, then he doesn't know, for example, that he's standing up. To put the point otherwise, and more naturally, they both agree that *if* Moore knows he's standing up, then he must know the dream-possibility is false. Moore and the skeptic part ways when deciding what to make of this condition they agree on.

Moore would have us reason like so:

1. If Moore knows he's standing up, then he must know the dream-possibility is false. (Premise)
2. Moore knows he's standing up. (Premise)
3. So he knows the dream-possibility is false. (From 1 and 2)

The skeptic would have us reason like so:

1*. If Moore knows he's standing up, then he must know the dream-possibility is false. (Premise)
2*. Moore doesn't know the dream-possibility is false. (Premise)
3*. So Moore doesn't know he's standing up. (From 1* and 2*)

Who gets the better of this exchange? The competing arguments are equally valid, with contradictory conclusions. They share their first premise. The whole question, then, boils down to whether it's more reasonable to accept 2 or 2*. It's obvious which Moore thinks is more reasonable. (Which do you think is more reasonable?) That wraps up Moore's implementation of option C while rejecting B.

Up till now, we've focused on ways that sense experience (or as Moore sometimes puts it, *the evidence of our senses*) might fail to enable knowledge of the external world, either because it was a mere figment of a dream or caused by an evil demon. Moore's discussion takes an unexpected turn when he contends that *sense experience doesn't exhaust the evidence* which enables his knowledge that the dream-possibility is false. In addition to sense experience, he has "memories of the immediate past."

It's at this point that Moore entertains option A, or something near enough. What reason, he asks, is there to think it's genuinely possible for him to be dreaming despite *both* having the sense experiences that he's having *and* remembering what he remembers? Moore reports that to him it seems impossible that he should be dreaming while having all those sense experiences and memories.

Notice that Moore doesn't say that the dream-possibility is impossible outright. He doesn't say it's impossible that he's merely dreaming. Instead he says it's impossible *given certain other things*. There's an important difference. Consider an analogy. The following claim is definitely possible: exactly two books exist. Call it the *two-books-possibility*. Yet the following claim is definitely impossible: exactly two books exist, *given that exactly one book exists*. And so while no one thinks that the two-books-possibility is impossible outright, it's obviously impossible *given certain other things* – for example, given that the one-book-possibility is actually true.

Another way of putting the same point is that while some things are possible *individually*, they might nevertheless be impossible *in combination*. The two-books-possibility and the one-book-possibility are obvious examples.

It's not clear why Moore thinks the dream-possibility is impossible given what he senses *and remembers*. He agrees that it's genuinely possible for all our sense experiences to be "mere dream-images," that is, mere figments of a dream. Why, then, couldn't all our apparent memories likewise be mere figments of a dream? And if all our sense experiences and all our memories could *individually* be mere figments of a dream, why couldn't they *collectively* be mere figments of a dream? Is there something special about memories, or memories in combination with sense experience, that makes them immune to apparent reproduction in a dream, whereas sense experiences, on their own, are not?

These are all good questions. But mere questions won't settle the matter. Moore challenges the skeptic to make a compelling case that the dream-possibility is possible not only outright, but also possible given the combination of sense experience and memories we have. Unless the skeptic succeeds, it remains more reasonable to accept 2 rather than 2*.

§5

Skeptic on skeptic (Klein, "How a Pyrrhonian Skeptic Might Respond to Academic Skepticism")

Peter Klein's response to external world skepticism differs greatly from Moore's. What we've been calling "skepticism about the external world" Klein calls "Academic" or "Cartesian" skepticism. That's because later members of Plato's Academy in ancient Athens were skeptics of this sort, and because of Descartes's enormously influential discussion of external world skepticism in his *Meditations on First Philosophy*.

There's one important nonverbal difference about the version of skepticism Klein confronts. Whereas we've been considering arguments for the view that we don't *know* (or don't *know for certain*) things about the external world, Klein considers an argument that our beliefs about the external world aren't even *reasonable* or *justified*.

Klein, Peter, "How a Pyrrhonian Skeptic Might Respond to Academic Skepticism," pp. 75–94 in Steven Luper (ed.), *The Skeptics: Contemporary Essays* (Aldershot: Ashgate, 2003). © 2003 by Steven Luper.

Epistemology: A Guide, First Edition. John Turri.
© 2014 John Wiley & Sons, Ltd. Published 2014 by John Wiley & Sons, Ltd.

Note a couple of important points about the relationship between knowledge and justification. On the one hand, it seems that knowledge requires justification. But on the other hand, justification does not in turn require knowledge. More precisely spelled out: if a belief of yours amounts to knowledge, then it certainly must also be justified; but it's not necessarily true that if your belief is justified, then it also amounts to knowledge. In support of the first point, we might note how absurd it would sound to claim, for example, that the coroner knows Michael Jackson died from a heart attack, but she's not justified in believing that he did. "If she's not justified in believing it," one wants to say, "then she certainly doesn't know it!" In support of the second point, we need only recall that knowledge requires truth (see §1), whereas justified belief doesn't. If all the abundant available evidence points toward one conclusion and you believe accordingly, then your belief is justified, even if it turns out that the evidence was misleading. You'd have a false justified belief, but since knowledge requires truth, your belief wouldn't amount to knowledge.

So it turns out that Klein confronts an even more radical form of skepticism than did Stroud or Moore. If skepticism about knowledge is true, skepticism about justification might still be false, because it's possible to have justified belief without knowledge. But if skepticism about justification is true, then skepticism about knowledge follows straightaway, because knowledge requires justification.

Here's a simplified version of the argument Klein considers.

1. If you're justified in believing that there's a table before you, then you're justified in believing that you're not merely dreaming there's a table before you. (Premise)
2. But you can't be justified in believing that you're not merely dreaming there's a table before you. (Premise)
3. So you aren't justified in believing that there's a table before you. (From 1 and 2)

Note that we focus on the simple example of a table, but the same reasoning applies generally to any claim about the external world.

One might think that the only reasoned reactions to the argument are:

A.   Accept the conclusion.
B.   Deny that the premises support the conclusion.
C.   Deny at least one premise.

Option A seems out of the question to most of us. B doesn't seem too promising, because the argument appears to follow a very simple, easily recognized logical pattern that guarantees its validity, namely: "if P is true, then Q is true; but Q can't be true; so P isn't true either." So it comes as no surprise that most people who encounter the argument end up opting for response C.

Klein discusses what he thinks is the most plausible way to implement C, namely, deny premise 1. The main idea of his discussion is that the most promising way to deny 1 is to deny the general "closure principle" that motivates it. (We'll look more carefully at the closure principle later in this book, especially in §§ 19–23 and 47). It's notoriously difficult to articulate the most plausible version of the closure principle, but for Klein it amounts to something like this: if you're "entitled" to believe some claim P, and you know that the truth of P *guarantees* the truth of some other claim Q, then you must also be entitled to believe Q. Klein judges that we've not yet seen a compelling argument against the closure principle, so we're left to conclude that the best of the standard responses to Cartesian skepticism fails to "settle matters."

A brief aside before pressing on. If you have trouble understanding or evaluating a general principle, such as the version of the closure principle just mentioned, it's best to consider *specific* examples that fit the general principle's pattern. Stop and review premise 1 of the argument in this section. It fits the closure principle's pattern. Do you find premise 1 plausible? Try to think of other claims that likewise fit the pattern. Do you find them plausible too? If so, that will tend to increase your confidence that the general principle is true. Can you think of any counterexamples – that is, can you think of any claims that fit the pattern but nevertheless seem *false*? If so,

21

that will increase your confidence that the general principle is also false. (Dretske's zebra/mule case, which Klein discusses, is often presented as a potential counterexample to the closure principle. We'll look more carefully at that example later in §19.)

Returning now to the main thread, given that Klein thinks the best standard response to the Cartesian skeptical argument fails, does he then endorse argument? No. Instead he develops a different, *nonstandard* response, namely

> D. Claim that the skeptic's argument settles nothing, because it's either based on an arbitrary assumption or simply begs the question.

We can represent Klein's basic argument for this assessment.

4. No argument with (i) a finite number of premises and (ii) a controversial conclusion ever settles anything, because it's either based on an arbitrary assumption or begs the question. (Premise)
5. The argument for Cartesian skepticism has (i) a finite number of premises and (ii) a controversial conclusion. (Premise)
6. So the argument for Cartesian skepticism settles nothing, because it's either based on an arbitrary assumption or begs the question. (From 4 and 5)

The argument is logically valid. Are its premises true? Premise 5 is clearly true. That leaves only 4, which is indeed the argument's crucial premise. Klein's complete defense of 4 involves us in his positive argument for *infinitism*, which we'll come to in §14.

Klein is a skeptic, but not a Cartesian skeptic. Instead, he's a *Pyrrhonian* skeptic. The Pyrrhonian thesis is that we never have enough evidence to *properly* conclusively affirm or deny anything that isn't completely and uncontroversially obvious. Cartesian skeptics conclusively affirm that we have no knowledge or justified beliefs about the external world. Pyrrhonian skeptics neither affirm nor deny this, at least not conclusively. Instead they *suspend* (i.e. *withhold* or *reserve*) *judgment* on all such claims. Consistent with all that, however, they may *provisionally* adopt a modest level of confidence in certain claims when presented with some apparently compelling evidence or argument. But further inquiry might overturn that.

Oddly enough, the Pyrrhonian thesis itself is not completely and uncontroversially obvious, so no self-respecting Pyrrhonian would conclusively affirm it!

§ 6

Realism in epistemology (Williams, "Epistemological Realism")

Imagine for a moment that we're in ancient China. Rumor is that the emperor has become quite eccentric lately. He issued a decree that no one besides the emperor and his handpicked animal caretakers may touch any animal that both belongs to the emperor and was born during a waning moon. Call these *prohibited animals*. The penalty for this "crime?" Death! As a result, all of us citizens want to become good at distinguishing the prohibited animals from the others.

But the combination of two significant facts prevents us from becoming good at making that distinction. First, the emperor owns specimens of all and only those animals native to the eclectic empire: giant pandas and Chinese alligators, dwarf blue sheep and red-crowned cranes, dholes and golden monkeys, silk moths and snow

Williams, Michael, "Epistemological Realism," pp. 83–93, 101–19, 121–4, 129–39 in *Unnatural Doubts* (Oxford, Blackwell Publishers, 1991). © 1991 by Michael Williams.

leopards, Pacific cod and tarantulas, long-eared jerboas and yaks, etc. Second, the emperor lets his animals roam free, refusing to house them in any type of park or enclosure. Any animal we encounter might be prohibited!

The emperor recognizes our dire predicament. Mercifully he directs his animal caretakers to equip all and only the prohibited animals with a special gold and purple tag. This makes life easier for us all, because now we're extremely reliable at distinguishing them from all the rest. And we take care to teach our children the distinction too, which isn't too difficult, given the distinctive colorful tags. And we lived happily ever after. The end.

Stepping out from our imaginary tale, let's note a few important points about it. First, there was indeed a group of prohibited animals, and a group of non-prohibited animals. In fact, all the animals in China sorted neatly into these two categories. Second, these categories tracked a distinction that was very important to the citizens. Third, the citizens were expert at sorting animals into the two groups. Fourth, the distinction was teachable – for example, they could teach their children how to reliably make the distinction. Fifth, the distinction was *projectible*, by which I mean: as the citizens came across *new* cases of animals from around the realm, they could effectively sort them into the preexisting groups.

This brings us to the sixth point, which is that despite the five points previously mentioned, the distinction in question is obviously *superficial*. It doesn't track any deep or essential differences, similarities, or relations among the animals classified. Consider three animals: a prohibited giant panda, a non-prohibited giant panda, and a prohibited silk moth. The two pandas obviously have much, much more in common than do the first panda and the moth. There's no *natural* or *genuine* kind of animal such as *animals the emperor owns that were born during a waning moon*. It's a mere *superficial* or *nominal* kind comprising a motley crew. By contrast, classifying animals by biological species (as we do with giant pandas, silk moths, etc.) or phyla (as we do with chordates, arthropods, and mollusks) does track deep and essential relations, similarities, and differences. *Giant panda* and *silk moth* are genuine kinds. The biological classifications track objective patterns among Earthling organisms. (From now on, instead of saying "similarities, differences, and relations," I'll just say "'patterns,'" intending exactly the same thing.)

Seventh, although it's perfectly understandable and predictable, given the circumstances, that the citizens would become proficient at applying the distinction, it's equally preposterous that anyone outside of that particular social and historical context would wish to classify animals that way.

Doubtless, the sixth and seventh points are closely related: no one else would want to employ the distinction precisely because it fails to identify a genuine kind. It identifies a merely superficial kind, marked by disunity, whose relevance is very narrowly restricted to a particular historical period of a particular society. There's no objective pattern there that could command our interest, enable understanding of life on Earth, or empower us to make helpful predictions or generalizations. (If all you knew about an animal was that it was prohibited, what could you reliably infer?) Compare that to the interest people in a wide variety of settings have in tracking the patterns marked out by biological species.

To come at the point from a slightly different angle, imagine trying to give a theory of prohibited animals. There's really nothing true and interesting you could say about the lot of them, beyond what's already contained in the description we used to pick out the kind, namely, "animals that belong to the emperor and were born during a waning moon." Lacking a (nontrivial) theory of prohibited animals evinces no defect in our understanding of the natural world. Again, compare that to all the important things paleontologists and zoologists tell us about the evolution, physiology, and genetic endowment of species. Lacking a theory of biological species would evince a serious defect in our understanding of the natural world.

Now here's a question for you. Do *our beliefs about the external world* form a genuine kind? Think of all the different things you believe about the external world. (Of course, it's impossible *in practice* to list all the things you believe, and it might even be impossible *in principle*, either because we have infinite beliefs or because there's no definite fact of the matter about how many beliefs we have.

But set that worry aside.) You probably believe things about the solar system, human prehistory, the constitution of matter, the weather, sports trivia, your health, your friends and family, important events from your childhood, popular culture, traffic laws, international affairs, agriculture, etc. There's certainly no *topical* unity here – the topics could be nearly as diverse as the world itself.

Might there be any other deep and important patterns binding our beliefs into a genuine kind? Other suggestions come to mind, but we'll need to put those aside for the moment because we've come as far as we profitably can without explicitly examining Michael Williams's argument in "Epistemological Realism." The groundwork we've laid thus far will help us along the way.

Williams's response to external world skepticism differs from Moore's and Klein's. The skeptic might ask how knowledge of the external world is possible at all. And she might go on to present arguments that we can't achieve such knowledge, or that we can never know whether we have such knowledge. Williams responds that the skeptic's question is defective. It's defective because *there's nothing really there to inquire about* – our beliefs about the external world don't form a genuine kind.

We can understand Williams's basic argument as follows:

1. If our beliefs about the external world don't form a genuine kind, then external world skepticism is a defective theory. (Premise)
2. Our beliefs about the external world don't form a genuine kind. (Premise)
3. So external world skepticism is a defective theory. (From 1 and 2)

The argument is valid, so let's see what can be said on behalf of the premises.

Start with 1. The aim of theory is to reveal deep and important patterns in some domain. But if there are no deep and important patterns there to be found, then no theory could reveal them. Genuine kinds are marked by deep and important patterns; they're not a mere "loose aggregate of more or less unrelated cases" (p. 54).

In order for our beliefs about the external world to be a proper object of theoretical inquiry, they would have to form a genuine kind of some sort. If they were a mere loose aggregate, then it'd be as hopeless to theorize about them as it is to theorize about prohibited animals. Yet the skeptic *does* theorize about our beliefs about the external world. She draws dramatic, sweeping conclusions about the entire range of them. So if our beliefs don't form a genuine kind, then her efforts are wasted. Her theory will be defective.

That brings us to premise 2. Earlier we noted that our beliefs about the external world exhibit no topical unity, so there's no hope to identify genuine patterns on that basis. The other promising suggestion, which Williams considers, is that they form a genuine *epistemological kind*. The idea here is that all our beliefs "naturally" and "inalienably" divide into two main kinds: basic and inferential. Basic beliefs possess "intrinsic" credibility – these are things we can just know, without needing to infer them from other things we believe. Basic beliefs include those beliefs about the properties of our current conscious experience – the ones that simply "record the data" of consciousness. Basic beliefs are "epistemologically prior" to inferential beliefs. Inferential beliefs lack intrinsic credibility; they must be justified based on an appropriate inference from basic beliefs. Inferential beliefs include those about external objects.

Epistemological realism is the doctrine that our beliefs fall into natural and inalienable kinds, some of which are essentially privileged and unproblematic, others of which essentially require "evidential support" from the privileged ones. *Substantive foundationalism* is historically the most widely held and influential version of epistemological realism. Both skepticism and traditional antiskeptical responses share a commitment to epistemological realism.

(You probably noticed that the basic/inferential distinction corresponds to the immediate/inferential distinction we met in §3. What Moore called "immediate," Williams calls "basic." You might also have noticed that Moore and Russell both agreed that knowledge of the external world is inferential, based on what we know immediately. Again this corresponds closely to the idea that basic beliefs are epistemologically prior to inferential beliefs.)

Williams rejects epistemological realism and argues that we should instead accept a view he calls "contextualism." Williams supports his preference for contextualism by appealing to obvious facts about our "ordinary practices." With his case against epistemological realism and for contextualism complete, Williams's defense of 2 is complete.

The realist's major mistake is to suppose that every belief has an utterly unchangeable epistemological character. But in everyday life, the evidential requirements for beliefs "shift with context." There are no fixed and immutable relations of epistemic priority. Multiple contextual factors determine which beliefs are beyond doubt and which inferences are acceptable. These contextual factors include the topic under discussion, what discipline we're practicing, and what problem we're trying to solve or question we're trying to answer. Independently of specifying contextual details, we cannot determine whether a belief is justified, or whether it requires any evidence to be properly held, or what inferences to and from the belief are acceptable. When it comes to these issues, there simply is "no fact of the matter" independent of context. That is the essence of contextualism.

Take the example "I have hands," made famous initially by Moore, and subsequently taken up by his student and colleague Ludwig Wittgenstein, the most celebrated twentieth-century philosopher, who in many ways inspires Williams's contextualism. In almost any context, no one would think that I need to infer my belief that I have hands from other beliefs. Rather, it's a basic claim that I know unproblematically. I'm as certain that I have hands as I am of anything else – there's nothing more certain for me from which I could infer it, or by which I could test it, which explains why it would be useless for me to go about inferring it that way. Nevertheless, in special circumstances I might need to investigate. For instance, suppose that upon waking up from a risky surgery to save my hands after a horrible car accident, the ends of my arms are still numb and wrapped in thick bandages so that I can't see whether I have hands or stumps. Then I might need to unwrap the bandages and look, or ask the nurse whether I have hands. I'd have to infer it from other things I believe.

Different fields of inquiry are defined by which beliefs stand in need of justification, which don't, and which inferences are acceptable. In a debate among archaeologists, it is simply beyond doubt that the Earth has existed longer than five minutes. We might wonder, for instance, whether a site excavated is really twenty-thousand years old, or whether the strata it was found in had been upset by glacial activity. That's a legitimate question in archaeology. But if we start questioning whether there really is an external world, then we've stopped doing archaeology and started doing a peculiar brand of epistemology. Likewise if we're debating whether to hire Harry or Sally, it is beyond doubt that Harry and Sally both exist. We might ask whether they're really as qualified as they claim to be. That's a legitimate question. But if we start questioning whether our evidence really does support the conclusion that other minds exist, then we've stopped having a business conversation and started having a philosophical one.

Beliefs have no epistemic status independently of the topic under discussion, the direction of our inquiry, and the broader needs and interests of those involved in the discussion. Context is the lifeblood of epistemology. Without it, there simply are no epistemological facts, contrary to what the epistemological realist would have us believe. And once we recognize that epistemological realism is false, Williams thinks, the response to skepticism is simple and straightforward, namely, that skepticism is deeply rooted in a badly mistaken theory of epistemological facts.

§ 7

Socratic questions and the foundation of empirical knowledge (Chisholm, "The Myth of the Given")

Roderick Chisholm was one of the most renowned American philosophers of the twentieth century. In his piece, "The Myth of the Given," he defends three theses about the structure of knowledge and justified belief. One thesis is purely formal, another substantive, and the last negative. All three theses pertain to what Chisholm calls "the doctrine of the given." More specifically, when combined the three theses constitute the most plausible version of that doctrine, which in turn, Chisholm believes, is the best theory of the structure of knowledge and justified belief.

A couple of brief points before we proceed. First, we'll discuss the doctrine of the given as a theory of the structure of *knowledge*, and leave *justified belief* (and *justified statements*) aside. The entire discussion about knowledge straightforwardly translates into an analogous discussion about justified belief (or justified statements). Second,

Chisholm, Roderick, "The Myth of the Given," pp. 261–86 in R. Chisholm, *Philosophy* (Englewood Cliffs, NJ: Prentice-Hall, 1964). © 1964 by Roderick M. Chisholm.

Epistemology: A Guide, First Edition. John Turri.
© 2014 John Wiley & Sons, Ltd. Published 2014 by John Wiley & Sons, Ltd.

Chisholm distinguishes between "foundational" and non-foundational knowledge (or between "self-justifying" and non-self-justifying beliefs). This is a mere verbal variation on a distinction we already seen made by Moore (§3) and Williams (§6).[1] Moore distinguished between "immediate" and "inferential" knowledge, and Williams distinguished between "basic" and "inferential" knowledge. "Foundational," "immediate," and "basic" all mean the same thing; "non-foundational" and "inferential" also mean the same thing. I will continue using the labels "basic" and "inferential."

We can state Chisholm's purely formal thesis as follows:

> A. Everything we know is either a self-justifying claim, or is (ultimately at least partly) justified by a self-justifying claim.

Recall one aspect of the relationship between knowledge and justification noted in §5, namely that any belief which counts as knowledge must also be justified. Everything we know must be justified in some way, and thesis A makes a general claim about the overall form such justification must take, but it doesn't say anything beyond that – that is, it doesn't say anything *substantive*. That's why it's a purely formal thesis.

In support of A, Chisholm appeals to our considered response to "Socratic questions" about our beliefs. Suppose I find myself believing that I know some claim P. Now I might wonder, "What justifies me in believing P?", or more naturally, "How *do* I know P?" In response I might say, "Because I know Q, which enables me to know P." But then I wonder, "Well, then, how *do* I know Q?," to which I might respond, "Because I know R, which enables me to know Q." You can see a pattern developing here. How will it all end? At some point – perhaps very early on in this line of questioning, or perhaps not for many more steps – I'll reach a point where I say of the claim in question, call it "X," "Well, I know X simply because it's a fact that X is true!" Here we reach what Chisholm calls a

---

[1] Klein also discusses the distinction, but I didn't cover that aspect of his discussion in §6. See §14 for more on that.

"proper stopping place" in the line of questioning. If describing our justification or evidence for believing X amounts to simply repeating "X," then we've reached a proper stopping point. Proper stopping points are called *self-justifying* for an obvious reason.

Some object to Chisholm's method on the grounds that these Socratic questions are defective. The critics charge that the questions either falsely presuppose that the claim in question is somehow doubtful, or improperly suggest that we really do know it after all. But for most things we believe, there simply are no legitimate grounds for doubt or for suggesting that they don't really amount to knowledge after all. And we of course cannot properly trust the results of a defective line of questioning, so Chisholm is wrong to draw conclusions based on these results.

Chisholm responds that the questions are not defective. They do not presuppose that the claims are doubtful or that we don't really know them. Indeed exactly the opposite is true. Here's a non-epistemological example to help clarify what Chisholm has in mind. Suppose we watch Tiger Woods make another fantastic shot. I turn to you and ask, "How *does* he strike the ball so well from that poor lie?" My question presupposes that he struck the ball well from a poor lie. Likewise, Chisholm imagines us asking the epistemological questions in a way that presupposes that we do know the claim in question. Of course, there are other ways of asking these same questions – we might adopt a certain stress pattern or an incredulous tone, which strongly suggests that we doubt that the belief amounts to knowledge. But again, that is not what Chisholm has in mind.

We can state Chisholm's substantive thesis as follows:

B. Some things we know are self-justifying claims about how things appear (that is, *seem*) to us.

Chisholm defends B by providing compelling examples, such as the following. Suppose that while eating a morello cherry I wonder, "How *do* I know that this seems to taste sour?" The only real answer I can offer simply repeats the claim in question: "I know because it seems to taste sour."

Some reject B on the grounds that claims about how things appear or seem are inherently *comparative*, which prevents them from being self-justifying. To say that something seems F – where "F" names some characteristic – is to say that it seems the way that F-things generally or ordinarily seem. For instance, to say that this cherry seems red is to say that this cherry seems the way red things generally seem: "seems red" just means "seems the way red things generally seem." But that involves a general claim that couldn't be self-justifying. If I do know that general claim, it is only because it justified by other things that I remember, in which case it's not self-justifying. (Notice: if I wonder, "How *do* I know that this is the way red things generally seem?," it won't do to answer, "Because that's the way red things generally seem.")

Chisholm responds that this is not the proper way to understand self-justifying claims about how things seem. The self-justifying ones are *non-comparative*, pertaining only to the intrinsic character of the way things appear *in this specific instance*. It's quite implausible that noticing the way this cherry seems requires me to relate it to red things generally. Of course, to communicate to you how this cherry seems to me, I might well have to compare it to other things. But that's a point about interpersonal communication, which doesn't apply to my beliefs about the way things appear to me, since I'm not trying to interpersonally communicate anything to myself.

This brings us to Chisholm's negative thesis:

    c.   Not all self-justifying claims are about the way things appear.

Chisholm provides examples to support C. His examples involve our mental states. For instance, suppose I wonder, "How *do* I know that I'm in pain?" I answer, "By the fact that I am in pain." Likewise, if I wonder, "How *do* I know that I believe philosophy is fascinating?," I will answer, "By the fact that I believe that philosophy is fascinating." These claims don't mention how things appear. Rather, they're categorical claims about the way things *are* in my mental life.

Chisholm doesn't believe that claims about the external world, such as "This is a dagger before me," can qualify as self-justifying.

Questioning reveals that our knowledge of such things depends on our knowledge of how things appear to us. "How *do* I know that this is a dagger?" "Because I see that it is a dagger." "And how *do* I know that I see that it is a dagger?" "Because it seems to me that I'm looking at a dagger." "And how *do* I know that it seems to me that I'm looking at a dagger?" "Because it seems to me that I'm looking at a dagger." It's only when we reach this last answer, Chisholm thinks, that we've found an appropriate stopping point.

That covers the major elements of Chisholm's explanation and defense of "the doctrine of the given." He also briefly indicates how he thinks epistemology should proceed. The challenge is to formulate a system of "criteria" or "rules of evidence," which specify when we are justified in thinking that we do know something, in particular when we know something through memory, perception, introspection, and rational (i.e., a priori) insight. (We'll look more at these sources of knowledge later, especially in §§42–45, 56 and 58–59.) The ideal is to construct the simplest and most satisfying system of rules which entail that we know most of the things that we ordinarily take ourselves to know.

§§ 8–9

The foundation of empirical knowledge? (Sellars, "Does Empirical Knowledge Have a Foundation?" and "Epistemic Principles")

Some believe that people two-hundred years from now will look back and regard Wilfrid Sellars as the most profound and systematic philosopher of the twentieth century. Sellars and Chisholm carried on a long debate about the status of basic knowledge. We've already taken a brief look at Chisholm's views. Now we'll study Sellars's. We'll focus on two aspects of his discussion: his critique of Chisholm, and his presentation of a positive alternative.

Sellars, Wilfred, "Does Empirical Knowledge Have a Foundation?" pp. 293–300 in H. Feigel and M. Scriven (eds.), *The Foundations of Science and the Concepts of Psychology and Psychoanalysis, Minnesota Studies in the Philosophy of Science*, Vol. 1 (Minneapolis: University of Minnesota Press, 1956). © 1956.

Sellars, Wilfred, "Epistemic Principles," pp. 332–49 in H. Casteneda (ed.), *Action, Knowledge, and Reality* (Indianapolis: Bobbs- Merrill, 1975). © 1975 by Wilfrid Sellars.

These two chapters have been included together because it was the most effective way to explain the complex common themes across Sellars' writings.

Epistemology: A Guide, First Edition. John Turri.
© 2014 John Wiley & Sons, Ltd. Published 2014 by John Wiley & Sons, Ltd.

Let's begin with three important terminological notes. First, Sellars often speaks of accepting "sentences" (or "sentence tokens" or "statements") and making "observation reports." We can understand him to mean the formation of *judgments* or *beliefs* which we would normally express by using those sentences or issuing those reports. So, for example, to accept the sentence, "This is green," or to sincerely report, "This is green," is to judge or form the belief that this is green. For the sake of simplicity and consistent terminology across sections, I'll speak simply of *beliefs* in interpreting Sellars.[1] Second, the "observational" knowledge Sellars speaks of is nothing other than the purported basic knowledge we get from our senses, which we've already seen Moore, Williams, Chisholm, and others speak of. Third, Sellars speaks of a belief being "justified," "reasonable," "correct," and "authoritative." These adjectives are used synonymously. I will limit myself to "justified" and "authoritative" and their cognates. It's also worth noting that Sellars, like Chisholm, appears to assume that knowledge and justification share the same structure, so that whatever we learn about basic and inferential knowledge applies equally to basic and inferential justification, and vice versa.

Recall that basic knowledge contrasts with inferential knowledge (see §3). Inferential knowledge is knowledge inferred from other things you believe. Basic knowledge isn't inferred from other things you believe, but instead forms the ultimate foundation for all your inferential knowledge.

Sellars, like Chisholm, uses explicit arguments to model the structure of knowledge. Suppose that I have inferential knowledge of some claim P. Something like the following argument might be offered to justify my belief in P.

1. I know that Q.
2. So Q is true.

---

[1] This glosses over potentially important subtleties in Sellars's formidably complex *overall* views about nature of thought and its relation to language use. For a helpful introduction to these complexities, consult Willem A. deVries's *Wilfrid Sellars* (McGill-Queen's University Press, 2005).

3. And if Q is true, then P must be too.
4. So I know that P.

In order for my knowledge to "transmit" from Q to P, I must, of course, know Q (a fact reflected in line 1 of the argument). My knowledge of Q might in turn be inferential because transmitted from my knowledge of R, after the same pattern. And this in turn might be inferential because transmitted from my knowledge of S. And so on. But, as Chisholm pointed out and Sellars concedes, it's extremely tempting to think that *not all* knowledge can be inferential in this way. At some point there must be some non-inferential or basic knowledge which, as they say, "gets the ball rolling."

What's required for basic knowledge? How does it derive its justification or authority?

Chisholm answered that it derives its authority from direct awareness of the fact known. Recall the Socratic questioning that ends at an appropriate stopping point – that is, when you answer the question "How *do* I know X?" by replying "Because it's a fact that X is true" (see §7). For Chisholm, appropriate stopping points include facts about our own mental states and facts about the way things appear to us. These facts are plausibly thought of as appropriate stopping points because we have direct, unproblematic access to them. They include the fact that I have a headache, or that I seem to be looking at something green, etc. Such facts *directly present themselves* to us – they are *given* to us – in our conscious experience. Sellars calls these direct presentations "nonverbal episodes of awareness," or more simply, "the given."

Sellars's main criticism is that citing these direct presentations provides us with a "merely verbal" and "ad hoc" solution, by which he means it appears shallow, contrived, and unpersuasive. When we arrive at one of these so-called stopping points, Sellars interprets us as providing something like this argument to justify our knowledge:

5. It is a fact (which I directly apprehend) that X.
6. So I know that X.

But, of course, there's a difference between *apprehending* and *merely seeming to apprehend*, just as there's a difference between *knowing* and *merely seeming to know*. So to know 5, I'd have to know that I satisfied whatever criteria distinguish *apprehending* from *merely seeming to apprehend*. So I've not really reached a proper stopping point after all! The chain of knowledge and justification continues. We have failed to locate an authoritative foundational basis.

Sellars's alternative account of basic knowledge's authority begins with two conditions: you must be reliable, and you must know that you're reliable. For example, suppose you look at a head of Romaine lettuce and instantly think *this is green*. For your belief to amount to knowledge, two things must be true of you. First, your forming the belief in that way must be a "reliable symptom" or "sign" of a green object's presence. Second, you must know that it's a reliable symptom of a green object's presence. (The way you form the belief is *by looking*.)[2]

These dual requirements lead to a puzzling predicament. To know that *this is green* is to know a particular fact. To know that *forming beliefs this way is reliable* is to know a general fact. Reflect for a moment about how we establish such general facts about a procedure's reliability. You need knowledge of many particular instances that conspire to form a good track record, a high success-to-failure ratio, thereby establishing reliability. So presumably you could know the general fact about the procedure's reliability *only if* you knew of many examples where (A) you believed *this is green* based on the way it looked and (B) a green object was indeed present. But how could you know B, which is a particular fact of the very sort we

---

[2] Sellars expresses himself inconsistently at a couple points. At times he writes as if the first condition, *being reliably formed*, is all that's required for the basic belief to "have authority," whereas the second condition, *knowing it was reliably formed*, is required for the further tasks of "expressing" the basic knowledge or gaining inferential knowledge by using the basic beliefs to help learn further things. At other times, he writes as if both conditions are required for the basic belief to have authority at all. Tension, confusion, or simple carelessness may underlie this inconsistency. Whatever the inconsistency's source, the second of these readings seems more prevalent in Sellars's writing, so I interpret his basic position accordingly – that is, as positing dual requirements for authority itself.

began by wondering about? The dual requirements tell us that in order to know B, we must know the general fact. And yet in order to know the general fact, we must know B.

So don't the dual requirements require us to do something impossible? Don't they tell us that we must know the general fact before we know the particular facts, when we must know the particular facts before we know the general fact?

No, the dual requirements require no such thing. They require us to know the general fact *in order to* know the particular fact, and they require us to know the particular fact *in order to* know the general fact. But the phrase "in order to" does not mean "before." The relation here is not *temporal* but rather, as Sellars puts it, *logical*. General knowledge and particular knowledge mutually presuppose one another, but neither precedes the other. To better appreciate this subtle distinction, consider a couple of non-epistemological examples. In order for this woman to be my mother, she must be my female parent, and in order for her to be my female parent, she must be my mother, but this obviously doesn't require her to be my mother *before* she's my female parent, or vice versa. Likewise, in order for this substance to be gold, it must have an atomic number of 79, and for this substance to have an atomic number of 79, it must be gold, but neither condition must precede the other. Indeed neither *could* precede the other, since they go together necessarily.

That should dispel the appearance of absurdity. It also positions us to say why Sellars thinks that Chisholm and other "foundationalists" are both right and wrong. They're right that at least some knowledge isn't inferred from other things we believe or know. Yet every bit of knowledge still "logically presupposes" knowledge of other facts, and so is not entirely independent of other things we know. The "foundation" metaphor obscures this important dimension of logical dependence. Being non-inferential isn't enough to be completely independent.

This brings us to perhaps the most intriguing aspect of Sellars's view, which is that the real foundation of all our worldly knowledge is the set of perceptual and inferential dispositions instilled in us through "a long history of acquiring piecemeal habits of response to various objects in various circumstances." We are gradually introduced into linguistic and conceptual practices, sometimes formally but more often informally through ordinary human society. These practices are essentially *normative* or *rule-governed*, and we are initiated into them by others who have already mastered the rules, and who train us through appropriate encouragement and criticism. (*Language use* is the paradigm example of such practices.) We become knowers only after sufficiently mastering these practices, which assures that we are at least minimally reliable at recognizing and classifying objects around us. As we reach that threshold, our knowledge of general and particular facts emerges concurrently as a whole package, all at once in a vast interlocking web.

Toward the end of §7, I mentioned that Chisholm thought the epistemologist's job was to formulate rules of evidence which would explain how we end up knowing most of the things we ordinarily take ourselves to know. Interestingly, Chisholm and Sellars might both agree on rules of evidence such as this:

> If I believe, based on the way things appear, that this is an orange pumpkin, then I'm justified in believing that this is an orange pumpkin.

Chisholm might defend such rules by claiming that they are necessary if we're to know most of the things we ordinarily think we know, and he has faith that we do know most of it. Or he might defend them by claiming that we know such rules innately.[3] Or he might defend them by claiming that they're necessary truths, discoverable through careful enough reflection, as are fundamental logical, mathematical, or ethical principles.

---

[3] The following passage, reminiscent of Plato's *Meno*, suggests (though it does not require) such an interpretation: "The truth which the philosopher seeks, when he asks about justification, is 'already implicit in the mind which seeks it, and needs only to be elicited and brought to clear expression'."

Sellars defends them by claiming that such rules are true by virtue of "the nature of" the conceptual and linguistic skills needed to make perceptual judgments, such as *this is an orange pumpkin*. You must be a reliable believer, and know that you are, in order to be a "language-using organism whose language is *about* the world in which it is *used*" to begin with. Indeed, *agency itself* requires as much. We would not be "acting beings at all" if such rules weren't true of us. Thus, the formation of such a perceptual belief, indeed *the mere act* of inquiring into how things seem to you, is enough to guarantee that you're a reliable believer, that you know you're a reliable believer, and that you know much else besides.

Suppose we ask Sellars, "How do you know all these facts about the nature of concept and language acquisition? And how do you know that you have sufficiently mastered the practices to be at least minimally reliable? How do you know that you're sufficiently reliable at applying the words and concepts you learned? And how do you know that you're an agent? Your argument relies on all these things, but in order to justify your acceptance of them, you need to rely on the very conceptual and linguistic resources whose authority is now in question. And isn't that just blatantly circular?" How could Sellars effectively respond? Is it even possible for him to respond without using the very words and concepts that have been called into question? And what might our answers to these questions reveal about the structure of knowledge and justification?

Or suppose we say to Sellars, "Okay, you've convinced us that reliability is built into the nature of concept and language acquisition, as well as agency. It's taken you years of careful, dedicated study to discover all that. But now you've figured it out, and those of us who believe you have the benefit of your insight. Yet how plausible is it that *ordinary people* believe all that, much less know it? It's overwhelmingly *implausible*! Most people have never even considered these interesting facts about the nature of concepts, language and agency. So how could such facts enable them to know? How could those facts imbue their beliefs with authority, if they're unaware of them? Could *the mere truth* of these facts be enough to imbue their beliefs with authority?"[4] Again, the answers to these questions promise to reveal much about knowledge and justification.

Reference

Willem A. deVries, *Wilfrid Sellars* (McGill-Queen's University Press, 2005).

---

[4] When considering how Sellars might respond to this last question, be sure to keep in mind what he says about the "second hurdle."

§ 10

It's not a given that empirical knowledge has a foundation (BonJour, "Can Empirical Knowledge Have a Foundation?")

More than once already we've encountered the basic idea behind an ancient puzzle known variously as "Agrippa's trilemma," "the Pyrrhonian problematic," and "the epistemic regress problem." We start with the very plausible assumption that if you know something, then you must have good reason to believe it. Now take any supposed piece of knowledge – for example, your knowledge that A is true (substitute whatever claim you like for "A"). The question then arises about how you know that A is true – what's your reason? Suppose your reason is that B is true, and B's truth guarantees A's truth. Fair enough. So you've inferred A from B. But unless you know that B is true, you can't knowledgeably infer A from B. So how do you know that B is true? Suppose your reason is that C is true, and C's truth guarantees B's truth. So you've inferred B from C.

Bonjour, Laurence, "Can Empirical Knowledge Have a Foundation?" pp. 1–13 in *American Philosophical Quarterly* 15, 1 (1978). © 1978 by *American Philosophical Quarterly*.

But now we'll want to know how you know that C is true. And so on. You can see a pattern developing. The question "How do you know … ?" will renew itself. The puzzle is to explain how, if at all, the pattern might unfold so as to vindicate the initial assumption that you actually do know that A is true.

There seem to be only three possible ways the pattern could unfold. The best way to see this is by asking simple questions which sort all possibilities into neat groups.

Does the pattern circle back? That is, as we trace back the chain of reasons for thinking that A is true, will A itself appear at any point? If it does, then the pattern is circular. If it doesn't, then it's noncircular. Suppose we have a noncircular pattern. *Does it ever end?* If it doesn't, then the pattern is infinite (and nonrepeating because it doesn't circle back). If it does, then the pattern is finite (and nonrepeating).

Those two questions neatly sorted all the possibilities into three nonoverlapping groups. We first divided them all into circular and noncircular, and then divided the noncircular ones into infinite and finite, leaving us with three basic patterns: circular, infinite, and finite.[1]

Infinitists say that infinite patterns enable knowledge. Klein is an infinitist. Coherentists say that circular patterns can. Sellars is a coherentist. Foundationalists say that finite patterns can. Moore and Chisholm are foundationalists. Skeptics say that none of the patterns can. If none of the three patterns can enable knowledge, then skepticism follows. We would know nothing, due to the impossibility of an appropriate structure or pattern of reasons.

In "Can Empirical Knowledge Have a Foundation?," Laurence BonJour argues that foundationalists have failed to make a convincing case that finite patterns can enable knowledge and thereby adequately resolve the regress problem. We can understand BonJour's main argument like so:

---

[1] BonJour says there are *four* options, because he breaks up the finite patterns into two groups: ones ending with a justified belief, and ones ending in unjustified belief. For simplicity I here ignore the finite chains ending in unjustified belief. Some things Michael Williams says in "Epistemological Realism" suggest that he might have sympathy for this option (see §6).

1. If basic knowledge isn't possible, then foundationalism doesn't solve the regress problem. (Premise)
2. Basic knowledge isn't possible. (Premise)
3. So foundationalism doesn't solve the regress problem. (From 1 and 2)

The argument is logically valid, so it remains to ask whether its premises are true.

Line 1 is very plausible. Foundationalists say that finite chains of reasons enable knowledge. Now if you don't know B, then you can't gain knowledge of A by inferring it from B. Ignorance doesn't beget knowledge. So a finite chain enabling knowledge must end in knowledge. Basic knowledge is precisely such knowledge at the end of a finite chain. So if basic knowledge isn't possible, then no finite chain enables knowledge, in which case foundationalism doesn't solve the regress problem.

Line 2 is the argument's key premise, and BonJour focuses mainly on defending it. His defense divides into two main parts. On the one hand, he presents a positive argument that basic knowledge is impossible. On the other, he anticipates and replies to two main objections to his positive argument.

Let's start with BonJour's argument that basic knowledge is impossible. Knowledge requires epistemic justification. Epistemic justification requires that you have good reason for thinking that your belief is true. Good reasons reliably indicate the truth. (BonJour calls them "truth-conducive.") And while you need not have *explicitly formulated* your good reasons for accepting the claim in question, you still must have them. (Good reasons *which you don't have* are epistemically useless to you.) In light of all this, BonJour thinks, to satisfactorily defend the claim that your belief in X amounts to basic knowledge, you must be able to knowledgeably demonstrate that your belief in X is likely to be true. This requires you to know, or at least reasonably believe, the premises of something like the following argument (what BonJour calls a "meta-justification" or a "justifying argument"), where "F" names whatever feature foundationalists say makes for basic knowledge.

4. My belief has the special foundationalist feature F. (Premise)
5. Beliefs with feature F are very likely true. (Premise)
6. So my belief is very likely true. (From 4 and 5)

But now it turns out that your belief in X doesn't constitute basic knowledge after all. It is, at best, *inferential* knowledge because it depends for its justification on other beliefs, namely, your belief in lines 4 and 5 of this argument. (BonJour's discussion here importantly resembles Sellars's argument in §§8–9 against Chisholm's "appropriate stopping points.")

Next, BonJour considers two objections to his argument that basic knowledge is impossible. The first is *the externalist response*. The externalist denies that you must know, or reasonably believe, the premises of a justifying argument in order for your belief to qualify as basic knowledge. It's enough that the premises of such an argument *be true*. It's enough that you *are* reliable about whether X is true; you do not also have to know that you're reliable.

The objection is called "externalist" because it allows factors relevant to knowledge and justification to be external to – that is, not included in – your perspective on the situation. Externalism is what Sellars earlier dismissed as the "thermometer view" of knowledge.

BonJour rejects the externalist response because, he says, it merely evades the regress problem rather than solving it. The "traditional notion" of knowledge requires you to actually *have* the reasons that enable knowledge. The reasons must be available from within your first-person perspective on the situation. That's because knowledge is "essentially the product of reflective, critical, and rational inquiry," and such inquiry obviously requires you to be aware of the reasons. How could you responsibly take into account factors which you're completely unaware of? Rather than actually address the regress problem, externalism takes the "radical" step of simply abandoning the traditional conception of knowledge. (See §28 for more on BonJour's treatment of externalism.)

That brings us to the second objection to BonJour's argument that basic knowledge is impossible. Taking a cue from BonJour, we can call it *the givenist response*. Here is the basic idea. BonJour is right that

47

you must be aware of the reasons that enable knowledge. But he is wrong that this awareness must take the form of *beliefs*. Instead, it can take the form of a *direct apprehension* or *awareness* of certain facts, which directly present themselves to us in conscious experience. This awareness can justify beliefs but needn't in turn be justified. For example, if I am experiencing a headache, I am consciously aware of this fact, and this awareness can directly justify my belief that I have a headache, without my needing to form beliefs about the nature of my experience. For instance, I wouldn't need to form the belief that (a) I'm having an experience with feature F, and (b) such experiences reliably indicate a headache. The experience of the headache itself enables basic knowledge that I have a headache. And no further question arises about whether the experience is justified – indeed, such a question doesn't even make sense – thereby ending the regress.

BonJour responds to the givenist by posing a dilemma. In what follows, "cognitive" means "like a belief, insofar as it represents some claim as being true." Either this so-called direct awareness is cognitive or it isn't. *If it is cognitive*, then it makes sense to ask how we know it's accurately representing the way things are, in which case the regress continues and we've not been given a proper solution to the regress problem. *If it isn't cognitive*, then although it's senseless to ask whether it's justified or how we know it's true, it's equally senseless to think that it could give us a reason to believe anything. If it really doesn't represent anything – if it doesn't depict the world as being one way rather than another – then how could it give us a reason to believe that the world is one way rather than another? It couldn't. So again we've not been given a proper solution to the regress problem. So either way givenism fails.

§ 11

Interpretation, meaning and skepticism (Davidson, "A Coherence Theory of Truth and Knowledge")

Imagine you wake up one day to find yourself in an utterly unfamiliar situation. You have no idea where you are or how you got here. The noontime sun is punishingly hot. You're uncomfortable, hungry, and thirsty. You slowly gaze around the unfamiliar countryside, shake your head in disbelief, and settle down on a nearby boulder in a thicket of trees to contemplate your situation. Before long you hear voices, distant and faint at first, but closer and clearer with each passing moment. The voices come from a small band of men traveling down the savannah along the forest's edge. Equipped with bow and arrow, they're obviously a hunting party. You're disappointed to hear that they speak a language utterly unfamiliar to you. You can't understand a word. Not knowing what to expect

Davidson, Donald, "A Coherence Theory of Truth and Knowledge," pp. 307–19 in Ernest Lepore (ed.), *Truth and Interpretation: Perspectives on the Philosophy of Donald Davidson* (New York: Blackwell, 1989). © 1989 by Ernest Lepore.

from them, you lie low and observe them. As they round the bend, their faces turn white as chalk. After an instant of stunned silence, they point energetically and yell, "Flarg! Flarg!," then dash madly for the trees and clamber up. "What's this all about?" you wonder as you shuffle sideways to get a look at what scared them so: a huge hippopotamus charging toward them! Apparently, they had surprised it while it was grazing. They keep track of it carefully while up in their perch, frequently pointing to it and saying, "Flarg." After it's gone, they creep down and continue on their way. You follow along behind for the remainder of the day. (They notice you but don't seem to care.) Whenever a hippo is in view, whether it be swimming, walking, grazing, or charging, they point and say "flarg," but otherwise they never say "flarg."

Let's reflect for a moment on what you would make of these people. In particular, how would you interpret the word "flarg?" And what beliefs would you attribute to them?

The best interpretation of "flarg" is that it means "hippo," because they appear to use it to refer to hippos, and only to hippos. Understanding "flarg" to mean "hippo" makes their assertions turn out true. But why not interpret "flarg" to mean "biscuit" or "pencil" or "lily?" Because that would be extraordinarily uncharitable – you'd then be interpreting them as making false assertions every time they pointed and uttered "flarg."

What beliefs you attribute to them depends on their behavior. When they point and say "flarg," you understand them to be expressing their belief that there's a hippo. When they flee from a charging hippo, you understand them to believe that a hippo is charging, and that a charging hippo poses a threat. (You consequently attribute to them a fear of charging hippos.) When they climb up the tree, you understand them to believe that climbing a tree is a way to escape the threat. (You also attribute to them a desire to not be injured, or else their escaping behavior makes no sense.) When they climb down after the hippo is no longer in sight, you understand them to believe that the hippo is gone and no longer threatens them. You also attribute to them belief in all the obvious and relevant consequences of all the beliefs just mentioned.

Notice something important: all the beliefs we just mentioned *are true*. You don't attribute false beliefs to them. You would not attribute to them the belief that a ground squirrel is charging, nor the belief that the hippo approaches to invite them to dinner, nor the belief that trees are lethally toxic to the touch. Of course, you might find it necessary to attribute some false beliefs to them as you follow them around all day. For example, suppose you knew that a maimed and emaciated adolescent elephant was approaching unseen by the group. Recently its ears and trunk were, tragically, cut off by vicious hooligans, making it impossible for it to nourish itself. Consequently, from afar it looks very much like a hippo. The hunters notice it from afar, scream "Flarg!," and head for the treetops again. In this case, you'd attribute to them the false belief that the animal is a hippo. But notice that this false belief is *reasonable*. It makes sense given the true background beliefs you attribute to them about a hippo's appearance, along with the true beliefs you attribute to them about the observable properties of the animal in question.

Notice something else important: you also attribute a well-rounded, consistent, and coherent set of beliefs to them. Because you attribute the belief that a hippo is charging, you also attribute the belief that an animal is charging, that hippos exist, that hippos can charge, etc. Because you attribute the belief that trees are nontoxic, you *avoid* attributing the belief that trees *are* toxic, or the belief that trees are probably toxic, or the suspicion that they are toxic.

To sum up, we find ourselves interpreting others' beliefs as being mostly true, reasonable, and coherent. A thoroughgoing *principle of charity* informs our interpretation. We came to this conclusion by studying a simple example of what Donald Davidson calls "radical interpretation." Radical interpretation occurs when we need to, as they say, "start from scratch" in understanding others. This would happen if we knew neither what their words meant nor what they believed. The example about the hippos was like this.

That's all very interesting, but how does it apply to epistemology? The application comes in two stages.

First, at least in the central and most basic cases, we as interpreters must "take the objects of a belief to be the causes of that belief."

51

Of course, *that's* just a methodological statement about how interpretation must proceed: we must interpret beliefs as being mostly true. But Davidson says its significance goes far beyond that, because *the way an interpreter must understand belief is the way beliefs must be.* The content of a set of beliefs must mostly reflect what causes them. This doesn't guarantee that all beliefs are true. But it does guarantee that most beliefs must be true, so any particular belief is at least likely to be true. "Belief is in its nature veridical," as Davidson puts it.

Second, any being capable of thought is in a position to appreciate that belief is by nature veridical. You need only "reflect" on the nature of belief to accomplish this. This guarantees that all thinkers have available a reason for thinking that their beliefs are mostly true, creating a "presumption in favor" of each particular belief being true. And now the external-world skeptic is in trouble.

We might understand Davidson's basic argument like so:

1. If all thinkers are in a position to know that most of their beliefs must be true, then skeptical worries (about justification, at least) are utterly unmotivated. (Premise)
2. All thinkers are in a position to know that most of their beliefs must be true. (Premise)
3. So skeptical worries are utterly unmotivated. (From 1 and 2)

That's Davidson's main argument in "A Coherence Theory of Truth and Knowledge,"[1] but a couple other comparative points are worth mentioning. First, earlier we saw that Sellars thought the nature of concept and language acquisition guaranteed that you were a reli-

---

[1] That this argument embodies the "take-home lesson" of Davidson's paper is confirmed by Davidson himself in the "Afterthoughts" he included in his collection of epistemological essays, *Subjective, Intersubjective, Objective* (Oxford, 2001), 154–157. There he says that "the important thesis for which I argue[d] is that belief is intrinsically veridical," that his "emphasis on coherence was misplaced," that he should not have said he was offering a "theory of truth," and that the main upshot of his whole argument was that "the correct account of the foundations" of language and thought would prevent skepticism from even "get[ting] off the ground" in the first place.

able believer (§§8–9). Davidson's view resembles Sellars's in this respect: something about the nature of beliefs, concepts, and the like guarantees reliability. And both Davidson and Sellars expressed confidence that all believers could somehow appreciate this important fact, though in both cases it seems fairly clear that ordinary people do not *in fact* base their beliefs on any such fact or the sophisticated reasoning that reveals it.

Second, earlier we saw BonJour pose a dilemma to foundationalists who favored *the given* as the ultimate basis of knowledge (§10). BonJour's dilemma was that the given must be cognitive or noncognitive; but if it's cognitive, then, like a belief, it stands in need of justification; and if it's noncognitive, then it cannot justify belief; so either way, the given fails to solve the regress problem. Davidson poses essentially the same dilemma: either sensory experiences can, in virtue of their content, stand in "logical" relations to beliefs, or they cannot; but if they can, then they "may be lying" and so, like beliefs, we need a reason to trust them; and if they cannot, then although they might be able to "cause" beliefs, they cannot justify them; so either way, foundationalism fails to solve the regress problem and skepticism threatens. This perceived failure of experiential foundations leads Davidson to conclude that "nothing can count as a reason for holding a belief except another belief." And this motivates him to seek the response to skepticism we reviewed earlier, culminating in the argument 1–3.

Reference

Donald Davidson, *Subjective, Intersubjective, Objective* (Oxford, 2001), 154–157.

§ 12

Blending foundationalism and coherentism (Haack, "A Foundherentist Theory of Epistemic Justification")

Imagine two jurors, Miss Knowit and Mr. Not, sitting in judgment of Mr. Mansour. Both paid close attention throughout the trial. The prosecution made a conclusive case that:

- Mansour had a motive to kill the victim.
- Mansour previously threatened to kill the victim.
- Multiple eyewitnesses place Mansour at the crime scene.
- Mansour's fingerprints were all over the murder weapon.

The defense simply rested its case. They contested nothing, called no witnesses. Each juror believes that Mansour is guilty. And he is indeed guilty. Do they know he's guilty? Do they at least reasonably believe it?

Haack, Susan, "A Foundherentist Theory of Empirical Justification," pp. 283–93 in Louis Pojman (ed.), The Theory of Knowledge: Classical and Contemporary Readings (Belmont, CA: Wadsworth, 1999). © 1999 by Susan Haack.

Epistemology: A Guide, First Edition. John Turri.
© 2014 John Wiley & Sons, Ltd. Published 2014 by John Wiley & Sons, Ltd.

You might be thinking, "Of course they know! He is guilty, they believe he's guilty, and the evidence is overwhelming." But things aren't so simple. We've not yet said *why* each juror believes Mansour is guilty. Miss Knowit believes he's guilty because of the facts presented at trial. And she believes those facts because she paid careful attention. She also considered alternative explanations for the victim's death, but none was nearly as good as the explanation that Mansour did it. By contrast, Mr. Not disregards the facts presented at trial and never considers alternative explanations. Instead, he believes that Mansour is guilty because he looks suspicious.

So although Miss Knowit knows, Mr. Not does not. Indeed Mr. Not doesn't even reasonably believe that Mansour is guilty. Why the difference? Causation. The evidence causes Miss Knowit's belief, but mere suspicion causes Mr. Not's. Being presented with good evidence isn't good enough. The evidence must also cause your belief. Susan Haack makes the same basic point when she says that "justification is a double-aspect concept, partly causal [and] partly logical."

On Haack's view, your belief in Q is justified to the extent that it's caused by good evidence for Q. That sounds simple. But complexity lurks just beneath the surface. She introduces many technical terms. We'll cover the most important points one by one. To the extent possible, I'll relegate technical terminology to parenthetical sentences. In what follows, let "Q" abbreviate the claim that it's raining. And let's suppose that you believe Q.

Many things help cause your belief, but the only things that count as *evidence* for your belief are your sensory experiences, introspective awareness, memories, and other beliefs. These are all mental states of yours. Take the whole set of mental states that help cause your belief in Q. (Haack calls these your "S-evidence" for Q.) It will turn out that, on Haack's view, what causes your belief isn't exactly the same as what justifies it. But the two are closely related.

As already mentioned, your S-evidence for believing Q will include other beliefs, memories, experience, and awareness. First take the other beliefs that help cause you to believe Q. (Haack calls these your "S-reasons" for Q.) A belief is always a belief in some proposition or claim, such as the claim that *the weather forecast calls for rain,* or the claim that *people outside are carrying umbrellas.* (I use "claim" and "proposition" synonymously.) When you believe a proposition, we call that proposition your belief's *propositional content.* For simplicity, let's suppose that there are only two beliefs in your S-evidence. Put those propositions on a list.

1.   The weather forecast calls for rain.
2.   People outside are carrying umbrellas.

(Haack calls these your "C-reasons" for Q.) An important feature of claims is that they have *truth values*: they are either true or false. The things we just put on the list have truth value.

Now let's consider the experiences that help cause you to believe Q. (Haack calls these your "experiential S-evidence" for Q.) The content of sense experience differs greatly from that of belief. Sense experience includes colors, shapes, sounds, tastes, tickles, and the like. Call this *sensory content.* An important feature of sensory content is that it lacks truth value. Colors can't be true or false, shapes can't be true or false, and likewise for the other forms of sensory content. The same goes for any combination of them. Now it's uncontroversial that sense experience has sensory content. But does it also have *propositional content*? Haack joins Davidson in saying that it doesn't. This explains why the relation between sense experience and belief can't be "logical," but only causal (compare §11). Only items with truth values can enter into logical relations.

But even though sense experiences don't have propositional content, you can still frame propositions *about* your experiences. So when you feel water drops pelt your skin, it's true that *you're feeling water drops pelting your skin.* When you hear a pitter-patter on the window sill, it's true that *you're hearing a pitter-patter on the window sill.* And when you see water drops falling, it's true that *you're seeing water drops fall.* These claims about your experience *can* enter into logical relations.

But Haack focuses on a slightly different sort of claim about your experience. She characterizes it not in terms of what is actually causing it, but by what would normally cause normal subjects to have an experience with that sensory content – in short, what normally causes such an experience. With this in mind, let's add these claims to our list:

3. You're having the sort of tactile experience normally caused by water drops pelting the skin.
4. You're having the sort of auditory experience normally caused by hearing a pitter-patter on the window sill.
5. You're having the sort of visual experience normally caused by water drops falling.

(Haack calls these your "experiential C-evidence" for Q.) Any claim that gets on the list this way *must* be true, because this part of the list simply describes the experiences that do in fact cause your belief.

Haack treats memory and introspective awareness the same as experience. When a memory or episode of awareness helps cause your belief, we add to the list claims that you're having a memory normally caused by such and such, or an episode of awareness caused by so-and-so. (These also count as "experiential C-evidence.") For simplicity we'll omit memory and introspective awareness from the present example.

When we've completed the list, we have a complete account of the evidence that determines how well-justified your belief in Q is. (Haack calls it your "C-evidence" for Q.) All this evidence is *propositional* and so is fully capable of standing in logical relations to Q. This allows Haack's view to avoid what she and Davidson think is a serious problem facing foundationalism. Foundationalism requires non-propositional items, such as experiences, to justify basic beliefs. But non-propositional items can't logically relate to beliefs. Yet a logical relation is necessary for justification. So since experiences don't logically relate to belief, they can't justify belief. All they can do is *cause* belief.

What causes your belief determines what your evidence is for holding the belief. We've just explained how that works. But what determines *how good* your evidence is? Three things, which we'll examine now.

First, it depends on how strongly your evidence supports the belief. One way to understand this is to imagine the list we created being used as premises in an argument whose conclusion is Q. Supposing those premises are true, how likely is the conclusion?

1. The weather forecast calls for rain. (Premise)
2. People outside are carrying umbrellas. (Premise)
3. You're having the sort of tactile experience normally caused by water drops pelting the skin. (Premise)
4. You're having the sort of auditory experience normally caused by hearing a pitter-patter on the window sill. (Premise)
5. You're having the sort of visual experience normally caused by water drops falling. (Premise)
6. So it's raining. (From 1–5) [Remember, in the present context "Q" abbreviates the claim that it's raining.]

The argument is not logically valid. The premises' truth doesn't *guarantee* the conclusion's truth. But their truth does seem to make the conclusion *very likely*, so the argument is still logically strong. In other cases, the argument might be more or less strong, ranging from the logically valid at one extreme, to no support whatsoever at the other.

Second, it depends on how "independently secure" your other beliefs are that help cause you to believe Q (i.e. how independently secure your "S-reasons" are). For you to know Q based on the evidence, all the S-reasons must themselves be well-justified independently of their relation to Q. In the present example, this means that you'd need to be justified in believing 1 and 2, without relying on Q. We would then need to see what causes you to believe lines 1 and 2, respectively, compile a list of your evidence, and see whether it provides a good argument for 1 and 2. Presumably, your evidence for 1 would be a memory of the weather forecast, and for 2 a visual experience. But if your evidence for 1 and 2 was a mere hunch or testimony from a source known to be unreliable, then your belief in 1 and 2 won't be justified and you won't know Q.

Third, it depends on how comprehensive your evidence is. It must include all relevant information, or at least all the relevant information you're aware of. For instance, suppose you knew that a film crew was in the neighborhood using sophisticated equipment to make it look like it was raining for a scene. If you ignore this information and believe Q anyway, then you don't know Q. On the present view, "ignoring it" requires it to be causally irrelevant to your belief in Q. Otherwise it would be part of your evidence.

That completes the explanation of Haack's view. I'll note three other points before moving on.

First, Moore claimed that you must know all the premises of an effective proof (§2). But on Haack's view, the same is not true of your evidence. She says that you needn't even *believe* the premises about your experiences (or your memories or introspective awareness – in short, your "experiential C-evidence"). So in the present example you wouldn't need to believe premises 3–5. And if you don't need to believe them, you don't need to know them either, because knowledge requires belief.

Second, Davidson characterized the meaning of speech and the content of thoughts by reference to what usually causes such speech and thoughts (§11). Haack chooses to characterize the believer's experiential evidence by reference to what normally causes such experiences. And just as Davidson thought his characterization established a truth-connection between belief and truth, you might think that Haack's characterization establishes a truth-connection between experiential evidence and truth. But that all depends on how we understand "normally."

Third, Haack does not categorically claim that her epistemology is non-skeptical. She claims only that *if we are able to* reliably get at the truth, then it's by following the principles of justification she lays out.

§ 13

Foundationalism, coherentism and supervenience (Sosa, "The Raft and the Pyramid")

The great Scottish philosopher David Hume once argued that *ambiguity* is the best explanation for persistent disagreement between parties to a long-standing debate. Wrote Hume,

> From this circumstance alone, that a controversy has been long kept on foot, and remains still undecided, we may presume that there is some ambiguity in the expression, and that the disputants affix different ideas to the terms employed in the controversy.[1]

But in his paper "The Raft and the Pyramid," Ernest Sosa takes a different approach to the debate between foundationalists and

[1] David Hume, *An Enquiry Concerning Human Understanding* (1748), Section 8.1.

Sosa, Ernest, "The Raft and the Pyramid," pp. 3–25 in *Midwest Studies in Philosophy*, Vol. 5: Studies in Epistemology (Minneapolis: University of Minnesota Press, 1980); an appendix to this paper is drawn from Ernest Sosa, pp. 113–22 "How Do You Know?" *American Philosophical Quarterly* 11 (1974). © 1980 by Midwest Studies in Philosophy.

coherentists over the structure of knowledge. Rather than assuming the sides are talking past one another, Sosa thinks that each side has identified part of the truth, but missed out on the bigger picture. Sosa proposes a new view, inspired by developments in ethical theory, which aims to capture what is attractive in both foundationalism and coherentism.

A key idea in Sosa's discussion is *supervenience*, and in particular the supervenience of the evaluative on the nonevaluative. It is widely accepted that all evaluative properties supervene on non-evaluative properties. To understand why this view seems so plausible, let's first clarify what we mean by "supervene," "evaluative" and "nonevaluative."

Supervenience can be neatly defined. Supervenience is a relation between two classes of properties. Let "A-properties" and "B-properties" name two distinct sets of properties. The A-properties supervene on the B-properties just in case no two things can differ in their A-properties without also differing in some of their B-properties. Put otherwise, there can't be an A-difference without a B-difference. When the A-properties supervene on the B-properties, we call the A-properties *supervenient* and the B-properties *subvenient* or *base properties*. It is also implied that the A-properties obtain because of or in virtue of the B-properties.

It isn't easy to informatively and uncontroversially define what counts as an evaluative property, but the following should suffice for present purposes. Evaluative properties are ones that feature centrally in evaluation, as when we judge something to be *right, wrong, proper, improper, good, bad, worthy, unworthy*, or the like. Nonevaluative properties are the ones that feature in what we might call a "neutral" description of something. For instance, if I hold forth a spade and say, "this is a spade," then I have described it neutrally. I haven't evaluated it or, as they say, "passed judgment" on it, although I have clearly classified it by placing it in the category of spades. By contrast, if I say "this is a good spade," then I have gone beyond merely classifying it to evaluating it. I have described it, but not neutrally.[2]

---

[2]   I do not intend to equate describing something *neutrally*, as I use that term here, with describing it *objectively* or *factually*. For all I've said reality might not be neutral, and evaluative descriptions might express objective facts.

Now we can see why it is widely assumed that the evaluative supervenes on the nonevaluative. First, if a spade is a good spade, it isn't just a brute fact that it's good. There must be an explanation of why it's good. And the explanation certainly seems to be that it's good because of its durability, strength, balance, comfortable grip, and other nonevaluative properties. Of course, in some cases one evaluative property could explain another. For example, it might be a worthy spade to purchase because it's good, but then its worthiness would still ultimately supervene on its nonevaluative properties. Second, it also seems that two things identical in their nonevaluative properties must also be identical in their evaluative ones. Consider how absurd it would be to maintain that although two spades were *indistinguishable* in terms of their strength, durability, balance, and so on, one of them is good but the other isn't. Surely such an outcome is impossible.

So all evaluative properties supervene on nonevaluative properties. And epistemic properties, including justification and knowledge, are evaluative properties. So epistemic properties, including justification and knowledge, supervene on nonevaluative properties. Call this *the epistemic supervenience thesis.*[3]

Sosa calls epistemic supervenience the "lowest" or most basic grade of "formal foundationalism" about epistemic properties. Notice that here "foundationalism" means something different from what we've encountered thus far (e.g. §10). All that supervenience requires is a nonevaluative basis which guarantees that the belief is knowledge. This leaves open what that nonevaluative basis is. A higher grade of formal foundationalism accepts the epistemic supervenience thesis, and further maintains that the subvenient base properties "can be specified in general." The highest grade of formal foundationalism accepts the epistemic supervenience thesis, and further maintains that the subvenient base properties can be simply and comprehensively specified.

---

[3] For detail on variations of the epistemic supervenience thesis, see the entry on epistemic supervenience in *A Companion to Epistemology*, 2nd edn, ed. Jonathan Dancy, Ernest Sosa, and Matthias Steup (Wiley-Blackwell, 2010).

Interestingly, coherentism and foundationalism, as we've understood those views thus far, both count as forms of formal foundationalism. They disagree merely about what the base properties are. Coherentists say the base property is coherence among a set of beliefs. By contrast, foundationalists say it is *being grounded in perception, introspection, memory, or rational insight.*

Sosa argues that this way of looking at epistemic properties sheds new light on the debate between coherentists and foundationalists, and ultimately suggests a way beyond it entirely. Start with coherentism. Some antifoundationalist arguments used by coherentists start to look suspicious. For example, BonJour and Sellars both argue that a true belief's being reliably produced isn't enough to ground knowledge. The subject would also have to know that it was reliably produced, they argue, and this is part of what makes the belief count as knowledge (see §§8–10). But this is not a good criticism because it conflicts with the epistemic supervenience thesis. The subvenient base properties must be nonevaluative. But *knowledge* is an evaluative property, so demanding knowledge in the subvenient base is illegitimate.

Similarly, sometimes antifoundationalists argue that a belief doesn't count as knowledge unless you also know that you wouldn't easily be misled about the claim in question. But then your belief isn't foundationally justified after all, because it's partly grounded in other knowledge. But this isn't a good criticism because it too conflicts with the epistemic supervenience thesis. Demanding knowledge in the subvenient base is illegitimate.

Sosa also criticizes coherentism for reasons independent of supervenience. One problem especially stands out, namely, its inability to account for justified beliefs only minimally integrated into our overall set of beliefs. Imagine that you have a splitting headache. You believe that you have a headache, and you have several other beliefs that cohere with this, such as the belief that you're in pain, that someone is in pain, and that you're presently aware of a headache. This is a nice coherent set of beliefs, and it's very plausible that you're justified in accepting all of them. So far, so good. But now Sosa asks us to imagine the following modified case, in which everything about you, "*including* the splitting headache," remains the same, except that we replace the belief that you have a headache with the belief that you *don't* have a headache, replace the belief that someone is in pain with the belief that someone *isn't* in pain, and replace the belief that you're aware of a headache with the belief that you *aren't* aware of a headache. Your beliefs in the modified case are just as coherent as they were in the original case, so coherentism entails that this set of beliefs is equally justified as the set in the original case. But it seems obvious that this set of beliefs isn't justified.

Even though coherentism's prospects look bleak, Sosa doesn't conclude that foundationalism carries the day. Contemporary foundationalists typically claim that true beliefs based on perception, introspection, memory, and rational insight count as knowledge. So they typically include these sources when specifying knowledge's subvenient base properties. The problem is that this list lacks unity. It seems like a *mere* list of conditions. Why just those sources? Call this *the scatter problem* for foundationalism. The question becomes more pressing when Sosa asks us to imagine "extraterrestrial beings" whose basic belief-forming processes are nothing like ours, but nevertheless work well in their native extraterrestrial environments. The foundationalist might well have to add more principles to his list, making it look even more scattershot. It would be better, Sosa proposes, "to formulate more abstract principles that can cover both human and extraterrestrial foundations."

This brings us to Sosa's positive proposal. He draws inspiration from the revival of virtue theory in the field of normative ethics. According to this view, moral virtues are the primary source of ethical justification. An action is right because it is produced by morally virtuous dispositions, or excellences of moral character, such as honesty and courage. A morally virtuous disposition is a character trait that enables the agent to promote good outcomes, or at least outcomes good enough under the circumstances and compared to the available alternatives. Sosa draws an important lesson from this "stratification of justification."

> The important move for our purpose is the stratification of justification. Primary justification attaches to virtues and other … stable

dispositions to act, through their greater contribution of value when compared with alternatives. Secondary justification attaches to particular acts in virtue of their source in virtues or other such justified dispositions.

Sosa proposes that we adopt the same strategy for epistemic properties. Primary justification attaches to *intellectual* or *epistemic* virtues, "through their greater contribution toward getting us to the truth." Secondary justification attaches to individual beliefs for having been produced by the virtues.

What reason do we have to adopt this strategy? Why think that this *virtue epistemology* is plausible? Because it allows us to appreciate what is right in both foundationalism and coherentism while avoiding their drawbacks. First, consider coherentism. It is intellectually virtuous to accept a claim based on its coherence with other things we believe, because doing so reliably enough helps lead us to the truth. So believing based on coherence can enhance justification. But virtue epistemology doesn't commit us to the view that coherence is the *only* thing required to gain justification or knowledge. Next consider foundationalism. We saw that it faces the scatter problem, a problem poignantly illustrated by the possibility of extraterrestrials who reliably form beliefs in ways utterly alien to us. Virtue epistemology offers a simple and principled explanation of why both our beliefs and the extraterrestrials' beliefs are justified: they spring from intellectual dispositions that are, relative to their normal environments, reliable. Similarly, we can explain why beliefs formed through perception, introspection, memory, and rational insight all tend to be justified for us, despite their superficial disunity: our dispositions to trust these sources are virtuous.

It is crucial to Sosa's view that the intellectual virtues have a non-evaluative basis, primarily in terms of how well they promote the acquisition of true rather than false beliefs. This is crucial because without it virtue epistemology can't respect the epistemic supervenience thesis. And if it violates the epistemic supervenience thesis, then much of Sosa's motivation for it, at least, won't withstand scrutiny. An important question to consider, then, is whether the virtues do have a fully nonevaluative basis, or whether they instead have an irreducibly evaluative element.

References

David Hume, *An Enquiry Concerning Human Understanding* (1748).
Jonathan Dancy, Ernest Sosa, and Matthias Steup, *A Companion to Epistemology*, 2nd ed. (Wiley-Blackwell, 2010).

§ 14

Infinitism (Klein, "Human Knowledge and the Infinite Regress of Reasons")

Recall the epistemic regress problem that we began §10 with. If you supposedly know that A, then the question "How do you know A is true?" arises and threatens to renew itself repeatedly. The puzzle is to explain how, if at all, the pattern might unfold so as to vindicate the initial assumption that you actually do know that A is true. We noted that there are three possible patterns, which can be sorted neatly by asking two questions. *Does the pattern circle back?* If it does, then the pattern is circular. If it doesn't, then it's noncircular. Suppose we have a noncircular pattern. *Does it ever end?* If it doesn't end, then the pattern is infinite and non-repeating. If it does end, then the pattern is finite and non-repeating. Coherentists say that circular patterns enable knowledge, foundationalists say that finite patterns

Klein, Peter, "Human Knowledge and the Infinite Regress of Reasons," pp. 297–325 in James Tomberlin (ed.), *Philosophical Perspectives*, 13 Epistemology, 1999. © 1999 by Philosophical Perspectives.

do, and infinitists say that infinite patterns do. Skeptics deny that any such pattern can. Who's right?

We've reviewed defenses of coherentism and foundationalism. But we've yet to see a defense of infinitism. In "Human Knowledge and the Infinite Regress of Reasons," Peter Klein offers a spirited defense of infinitism. Klein focuses on the structure of "rational belief." I will continue calling it "justified belief." And I'll assume that what is said about the structure of justified belief applies equally well to the structure of knowledge.

But we should note one important qualification before proceeding. Klein usually speaks simply of "rational belief" and "knowledge," but he is careful to qualify this at crucial moments in the discussion. The qualification is that Klein's version of infinitism pertains to "the distinctively adult human type of knowledge." He concedes that there might be types of knowledge that don't require infinite and nonrepeating chains of reasons. Presumably, these are the types of knowledge possessed by human children and non-human animals.

Klein's main argument is an argument from elimination. We have three alternatives: foundationalism, coherentism, and infinitism. Two of them are false. So the remaining one is true.

1. Either foundationalism, coherentism, or infinitism is true. (Premise)
2. Foundationalism is false. (Premise)
3. Coherentism is false. (Premise)
4. So infinitism is true. (From 1–3)

Strictly speaking, there are four alternatives. I left skepticism off the list just now. Klein suspects that skepticism is false, but he doesn't think that it is obviously false, and further work remains to be done on the issue.[1] So a painstakingly complete version of the argument would adjust line 1 to include skepticism as a possibility, and the conclusion would then be that *either* infinitism *or* skepticism is true.

---

[1] See especially the article's last four paragraphs and footnote 60.

But for the moment let's set skepticism aside and focus on the aforementioned version.

The argument is valid. So if its premises are true, its conclusion must be true too. Are the premises true? Line 1 is true, as shown by our opening discussion, which featured the two questions used to exhaustively sort all chains of reasons.

Line 3 is true, Klein argues, because coherentism violates the "Principle of Avoiding Circularity" by endorsing "question begging reasoning." The Principle of Avoiding Circularity (PAC) forbids the use of Q itself as a reason for believing Q. This principle forbids not only straightforwardly obvious instances of question-begging, such as the reasoning "Q, therefore Q," but also less obvious instances, where Q turns up as a reason in its own "evidential ancestry" indirectly and at many steps removed. For example, suppose that your reason for believing Q is R_1, and your reason for R_2 is R_3, and your reason for R_3 is R_4, and so on, until we reach R1000, where $R_{1000} = Q$. The principle forbids this too.

Line 2 is true, Klein argues, because foundationalism violates the "Principle of Avoiding Arbitrariness" by endorsing arbitrary foundations. The Principle of Avoiding Arbitrariness (PAA) forbids arbitrarily accepting beliefs. A belief is arbitrary if no good reason is available to hold it. One way for there to be no good reason is for there to be no reason at all. Another way is for there to be a reason, but "one for which there is no further reason" available.

Klein sums up his positive case for infinitism like so:

> Someone wishing to avoid infinitism must reject either PAC or PAA (or both). It is the straightforward intuitive appeal of these principles that is the best reason for thinking that if any beliefs are justified, the structure of reasons must be infinite and non-repeating.

The notion of *availability* features crucially in Klein's position. He doesn't claim that you must actually have an infinite and non-repeating series of reasons in order to be justified. He claims that the series of reasons must be available to you. In order for the series to be available to you, the series must exist. Klein calls this "objective availability." But objective availability isn't sufficient. The series must also be "subjectively available to you." A series is subjectively available to you just in case each of its members is such that either you believe it, or you are disposed to believe it under the appropriate circumstances.

After making his positive case, Klein answers four objections. Let's consider them each. First is the finite mind objection. The objection is that humans have finite minds. And if humans have finite minds, then they can't possess an infinite number of reasons. So humans can't possess an infinite number of reasons. But if they can't possess an infinite number of reasons, then infinitism entails that humans know nothing. But we do know some things. So infinitism is false.

Klein responds to this objection by denying that infinitism entails that we know nothing. He offers several reasons for the denial, but the basic idea seems to be this. On the one hand, infinitism doesn't require that you *actually have* all the reasons. It requires only that they *be available* to you. On the other hand, you needn't actually be disposed to accept the reason in order for it to be available to you. You need only be disposed to accept the reason under appropriate circumstances. And there's no trouble supposing that we have an infinite number of dispositions.

Second is Aristotle's objection. We can understand the objection as follows. If some knowledge results from inference, then some knowledge doesn't result from inference. And if some knowledge doesn't result from inference, then not all knowledge requires infinite chains of reasons. So if some knowledge results from inference, then infinitism is false. And some knowledge does result from inference. So infinitism isn't true.

Klein objects that this argument is invalid. It doesn't follow that if some knowledge results from inference, then infinitism is false. Klein admits that some knowledge does not result from inference, if we understand "result" causally; or alternatively, Klein admits that some knowledge might not be based on reasons. But it doesn't follow that infinitism is false. For all that has been said, it might still be that the subject has available to her an infinite and non-repeating set of reasons. And Klein thinks it is plausible that this is indeed the case, at least if we're talking about distinctively adult human knowledge.

Another of Aristotle's objections goes like this. If infinitism is true, then it would always be sensible to ask for a further reason, no matter how many reasons have been given. But it isn't always sensible to ask for a further reason. So infinitism is false. Klein responds that the sense in which it "isn't always sensible to ask for a further reason" isn't the relevant sense of "sensible." It isn't always *practically* sensible, because sometimes it's obvious that the participants to the conversation all accept certain presuppositions, and to ask for a reason would flout the common presuppositions. But given the right context, it can be intellectually respectable to challenge those presuppositions, and in turn it can be *intellectually* sensible to ask for a further reason. This is enough to preserve infinitism from the objection, Klein thinks.

Third is the regress objection, which comes in two versions. The more plausible version goes as follows. For every contingent proposition, there is an infinite chain of propositions that could serve as a justification for it. So if infinitism is true, then every contingent proposition is justified for us. (A contingent proposition is one that is possibly true and possibly false.) But not every contingent proposition is justified for us. So infinitism is false. Klein rejects the argument as invalid. From the fact that there is an infinite chain of propositions that could serve as a justification, it doesn't follow that the infinite chain is *available* to us. We've been given no reason to accept the claim that if infinitism is true, then every contingent proposition is justified for us.

Fourth is the objection from skepticism. The objection is somewhat elusive, but the basic idea seems to be this. If infinitism is true, then we can never be conclusively justified in accepting anything. And if we can never be conclusively justified, then skepticism is true. But skepticism is false. So infinitism is false. Klein's response is twofold. On the one hand, as already mentioned, he doesn't think that skepticism is obviously false. Skepticism is a serious challenge, so even if infinitism entailed skepticism, that wouldn't be automatically a decisive objection. On the other hand, Klein rejects the claim that if we can never be conclusively justified, then skepticism is true. Justification is never conclusive; it is always only provisional. Justification is provisional if it might turn out that the reason for holding it isn't backed up by a further, accessible reason. Klein nicely encapsulates this last response by saying that for beliefs we can expect only "limited guarantees," not "lifetime guarantees." But surely an infinite number of limited guarantees would be good enough to ward off the skeptic. If so, then it appears to beg the question against (anti-skeptical) infinitism to claim that skepticism follows from the lack of conclusive justification.

§ 15

The Gettier problem (Gettier, "Is Justified True Belief Knowledge?")

In 1963, Edmund Gettier published a very short paper entitled "Is Justified True Belief Knowledge?" Its brevity belied its significance, for it went on to become arguably the most influential epistemology paper of the twentieth century. The paper poses a simple but dramatic challenge to the traditional view that knowledge is justified true belief. Call the view that knowledge is justified true belief "JTB."

Gettier produced two cases in which, intuitively, a person gains a justified true belief but nevertheless fails to know. If the intuition is correct, then the cases demonstrate that JTB is false, because justified true belief doesn't suffice for knowledge. Examples of this kind are called *Gettier cases*. Before Gettier's paper, many philosophers accepted JTB. After Gettier's paper, philosophers have nearly unanimously rejected JTB. Some philosophers continue to believe that

Gettier, Edmund, "Is Justified True Belief Knowledge?" pp. 121–3 in *Analysis* (1963). © 1963 by Edmund Gettier.

Epistemology: A Guide, First Edition. John Turri.
© 2014 John Wiley & Sons, Ltd. Published 2014 by John Wiley & Sons, Ltd.

justified true belief is *necessary* for knowledge, even though it isn't sufficient. What follows are renditions (not exact replicas) of Gettier's two cases.

Call the first case "COINS." Job and Dimitri both applied for the same job. Near the water cooler at lunchtime, Job overhears someone ask The Boss, "Who will get the job?," and The Boss says, "Dimitri is going to get it." This justifies Job in believing that Dimitri will get the job. Distraught, Job heads over to the snack machine, where he sees Dimitri count ten dimes in change and put them in his pocket. This justifies Job in believing that Dimitri has at least ten dimes in his pocket. Job then goes through this argument to himself, "Dimitri will get the job. And Dimitri has at least ten dimes in his pocket. So the person who will get the job has at least ten dimes in his pocket." As it turns out, Job is correct: the person who will get the job has at least ten dimes in his pocket. But that's because Job will get the job, and Job has at least ten dimes in his pocket.

Job is perfectly justified in believing both premises of his argument, and the premises obviously entail the conclusion, so Job is justified in believing the conclusion too. Moreover, the conclusion is true. So if knowledge is justified true belief, then Job knows that the person who will get the job has at least ten dimes in his pocket. But, Gettier urges, it's obvious that Job does *not* know this.

Call the second case "FORD." Sarah observes her trusted colleague, Mr. Nogot, arrive at work driving a new Ford. Nogot reports to Sarah that he is ecstatic with his new Ford. Sarah has no reason to mistrust him, so this justifies Sarah in believing that Nogot owns a Ford. She then goes through this argument to herself, "Nogot owns a Ford. And Nogot works in this office. So someone in this office owns a Ford." As it turns out, Nogot is uncharacteristically playing a practical joke on Sarah. He doesn't really own a Ford. But Sarah is still correct: someone in the office owns a Ford. Unbeknownst to Sarah, Mr. Havit, the newly hired clerk on his first day in the office, does own a Ford.[1]

---

[1] This version of the case is adapted from Keith Lehrer, "Knowledge, Truth and Evidence," *Analysis* 25.5 (1965): 168–175.

Sarah is perfectly justified in believing the premises of her argument, and the premises obviously entail the conclusion, so she is justified in believing the conclusion. Moreover, the conclusion is true. So if knowledge is justified true belief, then Sarah knows that the conclusion is true. But again, the problem is that it seems obvious that Sarah doesn't know this. This case is structurally similar to COINS, and poses exactly the same problem for JTB.

Call a character like Job or Sarah a *Gettier subject*. We can represent the challenge to JTB with a simple argument.

(Anti-JTB)

1. If JTB is true, then the Gettier subject knows. (Premise)
2. The Gettier subject does not know. (Premise)
3. So JTB isn't true. (From 1 and 2)

Of course, when we say "the Gettier subject knows," we don't mean merely that the Gettier subject knows *some* unspecified claim or other. Rather we mean that the Gettier subject knows the relevant claim in question. The relevant claim will vary from case to case. In FORD, the claim is that someone in this office owns a Ford. In COINS, the claim is that the person who will get the job has at least ten dimes in his pocket.

Gettier cases aren't found exclusively in philosophical writings. One can find them even in children's literature. For example, consider Arnold Lobel's short story "Spring," featuring Frog and Toad.[2] After a long winter, Frog visits Toad's house to rouse him from hibernation. "Toad, Toad, wake up. It is spring!" Frog announces. But Toad doesn't want to get out of bed. "Blah," Toad grumbles, "I am not here." Frog enters the house, pulls Toad out of bed, and encourages him to enjoy "the clear warm light of April," to "run through the woods and swim in the river," and to sit on the "front porch and count the stars." Toad grumpily declines, "I am going

---

[2] *Frog and Toad are Friends* (Harper Collins, 1970).

back to bed. Come back again and wake me up at about half past May." Frog sadly watches Toad settle back down into a deep slumber. Then he has an idea. He goes into the kitchen, locates Toad's calendar, and tears off the pages for November through April, revealing the page for May. Now consider how Lobel concludes the story:

> Then Frog ran back to Toad's bed. "Toad, Toad, wake up. It is May now."
>
> "What?" said Toad. "Can it be so soon?"
>
> "Yes," said Frog. "Look at your calendar."
>
> Toad looked at the calendar. The May page was on top. "Why, it *is* May!" said Toad as he climbed out of bed. Then he and Frog ran outside to see how the world was looking in the spring.

As he sits up in his bed, Toad is justified in believing that it is May, based on the calendar and Frog's testimony. And Toad, of course, knows that if it is May, then it is spring (in the northern hemisphere, where they live). So Toad is justified in believing that it is spring. But Toad doesn't know that it is spring![3]

References

Arnold Lobel, *Frog and Toad are Friends* (Harper Collins, 1970).

Christina Starmans and Ori Friedman, "The Folk Conception of Knowledge," *Cognition* 124.3 (2012): 272–283.

John Turri, "A Conspicuous Art: Putting Gettier to the Test," *Philosophers' Imprint* (2013).

Keith Lehrer, "Knowledge, Truth and Evidence," *Analysis* 25.5 (1965): 168–175.

---

[3] For a fascinating experimental study suggesting that people tend to attribute knowledge in Gettier cases, see Christina Starmans and Ori Friedman, "The Folk Conception of Knowledge," *Cognition* 124.3 (2012): 272–283. For a related but subtly different approach, see John Turri, "A Conspicuous Art: Putting Gettier to the Test," *Philosophers' Imprint* (2013).

§ 16

Some principles concerning knowledge and inference (Harman, *Thought*, Selections)

In the selections from his book *Thought*, Gilbert Harman proposes a necessary condition on knowledge, which he motivates on the ground that it can explain what goes wrong in Gettier cases. The condition Harman defends is

(P)   Reasoning that essentially involves false conclusions, intermediate, or final, cannot give one knowledge.

A plausible defense of principle P begins with the observation that Gettier cases always seem to involve at least two inferences. The subject gathers some evidence that justifies her in accepting an intermediate conclusion. The intermediate conclusion, combined with some elementary logical insight, then justifies her in accepting

Harman, Gilbert, Selections from *Thought* (Princeton: Princeton University Press, 1973). © 1973 by Princeton University Press, 2001 renewed PUP.

the final conclusion. It is remarkable that the intermediate conclusion is *false* in Gettier cases. A natural conclusion to draw from this is that principle P is the key to solving Gettier cases. This is Harman's view.

Principle P can handle the Gettier cases presented in §15. Recall what happens in COINS. Job overhears his boss say that Dimitri will get the job, and Job sees Dimitri put ten dimes into his pocket. This justifies Job in inferring that Dimitri is the person who will get the job and has at least ten coins in his pocket. This is the intermediate conclusion. From here Job infers the final conclusion that the person who will get the job has at least ten coins in his pocket. But Dimitri won't get the job. So Job's reasoning to the final conclusion involves a false intermediate conclusion, and principle P consequently predicts that Job doesn't know the final conclusion. Similarly, recall what happens in FORD. Sarah receives abundant evidence that justifies her in inferring that Nogot owns a Ford. This is the intermediate conclusion. And Sarah knows that Nogot is someone who works in her office. From here she infers the final conclusion that a person who works in her office owns a Ford. But Nogot doesn't own a Ford. So Sarah's reasoning to the final conclusion involves a false intermediate conclusion, and consequently principle P predicts that she doesn't know the final conclusion.

The fact that principle P makes accurate predictions about these Gettier cases provides some evidence that it is true. But Harman worries that it can't handle some Gettier cases. In particular, he worries there are Gettier cases that don't involve inferring the final conclusion from a false intermediate conclusion. The following example is such a case, modeled on one of Harman's. Call it "LONER."

Monty is a loner living on a Montanan hilltop. He rarely enters the civilized world, except for an occasional visit to the Missoula General Store to refresh essential supplies. Today he arrives at the store at the crack of dawn, and takes a moment to connect his laptop computer to the store's freely available WiFi network. He loads up the homepage of the ever-reliable and widely respected *Missoula Times*. The front page reports that the governor was assassinated early that morning. The reporter witnessed the governor being shot and dying on the operating table soon thereafter. The report's every word is true. Monty checks the websites of other well-respected news agencies, and they all report the same thing. Flabbergasted, he prints a copy of the story, closes his laptop, gathers his supplies, and heads off into the wilderness. He will not have contact with civilization, including Internet access, for months. Moments after Monty departs, the *Times* retracts its story about the governor's death, and puts up a new story claiming that the governor survived. All the other news outlets do the same. Fearing a general revolt among Montanan farmers and ranch hands, the governor's aides and elite elements in Montanan society promoted this fake story, feverishly proclaiming that the governor survived the attack and would soon make a full recovery. They also kidnap the eyewitness reporter, drug him, and convince him that he imagined the whole thing. The news outlets are duped by these convincing lies and report them as fact. By midday, all Montanans except Monty and the conspirators believe the governor is still alive.

Harman denies that Monty knows that the governor is dead. Monty shouldn't be able to know just because he "lacks evidence everyone else has," namely, the evidence that all the major news outlets retracted their earlier stories and now report that the governor is alive. Rather, Harman contends, Monty's knowledge is "undermined by evidence [he] doesn't possess."

Why might this cause a problem for Harman's view? Because LONER is a Gettier case, Harman thinks, and principle P can't explain why Monty fails to know. Monty's final conclusion is that the governor is dead. But on any natural understanding of the case, Monty doesn't reason his way to this final conclusion from a false intermediate conclusion. One natural way to understand the story is that Monty's belief is an immediate or non-inferential belief based directly on testimony. On this understanding, Monty's belief in the conclusion can't be based on a *false* intermediate conclusion, because it isn't based on an intermediate conclusion *at all*. So principle P can't get a foothold here to explain why Monty lacks knowledge. Another natural way to understand the story – which seems to be the one Harman favors – is that Monty's belief in the final conclusion is based on the *true* intermediate conclusion that a wide range of reputable news outlets are consistently reporting that the governor is dead. So again, principle P can't get a foothold.

An initially attractive option is to adopt an alternative principle to explain the original Gettier cases as well as LONER.

(N) One knows only if there is no evidence such that if one knew about it one would not be justified in believing one's conclusion.[1]

In COINS, the evidence would be that Job's boss wasn't telling the truth when he said that Dimitri would get the job; in FORD, it would be that Nogot was lying about owning a Ford; and in LONER, it would be that the news outlets all retracted their stories. But Harman rejects principle N because it rules out too much. Take your belief about your grade in a course. You scored an A on every assignment, so you know that you earned an A for the course. But suppose your teacher thinks you've earned a failing grade. This is evidence such that if you knew about it you wouldn't be justified in believing that you earned an A. So principle N predicts that you don't know that you earned an A. But if your teacher believes this only because he has mistaken you for one of your classmates who is failing, then it presumably doesn't rob you of your knowledge.

What distinguishes your belief about your grade from Monty's belief about the dead governor in LONER? Why do you know, but Monty doesn't? Why does the evidence you don't possess fail to undermine your knowledge, but the evidence Monty doesn't possess does undermine his knowledge? If we could answer these questions, then we will have gone a long way toward bolstering Harman's approach to explaining what goes wrong in Gettier cases.

Harman's solution is to supplement principle P with a principle concerning permissible inference.

(Q) One may infer a conclusion only if one also infers that there is no undermining evidence one does not possess.

---

[1] Harman doesn't label the principle "N." He doesn't label it at all.

An inference is permissible only if it passes the test set by principle Q (call it "the Q-test"). And it stands to reason that an inference will yield knowledge only if it is permissible. So all inferential knowledge must pass the Q-test.

Now let's return to LONER and see if the combination of principles P and Q succeeds in giving Harman the result he wants. One might argue that the combination succeeds roughly as follows:

1.   Either Monty passes the Q-test or he doesn't. (Premise)
2.   If he doesn't, then principle Q predicts that he fails to know. (Premise)
3.   If he does, then principle P predicts that he fails to know. (Premise)
4.   So either principle P or principle Q predicts that Monty doesn't know. (From 1–3)

Line 4 would suit Harman's purposes perfectly, and it follows validly from the premises. Are the premises true? Line 1 of this argument is unassailable: it exhausts the logically possible options. Line 2 is supported by the reasoning from the previous paragraph ("all inferential knowledge must pass the Q-test"), along with the assumption that if Monty does know, then his knowledge is inferential. Line 3 could be supported as follows. Suppose for the sake of argument that Monty passes the Q-test. He infers the intermediate conclusion that the news outlets are all reporting that the governor is dead, and from this he infers the final conclusion that the governor is dead. So, because he passes the Q-test, at each step he must also simultaneously infer that there is no undermining evidence he doesn't possess. But then his reasoning violates principle P because it involves a false conclusion, namely, the false conclusion there is no undermining evidence. There is undermining evidence he doesn't possess: the governor's aides all vehemently deny that he is dead, and the news outlets are about to retract the earlier stories and report that the governor isn't dead after all.

Even supposing that the argument 1–4 succeeds, one question remains. Harman's strategy is to handle Gettier cases by identifying principles of inference and inferential knowledge, which Gettier subjects fail to satisfy. This strategy assumes that all Gettier cases involve inference. But is this assumption true?

Many philosophers would deny the assumption. Consider this version of a famous example. Call it "BARN." Barney and his son are driving through the country. Barney pulls over to stretch his legs, and while doing so, regales his son with a list of items currently in view along the roadside. "That's a tractor. That's a combine. That's a horse. That's a silo. And that's a fine barn," Barney adds, pointing to the nearby roadside barn. It was indeed a fine barn Barney saw. But unbeknownst to them the locals recently secretly replaced nearly every barn in the county with papier-mâché fake barns. Barney happens to see the one real barn in the whole county. Had he instead set eyes on any of the numerous nearby fakes, he would have falsely believed it was a barn.[2]

Many philosophers accept two things about BARN. First, it is a Gettier case: Barney doesn't know that there is a barn at the roadside, even though his belief is true and justified. Second, Barney's belief is noninferential. If both of those claims are true, then Harman's strategy can't handle all Gettier cases. Are both claims true?

Reference

Alvin Goldman, "Discrimination and Perceptual Knowledge," *The Journal of Philosophy* 73.20 (1976): 771–791.

[2] The case is adapted from Alvin Goldman, "Discrimination and Perceptual Knowledge." *The Journal of Philosophy* 73.20 (1976): 771–791. Goldman attributes the case to Carl Ginet.

§17

The essence of the Gettier problem (Zagzebski, "The Inescapability of Gettier Problems")

Gettier cases follow a recipe. Start with a belief sufficiently justified to meet the justification condition on knowledge. Then add an element of bad luck that would normally prevent the justified belief from being true. Lastly, add a dose of good luck that counteracts the bad luck, so that the belief ends up true anyhow. Bad luck is canceled by good luck. This double-luck structure, according to Linda Zagzebski, is the defining feature of Gettier cases.

Zagzebski argues that any view which posits "a small degree of independence" between the justification and truth components of knowledge will suffer from Gettier-style counterexamples. More generally, if we define knowledge as "true belief + X," then if we allow that true belief and X are tightly but imperfectly related, then

Zagzebski, Linda, "The Inescapability of Gettier Problems," pp. 65–73 in *The Philosophical Quarterly* 44, 174 (Oxford: Blackwell Publishers, 1994). © 1994 by The Editors of *The Philosophical Quarterly*.

our view will face Gettier-style cases. It doesn't matter whether X is *justification, produced by reliable faculties,* or some other intellectually good feature of beliefs. Given a close but imperfect relationship, we can construct cases where the normal relation between X and true belief is undermined (bad luck), but, for some accidental reason unrelated to X, a true belief gets produced anyway (good luck).

Zagzebski says there are two ways to try to avoid the Gettier problem. On the one hand, we might say that justification (or whatever we substitute for "X") *guarantees* truth. That is, we could "give up the independence between the justification condition and the truth condition." On the other hand, we might say that justification and truth are "almost completely independent." This approach allows a very large "element of luck" to be present in cases of knowledge. Such an approach would simply classify Gettier cases as genuine, even if peculiar, cases of knowledge, because "knowledge is mostly luck anyway."

§18

Knowledge is an unanalyzable mental state (Williamson, "A State of Mind")

There is a strong tradition in modern epistemology of offering *analyses* or *definitions* of knowledge. An analysis or definition is considered successful if it provides an informative and noncircular set of necessary and sufficient conditions for knowledge. The conditions featured in this analysis or definition should be simpler and better understood than knowledge itself. (Hereafter I will speak only of an "analysis" rather than repeating "analysis or definition.")

The JTB theory of knowledge is an excellent example of an attempt at analyzing knowledge. In the form of a proper analysis, JTB says:

A subject S knows that proposition P is true if and only if:

(i)   S believes that P,
(ii) S is justified in believing that P, and
(iii) P is true.

Williamson, Timothy, "A State of Mind," pp. 21–48 in T. Williamson, *Knowledge and Its Limits* (Oxford: Oxford University Press, 2000). © 2000 by Timothy Williamson.

Epistemology: A Guide, First Edition. John Turri.
© 2014 John Wiley & Sons, Ltd. Published 2014 by John Wiley & Sons, Ltd.

On this view, knowledge just is justified true belief. Each of the three conditions listed, i–iii, is necessary for knowledge, and all three combined is sufficient for knowledge. To put the matter in more familiar terms, each of the three conditions is an essential component of knowledge, and when you add them together, you get knowledge. Knowledge is thus a composite state, built up from simpler components.

Most philosophers accept that Gettier's famous counterexamples (§15) conclusively demonstrate that i–iii are not sufficient for knowledge. That is, having i–iii doesn't guarantee that you know that P. The initial temptation was to suspect that Gettier's clever examples would lead to the identification of some fourth condition that could be added to i–iii, leaving us with a minor adjustment to the very popular JTB analysis of knowledge.

But that initial temptation now appears to have been an illusion.[1] The simplest revisions to JTB were met with simple variations on Gettier's examples. Revisions become more complex; more complex Gettier cases doomed them. People began to suspect that JTB was fundamentally flawed, which inspired radical departures from the view, including views that eliminated the justification condition (i.e. condition ii) altogether, and replaced it with conditions that featured causal or counterfactual relationships (see, e.g. §21). Others concluded that knowledge really didn't matter so much, and what we should really care about is justification (e.g. §37).[2]

In the selection "A State of Mind," Timothy Williamson contends that the long history of failure to resolve the Gettier problem, as it has come to be called, should make us suspect that knowledge can't be analyzed in the desired way. The pursuit of an analysis in the mold of JTB is "a degenerating research program." Williamson also attempts to accomplish at least three other things. He argues

---

[1] For a different view, see John Turri, "Is Knowledge Justified True Belief?" *Synthese* 184.3 (2012): 247–259.

[2] See also Mark Kaplan, "It's Not What You Know That Counts," *Journal of Philosophy* 82.7 (July 1985): 350–363, and Laurence BonJour, "The Myth of Knowledge," *Philosophical Perspectives* 24 (2010): 57–83.

that knowledge is a mental state (i.e. a state of mind), that knowledge's status as a mental state dooms to failure the traditional project of analyzing knowledge, and that knowledge is a very special mental state.

Let's begin with Williamson's case that knowledge is a mental state.

1. If knowledge closely resembles paradigm cases of a mental state, then unless a special reason disqualifies it, knowledge is a mental state. (Premise)
2. Knowledge closely resembles paradigm cases of a mental state. (Premise)
3. So unless a special reason disqualifies it, knowledge is a mental state. (From 1, 2)
4. No special reason disqualifies it. (Premise)
5. So knowledge is a mental state. (From 3, 4)

The motivation for line 1 is that it's just a special case of a more general principle, namely, "we expect a concept to apply to whatever sufficiently resembles its paradigms." The motivation for line 2 is that belief is a paradigm mental state, and knowing and believing resemble one another. Moreover, prior to reflection, we seem to count knowledge as a mental state alongside belief, desire, fear, and other paradigmatic mental states. The motivation for line 4 comes from considering several purported disqualifying reasons, none of which is ultimately convincing. One purported disqualifying reason is that all mental states are transparent, but knowledge is not transparent. To say that a state is *transparent* is to say that whenever you are in that state, you are in a position to know that you are in that state. Williamson rejects the claim that all mental states are transparent, pointing to *hoping* as a clear example.

> I believe that I do not hope for a particular result to a match; I am conscious of nothing but indifference; then my disappointment at one outcome reveals my hope for another. When I had that hope, I was in no position to know that I had it (p. 215).

The fact that knowledge isn't transparent shouldn't convince us that knowledge isn't a mental state.

Next let's consider Williamson's case that the traditional project of analyzing knowledge is doomed. If knowledge is a mental state, then it stands to reason that the concept of knowledge is a mental concept in the fullest sense of "mental." But the concept of truth isn't a mental concept, because it "makes no reference to a subject" (i.e. a thinker or mind). And if *truth* is nonmental, then any complex concept that has *truth* as a component won't be a purely mental concept. At best, a complex concept containing *truth* will be a partly mental concept. This applies to the complex concepts *true belief* (which is just the conjunction of the concept of truth and the concept of belief) and *justified true belief* (which is just the conjunction of the concept of justification and the concept of true belief): these are, at best, only partly mental concepts. But the concept *knowledge* isn't only partly mental; rather, it is a mental concept in the fullest sense. So the tradition of analyzing knowledge as *true belief + something* — no matter what that "something" is – is doomed to failure.

Finally, let's consider Williamson's case that knowledge is a very special mental state. Knowledge is special because it is the most general factive stative attitude. It will take some unpacking to appreciate exactly what this means.

Mental states include general moods and conditions, such as being bored, depressed, or confused. They include sensations, such as pain and dizziness. Finally, and most centrally for present purposes, they also include *propositional attitudes*, or *attitudes* for short. Belief, desire, and hope, among others, are attitudes. Having a "bad attitude" is also a mental state, but it is more like a mood than a propositional attitude, and we shouldn't confuse it with the attitudes that concern us here.

A propositional attitude takes a *proposition* or *claim* as its object. ("Proposition" is the standard philosophical term, but "claim" is more natural.) Examples of propositions include:

- Tony lied to Parliament
- Penicillin was discovered in the twentieth century
- Ruth Barcan Marcus is a brilliant philosopher

Call an attitude that takes the proposition that Q as its object *an attitude that Q*. (Remember, we're using "P" and "Q" to abbreviate declarative sentences.) For example, the proposition that *Tony lied to Parliament* is the object of my belief that Tony lied to Parliament, and it is likewise the object of George's hope that Tony lied to Parliament, and Cherie's fear that Tony lied to Parliament. My belief, George's hope, and Cherie's fear have a common content.

Some attitudes are *stative* whereas some are or involve *processes*. Having a belief that Q is a state, but forgetting that Q is a process. To know that Q is a state, not a process.

An attitude is *factive* just in case it's impossible to have that attitude toward anything other than a true proposition. Conversely, if Q isn't true, then you can't have a factive attitude toward it. Intuitive examples of factive attitudes include seeing, remembering, recognizing, being aware, and knowing. That is, intuitively, none of the following is possible: to see that it's raining when it isn't raining, to recognize that it's raining when it isn't raining, to be aware that it's raining when it isn't raining, to remember that it was raining when it hadn't rained, or, finally, to know that it's raining when it isn't raining. An attitude is nonfactive just in case it *is* possible to have that attitude toward a non-true claim. Nonfactive attitudes include believing, hoping, and considering. Each of the following is certainly possible: to believe that it's raining when it isn't, to hope that it's raining when it isn't, and to consider whether it's raining when it isn't.

So far we been talking about mental states. We can also talk about *the language* that we use to ascribe mental states. Call *the verb* (or verb phrase) that we use to ascribe a factive attitude a *factive mental state operator* or "FMSO" for short. For example, "knows" is the verb that we use to ascribe the factive attitude of knowledge, so "knows" is an FMSO; "remembers" is the verb that we use to ascribe the factive attitude of remembering, so "remembers" is an FMSO; "perceives" is the verb that we use to ascribe the factive attitude of perceiving, so "perceives" is an FMSO. Williamson also stipulates that an FMSO must be *semantically unanalyzable*. By this he means that there is no way to analyze an FMSO into component parts, such that the combination of those parts is (literally) synonymous with the FMSO. Related to this stipulation is Williamson's suspicion that the traditional method of analyzing knowledge is doomed to failure, although strictly speaking the stipulation goes well beyond the content of the suspicion.

Finally, let's introduce the technical symbol "Φ." "Φ" may be replaced by any verb or verb phrase. For example, we could replace "Φ" with verbs that predicate physical actions, such as "run" or "jump," and we could also replace it with verbs that predicate mental states, such as "believes," "wishes," "senses," "is aware" or "knows."

Three principles summarize Williamson's views here:

W1. If Φ is an FMSO, from "S Φs that Q" one may infer "Q."
W2. "Know" is an FMSO.
W3. If Φ is an FMSO, from "S Φs that Q" one may infer "S knows that Q."

W1 encapsulates the essence of a factive attitude. W2 encapsulates the intuitive thought that knowledge is factive. W3 encapsulates the thought that knowledge is the most general factive stative attitude. W2 and W3 together constitute Williamson's "thin" and "modest positive account" of the concept of knowledge – a kind of Williamsonian successor to the traditional approach to analyzing knowledge.

But why believe that knowledge is the most general factive stative attitude (i.e. why accept W3)? Because we need a good explanation of "the importance of knowing." Knowledge is important because factive stative attitudes matter to us. Factive attitudes help us acquire goods and happiness, avoid dangers, and well-plan our lives. In a word, they're very useful. The various factive stative mental attitudes are all ways of knowing; for example, perceiving and remembering are ways of knowing. We value these useful matches between mind and world. And knowing is the most general attitude in which mind matches world – the general factive attitude such that you bear it toward Q just in case you bear any factive attitude toward Q – which makes it important.

Two questions about this last part of Williamson's project suggest themselves. First, is knowledge the most general factive stative attitude? Might it not be possible, for example, to perceive that Q without knowing that Q? Second, is this the only or best explanation of knowledge's importance? Might there not be other and better explanations? An affirmative answer to either question would pose a serious challenge to some but not all aspects of Williamson's view.[3] It might upset his modest account of knowledge or his views about what makes knowledge special, although it wouldn't threaten his argument that knowledge is a mental state or undermine his critique of the traditional project of analyzing knowledge.

References

John Turri, "Does Perceiving Entail Knowing?" *Theoria* 76.3 (2010): 197–206.
John Turri, "Is Knowledge Justified True Belief?" *Synthese* 184.3 (2012): 247–259.
Laurence BonJour, "The Myth of Knowledge," *Philosophical Perspectives* 24 (2010): 57–83.
Mark Kaplan, "It's Not What You Know That Counts," *Journal of Philosophy* 82.7 (July 1985): 350–363.

[3]   See John Turri, "Does Perceiving Entail Knowing?" *Theoria* 76.3 (2010): 197–206.

§19

Closure, contrast and semi-skepticism (Dretske, "Epistemic Operators")

I regret that I attended a play last night. I also know that if I attended a play last night, then I existed last night. Do those two facts guarantee that I regret that I existed last night? Far from it. Not only do those two facts not guarantee that I regret existing last night, they don't even seem to raise the probability that I regret existing last night.

What does this example show? Propositional attitudes aren't closed under known entailments. To say that a propositional attitude is closed under known entailment is to say that the following conditional claim is true: if you have an attitude toward P, and you know that P entails Q, then you also have that same propositional attitude toward Q. This conditional is false for regret, as we already saw. It's also false for happiness, surprise, anger, sadness, and many others. Gilmore might be happy that his sister's broken arm is healing

Dretske, Fred, "Epistemic Operators," pp. 1007–23 in *The Journal of Philosophy* 67, 24 (Dec. 24, 1970). © 1970 by The Journal of Philosophy, Inc.

quickly, and Gilmore knows that if her broken arm is healing quickly, then her arm was broken, but he's not happy that her arm was broken. I might be surprised (or angry, or sad) that James won the competition, and I know that if James won, then someone won, but I'm not surprised (or angry, or sad) that someone won. Similar remarks apply to other mental states, such as perceiving or remembering. Your friend tells you, "A copy of *Philosophical Investigations* is on the desk," so you hear that a copy of *Philosophical Investigations* is on the desk, and you know that *Philosophical Investigations* is a subtle and enigmatic book, but you didn't hear that a subtle and enigmatic book is on the desk.

In "Epistemic Operators," Fred Dretske argues that knowledge isn't closed under known entailment (or, as Dretske puts it, the epistemic operator "knows" doesn't fully penetrate the known consequences of the proposition known). To say that knowledge is closed under known entailment is to say that the following claim is true: if you know that P, and you know that P entails Q, then you know that Q. Or more simply, knowledge is closed under known entailment. Call this *the epistemic closure principle*.[1] Here is one way to understand Dretske's argument against the epistemic closure principle.

1. Propositional attitudes aren't closed under known entailment. (Premise)
2. Knowledge is a propositional attitude. (Premise)
3. So knowledge isn't closed under known entailment. (From 1 and 2)

Line 1 is supported by numerous examples of the sort discussed earlier. Setting knowledge aside for the moment so that we don't beg any questions, there doesn't seem to be a single example of a propositional attitude that is closed under known entailment. Line 2 seems very plausible on its own and is also supported by Williamson's discussion in §18.

---

[1] There are many versions of the epistemic closure principle in the literature. Here we focus on the simple version in the main text.

It is tempting to think that even if knowledge isn't closed under known entailment, surely reasons are. To say that a reason R is closed under known entailment is to say that the following claim is true: if R is a reason for you to believe P, and you know that P entails Q, then R is a reason for you to believe Q. Dretske rejects this *epistemic reasons closure principle* too. Consider a recently calibrated and reliably produced thermometer whose readout says "21° C." Its readout tells you that the ambient temperature is 21° C. Moreover, you know that if the ambient temperature is 21° C, then it's guaranteed that the thermometer isn't falsely representing the temperature as 21° C. Should we conclude that the thermometer tells you that it isn't misrepresenting the temperature as 21° C? Certainly not – the thermometer isn't equipped to tell you any such thing. It equipped to tell you what the temperature is, not to tell you that it isn't misrepresenting the temperature. A similar point holds for practical reasons, or reasons for action. The *practical reasons closure principle* is: if R is a reason for you to A, and you know that your A-ing entails that you B, then R is a reason for you to B. (Here "A" and "B" name types of actions.) That *dogs need exercise in order to be healthy* is a reason for you to walk your dog, and you know that you are walking your dog entails that you have a dog. But that *dogs need exercise in order to be healthy* is clearly not a reason for you to have a dog!

But why does it matter whether knowledge or reasons are closed under known entailment? Recall from §4 that Moore would have us reason like so:

1. If Moore knows he's standing up, then he must know the dream-possibility is false. (Premise)
2. Moore knows he's standing up. (Premise)
3. So he knows the dream-possibility is false. (From 1 and 2)

whereas, the skeptic would have us reason like so:

1*. If Moore knows he's standing up, then he must know the dream-possibility is false. (Premise)

2*. Moore doesn't know the dream-possibility is false. (Premise)
3*. So Moore doesn't know he's standing up. (From 1* and 2*)

When deciding who gets the better of this exchange, it seems initially that the whole question boils down to whether it's more reasonable to accept 2 or 2*. Dretske disagrees. Dretske's response to the apparent standoff is to accept *both* 2 *and* 2*. How can he do that? By rejecting the premise the arguments share in common, namely, that if Moore knows he standing up, then he must know the dream-possibility is false. Once we're convinced that the epistemic closure principle is false, we can in good conscience reject that shared premise. Moore is right about what he does know, the skeptic is right about what Moore doesn't know, and it's a mistake to think there's any conflict between those two claims.

Dretske also makes an ingenious positive proposal about how to best understand knowledge. The basic idea is that knowledge is a contrastive state. A full and proper description of your knowledge wouldn't just be "You know that P" but instead "You know that P *rather than* Q," where "Q" names a salient contrast class, or as Dretske puts it, a "range of relevant alternatives." Dretske's view is often described as a "relevant alternatives theory," but a better name is *epistemic contrastivism*.[2] Returning to the dispute between Moore and the skeptic, with this contrastivist theory of knowledge in hand, Dretske could diagnose the disagreement as merely apparent. Moore knows that he's standing up *rather than sitting down*. But Moore does *not* know that he's standing up *rather than merely dreaming that he's standing up*.

A vivid example ties together all the features of Dretske's view.

> You take your son to the zoo, see several zebras, and, when questioned by your son, tell him they are zebras. Do you know they are zebras? Well, most of us would have little hesitation in saying that we

---

[2] For a recent and wide-ranging defense of epistemic contrastivism, see Jonathan Schaffer, "Contrastive Knowledge," in *Oxford Studies in Epistemology*, Vol. 1. Edited by John Hawthorne and Tamar Gendler , 235–271 (Oxford University Press, 2005).

did know this. We know what zebras look like, and, besides, this is the city zoo and the animals are in a pen clearly marked "Zebras." Yet, something's being a zebra implies that it is not a mule and, in particular, not a mule cleverly disguised by the zoo authorities to look like a zebra. Do you know that these animals are not mules cleverly disguised by the zoo authorities to look like zebras? If you are tempted to say "Yes" to this question, think a moment about what reasons you have, what evidence you can produce in favor of this claim. The evidence you *had* for thinking them zebras has been effectively neutralized, since it does not count toward their *not* being mules cleverly disguised to look like zebras .... Granted, the hypothesis... is not very plausible, given what we know about people and zoos. But the question here is not whether this alternative is plausible, not whether it is more or less plausible than that there are real zebras in the pen, but whether *you know* that this alternative hypothesis is false. I don't think you do. In this I agree with the skeptic. I part company with the skeptic only when he concludes from this that, therefore, you do not know that the animals in the pen are zebras. I part with him because I reject the principle he uses in reaching this conclusion – the principle that if you do not know that Q is true, when it is known that P entails Q, then you do not know that P is true.

You know that it's a zebra rather than a giraffe (or an elephant, or a lion, or an alligator, and so on). But you don't know that it's a zebra rather than a cleverly disguised mule.

In what might be the most remarkable example of reality imitating philosophical fiction, *The Telegraph* (UK) ran an article in October 2009 entitled, "Gaza zookeepers draw crowds with painted donkeys after zebras die."[3] The article continues,

> A zoo in Gaza has painted two white donkeys with stripes in order to replace two zebras that died of starvation earlier this year during the

[3] For the full article and video of the cleverly disguised donkeys, see http://www.telegraph.co.uk/news/worldnews/middleeast/israel/6274874/Gaza-zookeepers-draw-crowds-with-painted-donkeys-after-zebras-die.html.

Israel-Hamas war. Israel restricts the importing of animals into Gaza, so the Marah Land Zoo's keepers covered the pair of donkeys in black and white stripes instead.

Mohammed Bargouthi, the owner of the zoo, said it would have cost $40,000 to smuggle… a real zebra into Gaza. So, instead, he used French-manufactured hair dye.

Mr Barghouthi's son, Nidal, said the two female donkeys were striped using masking tape and hair dye, applied with a paint brush.

"The first time we used paint but it didn't look good," he said. "The children don't know so they call them zebras and they are happy to see something new."

If Dretske's view is correct, then knowledge would be very similar to explanation. Explanation is also contrastive and not closed under entailment. To see that explanation is contrastive, suppose that you and Jane meet for lunch at the restaurant Thai Gardens. Jane is deciding between the vegan Pad Thai and the Pork Panaeng, when she announces, "I'll have the Pad Thai." Curious, you ask why she ordered that. She answers, "Because it's vegan, and I'm trying to keep to a vegan diet." That's a perfectly good explanation, clearly setting the Pad Thai apart from the other option it was being weighed against. But suppose that Jane had instead been deciding between the vegan Pad Thai and the vegan Panaeng, when she announced, "I'll have the Pad Thai." In that case, if you asked her why she ordered that, it would be no explanation at all for her to answer, "Because it's vegan, and I'm trying to keep to a vegan diet." This does nothing at all to set the vegan Pad Thai apart from the vegan Panaeng. This shows that explanations are sensitive to salient contrasts: a vegan dish is distinguished from a carnivorous dish simply in virtue of being vegan, but it obviously can't be distinguished from another vegan dish simply in virtue of being vegan. As Dretske puts it, if you change the contrast, you thereby "change what it is that is being explained and, therefore, what counts as an explanation."

We can work with the same example to demonstrate that explanation isn't closed under entailment. The fact that *Jane ordered the Pad*

Thai guarantees that *Jane ordered something*. But the explanation for *why Jane ordered something* is not going to be the same as the explanation for *why Jane ordered the Pad Thai*. That is, the explanation for why Jane ordered something isn't going to be that *the Pad Thai is vegan*. Consider how puzzled you'd be if you asked, "Jane, why did you order something?," and she answered, "Because the Pad Thai is vegan." Such a response would be ridiculous. Rather, the explanation for why Jane ordered something is likely to be that she was hungry, or that the server asked her to order, or that it would be rude to meet you for lunch but order nothing.

Dretske's view, thus, has at least two noteworthy virtues. On the one hand, it provides a novel and vigorous response to a formidable skeptical argument. On the other hand, it identifies (or, at least, purports to identify) deep and unexpected similarities between knowledge and explanation. Identifying such similarities between independently interesting and important phenomena is a theoretical virtue.

Reference

Jonathan Schaffer, "Contrastive Knowledge," in *Oxford Studies in Epistemology*, Vol. 1. Edited by John Hawthorne and Tamar Gendler, 235–271 (Oxford University Press, 2005).

§ 20

Closure, contrast and anti-skepticism (Stine, "Skepticism, Relevant Alternatives, and Deductive Closure")

Gail Stine thinks that the "relevant alternatives" view of knowledge is correct, so she agrees with Dretske (§19) about that. But she isn't convinced that we need to give up the epistemic closure principle in order to avoid skepticism, so she disagrees with Dretske about that.

There are five main features of Stine's view. First, her relevant alternatives theory of knowledge says: you know Q just in case you can rule out all alternatives to Q that are relevant in the context. Importantly, an alternative is relevant in a context "only if there is some reason to think that it is true." Second, she would prefer to retain the epistemic closure principle, if at all possible. The epistemic closure principle says: if you know that P, and you know that P entails Q, then you know that Q. Third, she thinks that the skeptic

Stine, Gail, "Skepticism, Relevant Alternatives and Deductive Closure," pp. 249–61 in *Philosophical Studies* 29 (Dordrecht, Netherlands: D. Reidel Publishing Co., 1976). © 1976 by *Philosophical Studies*.

is ordinarily wrong when he says that we "don't know" the things we typically take ourselves to know. Fourth, normally if you say that someone knows Q, then you are presupposing that the denial of Q – that is, not-Q – is a relevant alternative in the context. In virtue of this, if you say, for example, "Fred knows that Q," you thereby *suggest*, though you do not explicitly state, that not-Q is a relevant alternative. Fifth, you can know some claims without any evidence at all. In particular, if P is *not* a relevant alternative in the context, then you know not-P, even if you have no evidence for accepting not-P.

How does Stine make all these things fit together into a coherent whole? The best way to see how is to focus on her treatment of Dretske's famous zebra/mule case. Recall that Dretske says that if you went to the zoo, ordinarily you would know that the striped animals in the pen marked "Zebras" are zebras. You know this because ordinarily the relevant alternatives are that the animals in the pen are giraffes, or elephants, or lions, or some other animal typically found in zoos. You have conclusive evidence that these animals are zebras rather than giraffes (or elephants, lions, etc.), so we don't hesitate to attribute this knowledge to you. But suppose it became a relevant alternative that the animals were actually just cleverly disguised mules made to look just like zebras. You have no evidence for the claim that the animals are zebras rather than cleverly disguised mules, so you don't know that they are. In such a case, it would be false to say that you know the animals are zebras.

Suppose Dretske is right about this last point – that is, suppose he's right that in the odd case when it becomes relevant whether the animals are cleverly disguised mules, you don't know that they're zebras. This causes trouble for an anti-skeptical advocate of epistemic closure *only if* it shows that *in the ordinary case* you fail to know that the animals aren't cleverly disguised mules. And Stine denies that it shows any such thing. On her view, in the ordinary case, when you know that they're zebras, you know that they're not giraffes, and you also know that they're not cleverly disguised mules. Thus, she resists skepticism and preserves closure.

But wouldn't it sound odd to say, even on an ordinary trip to the zoo, that you "know that the animals are not cleverly disguised mules?" Yes, Stine agrees, it would sound odd. But a statement might sound odd for many reasons, and not necessarily because it's false. Sometimes a statement sounds wrong because it suggests something that is false, or because it is irrelevant, inappropriate, or misleading. Ordinarily, if we were to say that you know the animals are not cleverly disguised mules, it would suggest that *the animals are cleverly disguised mules* is a relevant alternative. But it isn't a relevant alternative, because we have no reason to think that it is true. So it sounds wrong because it falsely suggests that something is relevant when it's not. Moreover, because *the animals are cleverly disguised mules* is not a relevant alternative, you know, without needing any evidence, that the animals are not cleverly disguised mules. So despite the fact that it would sound odd that you know the animals aren't cleverly disguised mules, it's nevertheless literally true.

We're left with several questions about Stine's original and stimulating view. First, it's a centerpiece of her view that "the evidence picture of knowledge has been carried too far." Not only does she say that you know without evidence that irrelevant alternatives are false, so that you know without evidence that the animals aren't cleverly disguised mules, she also says that you know without evidence that the animals are zebras. She even goes so far as to say that if you "take [P] for granted in normal circumstances," then you do know that P in those circumstances. Is she right about the possibility and extent of such *baseless* or *nonevidential* knowledge, as we might call it? Second, Stine sometimes slides back and forth between denying that *having evidence* is required in order to know something, on the one hand, and denying that *producing evidence* is required in order to know it, on the other. But as we saw earlier in our discussion of G.E. Moore (especially §2), producing evidence might be much harder than merely having it, so we should be mindful of the distinction. Third, Stine sometimes slides back and forth between what is required to *have knowledge*, on the one hand, and what is required to "support a *knowledge claim*," on the other. (To make a knowledge claim is to claim that somebody knows a certain proposition.) But the requirements for having knowledge aren't guaranteed to match the requirements for adequately supporting a knowledge claim, so we should be wary of sliding back and forth between the two.

§ 21

Keeping close track of knowledge (Nozick, "Knowledge and Skepticism")

Just before 11 p.m. on December 8, 1980, John Lennon was walking toward his apartment building in New York City when a seriously disturbed young man, Mark David Chapman, approached him from behind and shot him four times in the back. Lennon died within minutes from the massive injuries he sustained. Chapman was arrested at the scene, charged with Lennon's murder, pleaded guilty, and is currently still serving a life sentence in prison. Chapman has since explained in great detail his motivation for murdering Lennon.

While there is little doubt that Chapman killed Lennon that night, there is even less doubt that *someone* killed Lennon that night. You needn't be a conspiracy theorist or harbor any doubt whatsoever

Nozick, Robert, "Knowledge and Skepticism," pp. 172–85, 197–217 in *Philosophical Explanations* (Cambridge, MA: Harvard University Press, 1981). © 1981 by Robert Nozick.

Epistemology: A Guide, First Edition. John Turri.
© 2014 John Wiley & Sons, Ltd. Published 2014 by John Wiley & Sons, Ltd.

about Chapman's guilt in order to accept the following conditional, which is certainly true:

(A) If Chapman didn't kill Lennon on December 8, 1980, then someone else did.

Any reasonable person who agrees that somebody killed Lennon that day will accept A, even those who accept Chapman's guilt. And yet the following conditional seems clearly false to all but the most ardent conspiracy theorist:

(B) If Chapman hadn't killed Lennon on December 8, 1980, then someone else would have.

In some ways, A and B closely resemble one another. They are both conditionals – that is, they are both "if … then … " statements. And they both express a relationship between the same two states of affairs, namely

- *Chapman's not killing Lennon on December 8, 1980,*

and

- *Someone other than Chapman's killing Lennon on December 8, 1980.*

Yet despite their similarities, A and B have very different meanings, because they express *different relationships* between those two states of affairs. This results in A and B having different truth conditions, and as things turn out, different truth values.

Statements like A are called *indicative conditionals*. Statements like B are called *subjunctive conditionals*. For either type of conditional, the if-clause is called its *antecedent*, and the then-clause is called its *consequent*. A distinguishing feature of subjunctive conditionals is that they feature "would" in the consequent. The relationship between indicative and subjunctive conditionals is a vexed and controversial topic that falls far outside the scope of this text.[1] But a few words about the truth conditions of subjunctive conditionals are in order.

A good way of proceeding in the present context is to ask, why does B seem false? Suppose, contrary to fact, that the world is the way that B's antecedent would have it. That is, suppose that Chapman hadn't killed Lennon. In making this counterfactual supposition, let's make no more changes than are needed to make the counterfactual supposition true. That is, make no more changes than are needed for Chapman to have not killed Lennon on December 8, 1980. Here we come to the crucial point: that minimal set of changes does *not* include someone else killing Lennon on that day – someone waiting in the wings, as it were, who beat Chapman to it, or acting as a "backup assassin" in case Chapman somehow failed. Rather, the minimal set of changes includes something much more simple and mundane: for example, that Chapman's gun malfunctioned, or that he dozed off and so missed his chance that day, or that he decided at the last second to not harm Lennon. In short, B is false because *the easiest way* for its antecedent to have turned out true is *not* a situation in which its consequent is also true.

By the same token, the following subjunctive conditional seems true:

(C) If Chapman hadn't killed Lennon on December 8, 1980, then Lennon wouldn't have been killed that day.

Conditional C seems true because the easiest way for its antecedent to have turned out true is a situation in which its consequent is also true. Remove Chapman's lethal actions, and Lennon lives.

Robert Nozick develops a theory of knowledge based on subjunctive conditionals. Subtleties aside, his basic proposal is to analyze knowledge as follows:

[1] For a detailed introduction on this and related issues, see Jonathan Bennett, *A Philosophical Guide to Conditionals* (Oxford University Press, 2003).

You know that P if and only if:

(1) P is true.
(2) You believe that P.
(3) If P weren't true, then you wouldn't believe that P.
(4) If P were true, then you would believe that P.

Nozick intends conditions 1–4 to be individually necessary and jointly sufficient for knowledge. Or to put the matter in more familiar terms: each of the four conditions is an essential component of knowledge, and when you add them together, you get knowledge. (See §18 for more on the analysis of knowledge.)

Nozick's proposal is orthodox in some ways and unorthodox in others. Conditions 1 and 2 of Nozick's analysis are orthodox. But the analysis doesn't mention anything about justification or evidence, which is unorthodox. Instead of viewing knowledge as a special kind of justified belief, Nozick views knowledge as a special "way of being connected to the world," as a "real factual relation, subjunctively specifiable," which he calls *tracking*. To know that P is to *track the truth of P*. Conditions 3 and 4 together spell out the truth-tracking component of Nozick's view, which replaces the traditional justification condition on knowledge. Nozick calls condition 4 the "adherence condition," and condition 3 the "variance condition." (Condition 3 is frequently called the "sensitivity condition" in the literature, and I'll use this terminology in what follows.)[2] "To know that *p* is to be someone who would believe it if it were true, and who wouldn't believe it if it were false."

Why accept Nozick's truth-tracking account of knowledge? Nozick presents two main reasons. Nozick's first reason is that it handles a range of standard Gettier cases (see §§15–17). To illustrate, reconsider the case FORD. Sarah observes her trusted colleague, Mr. Nogot, arrive at work driving a new Ford. Nogot reports to Sarah that he is ecstatic with his new Ford. Sarah has no reason to

---

[2] This is unfortunate, since Nozick himself used "sensitivity" to refer to the conjunction of adherence and variance (cf. p. 257).

mistrust him, so this justifies Sarah in believing that Nogot owns a Ford. She then goes through this argument to herself, "Nogot owns a Ford. And Nogot works in this office. So someone in this office owns a Ford." As it turns out, Nogot is uncharacteristically playing a practical joke on Sarah. He doesn't really own a Ford. But Sarah is still correct: someone in the office owns a Ford. Unbeknownst to Sarah, Mr. Havit, the newly hired clerk on his first day in the office, does own a Ford.

Intuitively, Sarah doesn't know that someone in her office owns a Ford. Nozick's account thus gives the intuitively correct verdict, because she doesn't satisfy condition 3 of Nozick's analysis, the sensitivity (i.e. the "variance") condition. To see that she doesn't satisfy the sensitivity condition, consider this subjunctive conditional.

(D)   If it were false that someone in Sarah's office owns a Ford, then Sarah wouldn't believe that someone in her office owns a Ford.

Given the way the case is described, conditional D seems clearly false. The easiest way for the antecedent of D to have turned out true would have been, say, for the clerk to have purchased a Honda rather than a Ford when shopping for a vehicle, or for the clerk to have started working in the office the following day.[3] But Sarah would still have believed that someone in her office owns a Ford, so the consequent of D would be false. That is, the easiest way for it to have turned out true that *it is false that someone in Sarah's office owns a Ford* – or, more naturally, for it to have turned out true that *no one in Sarah's office to own a Ford* – would not change the fact that Sarah believes that someone in her office owns a Ford. It wouldn't change that fact because it wouldn't have changed the fact that Nogot tricks Sarah into believing that someone in her office owns a Ford.

---

[3]   We would have to fill in further details of the story to make it perfectly clear what would be the easiest way to make the antecedent of D true, though the same is generally true for the subjunctive conditionals we encounter in everyday life. We could simply stipulate such details in FORD; I've made a couple natural suggestions in the text for how to do this.

Nozick's second reason is that his account strikes just the right balance between skepticism and anti-skepticism. On the one hand, Nozick claims that his account is appropriately anti-skeptical because it rules that we know most of the things we ordinarily take ourselves to know. For example, it rules that I know that I have hands, that you know that you're reading a book, and that Fred knows the black-and-white striped animals in the zebra pen are zebras. To see that Nozick's account does this, let's focus on your belief that you're reading a book. You know this because:

(Y1)   it is true that you're reading a book,
(Y2)   you believe that you're reading a book,
(Y3)   if you weren't reading a book, then you wouldn't believe that you were reading a book, and
(Y4)   if you were reading a book, then you would (still) believe that you were reading a book.

Why think that Y4 is true? Because in nearby possibilities where you continue reading a book, you're attuned enough to this fact to keep track of it, and so continue believing that you're reading a book. (There might be abnormal situations in which Y4 wouldn't be true, but it's worth focusing, at least initially, on whether Nozick's account gets the normal cases right, as it seems to do.) Why think that Y3 is true? This is usually where skeptical worries arise. But such worries are simply misplaced. To see why, we need only answer the question, what would be the minimal set of changes needed to make the antecedent of Y3 true? That is, what is the easiest way for it to have turned out false that *you're reading a book right now*? The answer is likely to be something simple and mundane: for example, you put the book down a moment ago to rest your eyes, or to answer the phone, or to get a glass of water. In such a case, you wouldn't believe that you were (at that very moment) reading a book.

On the other hand, Nozick claims that his account is appropriately skeptical because it rules that we don't know things that we ordinarily take ourselves to not know. In particular, it rules that we don't know that various clever skeptical hypotheses are false. For example, I don't know that I'm not merely dreaming that I have hands, you don't know that an evil demon isn't expertly deceiving you into thinking that you're reading a book, and Fred doesn't know that the animals in the zebra pen aren't mules cleverly disguised to look exactly like zebras. To see that Nozick's account does this, let's focus on Fred's belief that the animals aren't cleverly disguised mules. In order for Fred's belief to count as knowledge, Nozick's account requires the following sensitivity condition to be met: if it were false that the animals weren't cleverly disguised mules, then Fred wouldn't believe that they weren't cleverly disguised mules. Put more simply, and canceling out a potentially confusing double-negative, the sensitivity condition in this case is:

(F3)   If the animals were cleverly disguised mules, then Fred wouldn't believe that they weren't.

But this subjunctive conditional isn't true. If the animals were cleverly disguised to look exactly like zebras, then Fred would still believe that they weren't.

More generally, for any "carefully chosen" radical skeptical hypothesis, such as the dream-possibility and the demon-possibility, our belief that it is false will be insensitive. There simply "is no way we can know" that such things aren't happening, Nozick claims, and the fact that these hypotheses make us "uneasy" reveals that we intuitively acknowledge this. To assert, as G.E. Moore did (§4), that we do know that these skeptical hypotheses are false is a "suspicious" exercise in "bad faith" that is "bound to fail."

But if we don't know that the radical skeptical hypotheses are false, then how can I know that I have hands, and how can you know that you're reading a book, and how can Fred know that the animals are zebras? How does Nozick reconcile all of this? Following Dretske, Nozick denies the epistemic closure principle. Moreover, he offers the sensitivity condition on knowledge as an explanation for why the closure principle fails. Knowledge is closed under known entailment only if all its necessary conditions are closed under known entailment. But the sensitivity condition isn't closed under known entailment. So knowledge isn't closed under known entailment either.

To a large extent, one's estimation of Nozick's account will be determined by whether one agrees with Nozick that "it is pleasant to grant the skeptic a partial victory after all."

Reference

Jonathan Bennett, *A Philosophical Guide to Conditionals* (Oxford, 2003).

§ 22

Moore wins (Sosa, "How to Defeat Opposition to Moore")

In a broad sense of "possible", it seems possible that I am nothing more than brain in a vat, floating serenely in a nourishing amber liquid, hooked up to electrodes feeding me a constant flow of radically misleading sensory stimuli, the unwitting subject of an elaborate cognitive scientific experiment by an advanced species of extraterrestrials. If I were in such a situation, I wouldn't have hands. I would be a handless brain in a vat (a "BIV" for short). Call this the BIV-possibility. It is a skeptical hypothesis similar to the dream-possibility and the demon-possibility discussed by Stroud, Russell, and Moore (see §§1–4).

The BIV-possibility is reminiscent of the one depicted in the modern science fiction film *The Matrix*. The main differences are, first, that *The Matrix* isn't a perfect deception because there are occasional internal

Sosa, Ernest, "How to Defeat Opposition to Moore," pp. 141–53 in *Philosophical Perspectives* 13, Epistemology (1999). © 1999 by *Philosophical Perspectives*.

Epistemology: A Guide, First Edition. John Turri.
© 2014 John Wiley & Sons, Ltd. Published 2014 by John Wiley & Sons, Ltd.

signs of deception that the humans ensnared in *The Matrix* can detect, and second, that the humans in *The Matrix* still have bodies, including hands. By contrast, the BIVs are mere brains without appendages, and are perfectly deceived by their extraterrestrial captors.

The following trio of claims is inconsistent.

1. I know that I have hands.
2. If I know that I have hands, then I know that I'm not a handless BIV.
3. I don't know that I'm not a handless BIV.

At least one of these three claims is false. But which? The skeptic argues that since 3 and 2 are both true, 1 is false. Dretske and Nozick argue that since 1 and 3 are both true, 2 is false (§§19 and 21). Moore argues that since 1 and 2 are true, 3 is false (§4). Who is right?

In "How to Defeat Opposition to Moore," Ernest Sosa sides with Moore and against a growing trend to decry Moore's staunch and thoroughgoing anti-skepticism. Nozick in particular singles out the Moorean stance for criticism, labeling it a "suspicious" exercise in "bad faith" that is "bound to fail" (§21). Nozick opts for a sensitivity-based theory of knowledge, which motivates a rejection of 2, thus freeing him to embrace both 1 and 3. Nozick motivates his rejection of 2 by rejecting a more general principle from which 2 follows, namely, the epistemic closure principle, which says that if you know that P, and you know that P entails Q, then you know that Q.

Nozick's *sensitivity condition* on knowledge says that you know that P only if the following subjunctive conditional is true:

If P weren't true, then you wouldn't believe that P.

My belief that I have hands is sensitive because if I didn't have hands, then I wouldn't believe that I did. (If you're confused as to why this belief is sensitive, see §21 for an intuitive explanation of how to evaluate subjunctive conditionals.) And, of course, I know that my having hands entails that I'm not a handless BIV. But my belief that I'm not a handless BIV is insensitive because if I were a handless BIV, I would still believe that I wasn't.

Sosa denies that knowledge requires sensitivity. The sensitivity condition has at least two implausible consequences. The first is that it would prevent us from having second-order knowledge of a sort that we often have. (*Knowledge that you know something* is second-order knowledge; *a belief that you believe something* is a second-order belief.) Take any mundane sensitive belief, such as Angelo's belief, "I just finished brushing my teeth." (Let "Q" abbreviate this proposition that Angelo believes). Even by Nozick's lights, Angelo knows Q. Now suppose that Angelo also believes, "My belief that Q is true." This second-order belief is going to be insensitive. For if it were sensitive, the following conditional would be true:

> If Angelo falsely believed that Q, then Angelo wouldn't believe that his belief that Q is true.

But if Angelo is even "minimally rational and attentive," Sosa argues, then that conditional is going to be false, because any way of making the antecedent true will make the consequent false. If Angelo falsely believed that his belief that Q is true, then he would believe Q, for he isn't so inattentive as to think he believes Q when he doesn't. And if Angelo believed Q, then he would of course believe that his belief is true, for to do otherwise would be incoherent. So Angelo's second-order belief is insensitive, and the sensitivity condition implies that it doesn't count as knowledge. But, Sosa contends, it's totally implausible that Angelo could know *that Q is true* but be unable to know *that his belief that Q is true*. (Sosa's discussion here is subtle and somewhat terse, but he judges this to be a "conclusive" objection to the sensitivity theorist, so it's worth pondering carefully.)

The second implausible consequence is that the sensitivity condition would prevent us from having knowledge in the following sort of case, which I'll call "CHUTE". Ernie lives in a high-rise condo. On his way to the elevator from his condo, he drops a trash bag down the garbage chute. Ernie believes that the bag will soon reach the basement, and indeed it does, traversing the chute in short order, just as it always does.

Intuitively, Ernie knows that the bag will soon reach the basement. But Ernie's belief that it will soon reach the basement isn't sensitive. For if it had been false that the bag would soon reach the basement, then Ernie would still have believed that it would soon arrive. This is because if the bag had failed to soon reach the basement, it would have been because someone many floors down jammed the chute with an overstuffed bag of trash – a previously unheard of occurrence in this exceptionally well-maintained community of responsible citizens – and Ernie would have been unaware of this.

Sosa proposes an alternative condition on knowledge, *safety*, in place of sensitivity. The *safety condition* says that you know that P only if the following, different subjunctive conditional is true:

You would believe that P only if it were true that P.

Sosa actually proposes several different versions of safety for our consideration. One very promising alternative formulation, which I'll call the *weak safety condition*, says that you know that P only if:

Not easily would you believe that P without it being true.

The weak safety condition has at least two noteworthy benefits. First, it handles standard Gettier cases. The Gettier subject would easily believe P without it being true, so the Gettier subject doesn't know. Second, in good Moorean fashion, the weak safety condition doesn't prevent us from knowing that radical skeptical scenarios are false. Why? Because the truth of such scenarios would require the world to be radically different, and such radical differences would not easily occur. Since they would not easily occur, not easily would we falsely believe that they don't occur. *An awful lot* would have to change in order for us to *falsely* believe that we're not handless BIVs!

Related to its handling of skeptical possibilities, the weak safety condition also avoids the first implausible consequence of the sensitivity condition noted earlier. The sensitivity condition allows that

Angelo knows he just finished brushing his teeth, but prevents him from knowing that he's not wrong about having just finished brushing his teeth. This is a very odd result. By contrast, weak safety allows that Angelo knows both things. For just as he wouldn't easily be wrong about having just finished brushing his teeth, by the same token he wouldn't easily be wrong about his being right that he just finished brushing his teeth.

§ 23

The closure principle: dangers and defense (Vogel, "Are There Counter examples to the Closure Principle?")

In "Are There Counterexamples to the Closure Principle," Jonathan Vogel argues for three main points. First, the most serious challenges to the epistemic closure principle involve what Vogel calls *lottery propositions*. Dretske's zebra/mule case (§19) doesn't involve a lottery proposition, and so doesn't pose a serious challenge to the closure principle. Second, even if the closure principle fails in lottery cases, this won't, contra Dretske, help us handle Cartesian skepticism. Third, there are ways to interpret our intuitions about lottery cases so that the closure principle is preserved.

A lottery proposition has three essential features. First, although it is very likely to be true, it wouldn't be "abnormal" if it turned out to be false. Second, despite its high unlikelihood, we have statistical

Vogel, Jonathan, "Are There Counter examples to the Closure Principle?," pp. 13–27 in M. D. Roth and G. Ross (eds.), *Doubting*, (Kluwer Academic Publishers, 1990). © 1990 Kluwer Academic Publishers.

Epistemology: A Guide, First Edition. John Turri.
© 2014 John Wiley & Sons, Ltd. Published 2014 by John Wiley & Sons, Ltd.

evidence that there is a real chance that it could be false. Third, it is a member of a set of propositions such that (a) each member is roughly equally likely, (b) it would be arbitrary for you to accept one of them but not the others, and (c) accepting them all seems inappropriate.

Vogel calls these "lottery propositions" because the paradigm case is the proposition that you will not win the lottery (when you own a ticket in a large, fair lottery, whose results haven't yet been announced, and regarding which you have no inside information). In general, says Vogel, we tend to have the intuition that you don't know lottery propositions.[1]

Lottery propositions aren't restricted to their namesake. That is, they aren't restricted to propositions about lotteries, such as *my ticket is a loser*, or *you're not going to win the lottery*. Other examples include: I won't have a heart attack in the next 5 min, my car hasn't been stolen since I last saw it this morning, and I won't get a hole-in-one on the next par-3 hole I play in golf. Each of these propositions is highly likely, but it wouldn't be abnormal if it turned out to be false; we have statistical evidence that there is a small but real chance that it will turn out false; and it is a member of an appropriate set with features (a–c). This last point requires some explanation.

Take the heart-attack example. Let "H_0" name the proposition that I won't have a heart attack in the next five minutes, let "H_1" name the proposition that healthy adult 1 won't have a heart attack in the next five minutes, let "H_2" name the proposition that healthy adult 2 won't have a heart attack in the next five min, and more generally let "H_n" name the proposition that healthy adult n won't have a heart attack in the next five minutes. This gives us a set of related heart-attack propositions,

$$\{H_0, H_1, H_2, \ldots H_n\}$$

[1] For a study of people's epistemological judgments in lottery cases, see John Turri and Ori Friedman, "Winners and Losers in the Folk Epistemology of Lotteries," in *Advances in Experimental Epistemology*. Edited by James Beebe (Continuum, Forthcoming).

such that any two members of the set are roughly equally likely to be true. That is, for any two members of this set, *h* and *h**, the probability that *h* is true ≈ the probability that *h** is true. In short,

$$\Pr(h) \approx \Pr(h*)$$

If *h* and *h** are roughly equally probable, then it's clearly arbitrary to accept one but not the other. So it's arbitrary for you to accept H_0 but not accept H_1, H_2,…, H_n. You must treat them all similarly. To avoid arbitrariness, you must either *accept all* of the H-propositions or *accept none* of them. But accepting all the H-propositions seems unreasonable, so it seems that you should accept none of them.

Moreover, it seems plausible that if you shouldn't accept a proposition, then you don't know that proposition, even if it's true and you do accept it. So since you shouldn't accept H_0, you don't know H_0.

From this perspective, it's easy to see the deep relationship between heart attacks and the classic lottery case. Let "L_0" name the proposition that my ticket is a loser, let "L_1" name the proposition that ticket 1 is a loser, let "L_2" name the proposition that ticket 2 is a loser, and more generally let "L_n" name the proposition that ticket *n* is a loser. This gives us a set of related loser propositions,

$$\{L_0, L_1, L_2, …, L_n\}$$

such that any two members of the set are roughly equally likely to be true.[2] That is, for any two members of this set, *l* and *l**, the probability that *l* is true is roughly equal to the probability that *l** is true. In short,

$$\Pr(l) \approx \Pr(l*)$$

---

[2]   In a standard lottery case, each ticket is not just *roughly* but also *precisely* equally likely to lose. But since *precisely equally likely* entails *roughly equally likely*, this is not a problem. And presumably any tendency to deny knowledge in a lottery case would persist if we found out that the tickets weren't all *precisely* equally likely to lose but were instead *roughly* equally likely to lose, within a *very* small interval, say, within 0.000000001.

In light of their equiprobability, you must treat all the loser propositions similarly. So since you can't sensibly accept them all, you must accept none of them, and thus you shouldn't accept that your own ticket is a loser. And if you shouldn't accept it, then you don't know it.

The most serious challenges to the epistemic closure principle, Vogel claims, feature lottery propositions. Recall that epistemic closure says that if you know that P, and you know that P guarantees Q, then you know that Q. The challenge, as Vogel sees it, is that we ordinarily take ourselves to know many things that obviously entail lottery propositions, yet it seems that we can't know these lottery propositions. Vogel has in mind examples of the following sort.

I know that I can't afford a $5,000,000 private jet. After all, my bank account and assets are far from adequate, and there's no prospect of financing it because I earn a professor's salary. I also know that if I can't afford a $5,000,000 private jet, then I haven't just unexpectedly inherited a vast fortune from an unknown relative. (Let's just stipulate that *a vast fortune* is greater than $10,000,000, after all taxes, encumbrances, etc., are handled.) But, intuitively at least, I *don't* know that I haven't just inherited a vast fortune. (How could I know such a thing?) Yet we would expect exactly the opposite if epistemic closure were true.

To substantiate this last point, consider the following, where "A" abbreviates the proposition that I can't afford the jet, and "F" the proposition that I haven't inherited a vast fortune.

1. I know that A.
2. I know that A guarantees F.

Now if the epistemic closure principle were true, then it would also be true that

3. If I know that that A, and I know that A guarantees F, then I know that F.[3]

---

[3] Here we set aside quibbles about how best to formulate the closure principle and focus simply on the most straightforward version.

And from 1–3, it obviously follows that

4.   I know that F.

But as we have already said, 4 is counterintuitive.

The proposition *I haven't just inherited a vast fortune* is a lottery proposition. First, despite its extremely high probability, it wouldn't be *abnormal* if it turned out to be false. Second, there is a statistical chance that any one of us has just been the beneficiary of such a ser-endipitous bequest. Third, it would be arbitrary for me to deny that I just inherited a vast fortune, but not deny that others just inherited a vast fortune. After all, I have no evidence that I'm any less likely to inherit a vast fortune than anyone else is.

Now return to Dretske's zebra/mule case. You're viewing the black-and-white striped equine animals in the zoo exhibit marked "Zebra." We're inclined to say that you know that the animals are zebras. And of course you know that if they're zebras, then they aren't mules cleverly disguised to look just like zebras. Nevertheless, Dretske says, you don't know that the animals aren't cleverly dis-guised mules.

Vogel rejects this verdict. If you really do know that the animals are zebras, then that's because you have "background information" which enables you to know that "zoos generally exhibit genuine specimens" and that "only under the most unlikely and bizarre cir-cumstances, if at all, would" a convincing and undetected "substitution" of cleverly disguised mules for zebras occur. And since you have "no reason whatsoever to think that any such circumstances obtain," you can know *both* that the animals are zebras *and* that they're not cleverly disguised mules. Any background information enabling you to know that the animals are zebras will also enable you to know that they're not cleverly disguised mules. Indeed, it would enable you to know that they're zebras, in part, *by* enabling you to know that they're not cleverly disguised mules.

The proposition *the animals aren't cleverly disguised mules* isn't a lottery proposition. First, it would be abnormal if it turned out to be false – that is, it would be abnormal for cleverly disguised mules to be displayed in a zebra exhibit at a reputable zoo. Second, we don't have statistical evidence that such substitutions take place from time to time. Third, the proposition that they aren't disguised mules is not a member of a set of propositions with the relevant features. What would the set of zoo propositions be? By analogy with the heart-attack and lottery cases earlier, we would start by letting "Z_0" name the proposition that the animals in this zoo that look just like zebras aren't cleverly disguised mules. But it's difficult to see how to proceed from here.[4]

Similar remarks apply to the skeptical hypothesis that I'm nothing more than a handless brain in a vat, radically deceived by some evil genius (cf. §22). First, it would certainly be abnormal if that proposition turned out to be false! Second, we have no statistical evidence that sometimes people are ensnared and envatted. Third, the proposition that I'm not a handless brain in a vat is not a member of an appropriate set of propositions: in order for it to be, "I would have to be an indistinguishable member of a class of subjects of which it is known that at least one member is a brain in a vat (making it arbitrary for me to believe that I'm not such a brain)" (p. 294).

In light of these points, Vogel argues, *even if* epistemic closure fails in cases involving lottery propositions, simply denying epistemic closure isn't enough to overcome traditional Cartesian skeptical challenges. For those skeptical challenges don't involve lottery propositions, and we haven't been given "a convincing basis" that epistemic closure fails in cases that don't involve lottery propositions.

But are lottery cases genuine counterexamples to the epistemic closure principle? Vogel admits that it's tempting to conclude that they are, but he also thinks that there are alternative explanations of

---

[4] See footnote 12 of Vogel's paper where he describes how the Zebra case could be made more like a lottery case. We begin by asking, "Do you know that members of some college fraternity didn't steal the zebra last night as a prank, leaving behind a disguised mule?" Then we note that "there is some reason to think that successful, temporarily undetected college pranks are brought off from time to time." In light of this, you might not "be entitled to say that you know that there isn't a cleverly disguised mule before you." Vogel concedes that if the case is "properly filled out," then *the animals aren't cleverly disguised mules* could be a lottery proposition.

our intuitions about the cases, which do preserve epistemic closure. The alternatives posit that "some kind of shift takes place" between the circumstance where we have the intuition that, say, I know that I can't afford a private jet, and the circumstance where we have the intuition that I don't know that I haven't just inherited a vast fortune. There is never one *"fixed* set of circumstances" – there is "no *one* time" – where we have both intuitions. It is only by confusing intuitions had in different circumstances that we're led to think that closure fails. Our intuitions in any one circumstance don't conflict with the closure principle. We'll encounter related proposals when we discuss epistemic contextualism in §§47–49.

Reference

John Turri and Ori Friedman, "Winners and Losers in the Folk Epistemology of Lotteries," in *Advances in Experimental Epistemology*. Edited by James Beebe (Continuum, Forthcoming).

§ 24

Evidentialist epistemology (Feldman and Conee, "Evidentialism")

When Carl Bernstein and Bob Woodward were investigating the Watergate scandal in the early 1970s, their secret informant, Deep Throat, is reputed to have admonished them to "follow the money." Bernstein and Woodward did just that, and a rich tapestry of criminality and deceit continued unraveling, ultimately contributing to the downfall of Richard Nixon's presidency. When it comes to detective work, "follow the money" is good advice indeed.

Richard Feldman and Earl Conee advocate a similar position when it comes to forming justified beliefs, namely, *follow the evidence*. But whereas Deep Throat would presumably not have told Woodward and Bernstein follow *only* the money – things other than money were, after all, relevant to the central intrigues of Watergate –

Feldman, Richard and Earl Conee, "Evidentialism," pp. 15–34 in *Philosophical Studies* 48 (Kluwer Academic Publishers, 1985). © 1985 by *Philosophical Studies*.

Feldman and Conee go an extra step and say "follow the evidence, and *only* the evidence." For on their view, whether believing a proposition is justified for you is determined *entirely* by the evidence you have. They call this view *evidentialism*.

A couple clarifications about evidentialism are in order. First, Feldman and Conee cast the net of evidentialism broader than just belief. They generalize it to all "doxastic attitudes." There are three main doxastic attitudes: belief, disbelief, and suspension of judgment (also known as "withholding judgment"). To believe P is to accept that P is true, to disbelieve P is to accept that P is false, and to suspend judgment on P is the attitude you adopt when it's just unclear to you whether P is true or whether it is false. A familiar example might help clarify these attitudes. When it comes to the proposition *God exists*, theists believe it, atheists disbelieve it, and agnostics suspend judgment. Stated generally and precisely, evidentialism is the view that:

> You are epistemically justified in adopting a doxastic attitude toward a proposition at a certain time *if and only if* having that attitude toward that proposition fits the evidence you have at that time.

The "if and only if" indicates that Feldman and Conee are attempting to provide a necessary and sufficient condition for epistemic justification. (See §18 for more on what necessary and sufficient conditions amount to.)[1]

Second, what do Feldman and Conee mean by the qualifier "epistemic" in "epistemic justification?" There are two aspects to this. On the one hand, they clearly intend to distinguish it from moral, prudential, and legal justification. Moral justification pertains to whether an act is morally permissible, a status sensitive to factors such as the

---

[1] Strictly speaking, Feldman and Conee say things that indicate an even *stronger* characterization of epistemic justification, beyond the identification of a necessary and sufficient condition. They claim that epistemic justification is also *"determined by"* your evidence. But this subtle difference needn't occupy us here. For more, see my entry "Epistemic Supervenience" in *A Companion to Epistemology*. Edited by Jonathan Dancy, Ernest Sosa, and Matthias Steup (Wiley-Blackwell, 2010).

likely expected consequences of the action, the rights of other parties affected, and the intentions motivating the action; prudential justification pertains to how an action affects the agent's own interests and desires; and legal justification pertains to what the relevant laws forbid and permit within a jurisdiction. No doubt acts of cognition and inquiry can be morally, prudentially, and legally evaluated, but Feldman and Conee aren't concerned with any of that here.

On the other hand, it is natural to suppose that they're offering a theory of the sort of justification most closely connected to knowledge, and which features in the classic JTB theory of knowledge (see §§15–18), since they compare their account with other accounts of justification that are attempts to analyze the J in JTB. For example, they claim that evidentialism is "nearly equivalent" to a view of Roderick Chisholm's, which is a traditional view of justification. They also point out that evidentialism doesn't conflict with a view of Alvin Goldman's because Goldman isn't concerned with "the traditional concept of epistemic justification." And they respond to an objection due to Hilary Kornblith, on the assumption that Kornblith's objection is directed at "the traditional analysis of justification" (footnote 15).

Given all this, it might seem obvious that Feldman and Conee are offering evidentialism as an analysis of justification, in the JTB tradition. In the end, I think this is the best way to understand their presentation. Yet it's worth mentioning that at the very beginning of their article they say something that apparently conflicts with this interpretation. They say that their view is *not* offered as "an analysis," but rather "to indicate the kind of notion of justification that we take to be characteristically epistemic – a notion that makes justification turn entirely on evidence." This makes it sound as though they're simply *stipulating* a conception of a certain kind of epistemic merit, which they then proceed to defend from recent trends in epistemology. But if this were all they aimed to accomplish – that is, defending some stipulative definition – then their paper would hold little interest.

Feldman and Conee's argument in "Evidentialism" is defensive. They take evidentialism to be "the basic concept of epistemic justification," one that is neither "surprising" nor "innovative," and which has "the most initial plausibility." So, they reason, if there are no good objections to the view, then we should accept evidentialism as the correct view.

One objection they consider is that an attitude is epistemically evaluable only if it is voluntarily adopted, but evidentialism implies that some involuntarily adopted attitudes are epistemically evaluable, so evidentialism is false. An attitude is voluntarily adopted just in case it is "up to you" whether you adopt it, rather than being something that merely happens to you. Feldman and Conee concede that evidentialism implies that some involuntary attitudes are evaluable, but they deny that this is a genuine problem for their view. They deny that it's a genuine problem because we have reason to reject the general principle that an attitude is evaluable only if it is voluntary (call it "the voluntariness principle"). They give two types of counterexample to the voluntariness principle. On the one hand, they point to involuntary justified perceptual beliefs, such as when you spontaneously and involuntarily believe that the lights are on (when you're awake and alert in a well-lit room). On the other hand, they point to involuntary unjustified beliefs, such as the belief of a delusively paranoid man who just can't stop himself from believing that he's being spied on, no matter what the evidence. Feldman and Conee suggest that the voluntariness principle might seem plausible to us if we fail to distinguish between an *evaluation of an attitude* and an *evaluation of the person*. We don't praise you for believing that the lights are on, and we might not blame the paranoid man who can't help himself, but that doesn't prevent us from recognizing that your *belief* has epistemic merit, or that the paranoid man's *belief* has demerit.

Another objection is that an attitude is justified for someone only if having that attitude is within the power of a normal person, but evidentialism implies that at least some attitudes are justified despite not being within the power of a normal person to have, so evidentialism is false. Feldman and Conee again concede that evidentialism implies that some attitudes are justified despite not being within a normal person's power to have, but they deny that this is a genuine problem for their view. It is an "unfortunate" fact that sometimes meeting the relevant standard requires exceeding normal human limits, whether the standard is epistemological, academic, or artistic. Some teachers set a standard for an "A" in a course that is "unattainable for most students," and some standards of artistic evaluation are far beyond a normal person's capabilities. Feldman and Conee think that we shouldn't expect epistemic standards to differ from academic or artistic standards in this respect.

Another objection goes as follows. Suppose a person, call her Laura, is very sloppy and irresponsible in gathering evidence on a certain question, say, who was president of the United States in 2010. And suppose further that, as a result of her sloppy and irresponsible performance, Laura's evidence currently "fits" the claim that George W. Bush was president of the United States in 2010. Laura got herself into this position by reviewing notes from various news reports published in 2001, a dateline she repeatedly and carelessly transposed in her notes to "2010." And she otherwise leads a very sheltered life, never discusses politics, etc., so doesn't have the sort of counterevidence we would usually expect someone to have, to the effect that Barack Obama was president in 2010. Is Laura's belief that George W. Bush was president in 2010 justified? Of course it's not justified, the objection goes, because she's basing her belief on irresponsibly acquired evidence. But evidentialism implies that it is justified, because it fits her evidence. So evidentialism is false. In response, Feldman and Conee say that evidence can justify belief, regardless of how it was gathered. So in the example just considered, they would say that although Laura's sloppy evidence-gathering reveals an intellectual vice of hers, her belief is nevertheless justified.

Consider finally the following objection to evidentialism, which pertains to how *the basis upon which a belief is held* relates to justification. Imagine a juror, call him Jude, who has paid careful attention during the entire trial. The prosecution presented an overwhelming case that the defendant is guilty. Jude is aware of the prosecution's case in all its details and has no reason to mistrust any of it. The defense simply rested its case, having despaired of rebutting the prosecution. It seems obvious that *believing that the defendant is guilty* fits Jude's evidence, and that Jude is justified in believing that the defendant is guilty. So far, so good for evidentialism. But now add an unexpected twist to the case: despite all this powerful evidence and justification that Jude has, his belief that the defendant is guilty is based on something totally unrelated and ridiculous – a fortune-teller's vague prediction from years ago. Clearly, if Jude bases his belief on such rubbish, then his belief is unjustified. But his belief fits the evidence that he does have, so evidentialism implies that his belief is justified. So evidentialism is false.

In response, Feldman and Conee make an important distinction between *having justification to believe a proposition* and *having a well-founded belief in that proposition*. Evidentialism, as we characterized it earlier, says that having justification to believe a proposition amounts to having evidence in favor of believing it. But merely having the evidence and believing what the evidence supports isn't enough for your belief to be well-founded. A belief is well-founded only if the evidence you have supports holding that belief, *and* you form the belief *based on* the evidence. Feldman and Conee then use this evidentialist conception of well-foundedness to explain what's wrong with Jude's belief: Jude is justified in believing that the defendant is guilty, but Jude doesn't have a well-founded belief that the defendant is guilty. In fact, Jude's belief is ill-founded. The evidentialist has no trouble accommodating this fact.

Reference

John Turri, "Epistemic Supervenience" in *A Companion to Epistemology*. Edited by Jonathan Dancy, Ernest Sosa, and Matthias Steup (Wiley-Blackwell, 2010).

§ 25

Non-defensive epistemology (Foley, "Skepticism and Rationality")

Imagine that you're fascinated with tightrope-walking. You dream of staring down at the crowd of faces staring in amazement up at you as you slide along the high wire with ethereal grace. But you have no training in tightrope-walking, so it would be extremely unwise to just climb up and give it a try! So you decide to start training so that you can one day walk the high wire. You hire a coach and spend hours every day practicing in your backyard, on a wire stretched between two short poles. Over several months you become highly skilled and can traverse the rope hundreds of times without incident. You're a real expert now; further training is pointless. You're as ready as you'll ever be to walk the high wire.

Foley, Richard, "Skepticism and Rationality," pp. 69–81 in M. D. Roth and G. Ross (eds.), *Doubting* (Dordrecht, Netherlands: Kluwer Academic Publishers, 1990). © 1990 by Kluwer Academic Publishers.

Epistemology: A Guide, First Edition. John Turri.
© 2014 John Wiley & Sons, Ltd. Published 2014 by John Wiley & Sons, Ltd.

Or are you? If you're ready, then why have you been having nightmares, filled with grisly scenes in which you fall to your doom – twenty, thirty, forty feet and more? "That's why they invented safety," your friends remind you impatiently, "so that you can walk the highwire without fear of falling to your death!" "Of course," you think to yourself, "even if I do slip – which is unlikely with my skill – the net will gently corral me without incident."

Or will it? If you're so confident that the net will save you, then why are you beset by the unwelcome thought of the safety net failing at the moment you need it most, tearing apart as you hurtle through it to a very sticky end? In response, you decide to use a *double* net, one safety net atop another. "Surely that will put my mind at ease," you think. But then another thought grips you: what about the net's moorings? Will they hold? You could double-thread the net through the eyelets, and even double the number of eyelets. Right, that will work. But what about the posts into which the eyelets are bolted? Have them reinforced and set in concrete. And if the concrete cracks? Use the latest and greatest mix, blended with a space-age polymer that resists cracking even under the most extreme earthly conditions. "At last," you exhale, "I can rest assured that I won't be falling to my death."

Or can you? If you're so sure, then why does it keep occurring to you that someone might sabotage your well-laid plans? A malicious and ruthless saboteur could, just by nicking the wire and weakening the nets, send you careening to oblivion. "I'll hire the best security detail to foil any would-be saboteur," you resolve defiantly.

All this worrying and planning has left you frustrated and exhausted. But you're not done worrying yet. One last shadow of doubt crosses your mind, and it is an ominous doubt indeed. At first you dismiss it as silly. "It's pointless to worry about such things," you admonish yourself, "I could never guard against *that* possibility, so just ignore it." But you can't ignore. The seed of this doubt has penetrated deep, and its roots grown strong on the nectar of fear it has incited. Unable to bear it any longer, you ask yourself aloud, "What if … *I'm cursed*? Cursed so that no matter what precautions I take, I will – somehow, some way – end up plummeting to my death from the highwire?"

If you're ever going to achieve your goal of walking the high wire, then at some point you're just going to have to *trust* that your abilities won't fail, that the environment will cooperate, and that others won't conspire to ruin you. At some point it's rational for you to accept that you've done enough to prevent a terrible accident. And at some point it's irrational for you to continue letting these increasingly preposterous possibilities scare you into delaying action, at great expense to yourself. To live a healthy human life, you must learn to live with risk. You must accept that it isn't within your power to guarantee success. All you can do is to proceed in a way that, by your own lights, seems likely enough to be satisfactory.

Richard Foley argues that modern epistemology suffers from a defect analogous to the one manifested in this story about tightrope-walking. This defect is on display most dramatically in Descartes's response to skepticism. If only we were careful and thoughtful enough in our inquiry, Descartes claimed, each of us would be guaranteed to avoid error entirely, while at the same time grasping many of the most important truths. Descartes proposed a rule: accept a proposition if and only if you clearly and distinctly perceive its truth. Rigorous observance of this rule, he thought, enabled him to prove that God exists, that God is no deceiver, and thus that our cognitive powers and dispositions are reliable guides to the truth, at least if we're careful to try our best when exercising them. A rational belief *must* be true and amount to knowledge. And it is entirely within our power to proceed rationally. So it is entirely within our power to know. Thus, the skeptic is refuted. Dutiful intellectual effort guarantees intellectual success.

There is a glaring error here, as Foley sees it. It neglects an unavoidable feature of "the human condition," namely, that *there are no guarantees in life*. For any nontrivial endeavor, no amount of natural ability, training, precaution, effort, and cooperation will ever guarantee success. Inquiry is no different from tightrope-walking in this respect. Success is never entirely within our power to achieve. We're always at least partly at the mercy of forces beyond our control. Whether we succeed depends on many things that we

131

aren't responsible for. We can't ever fully control these things, and in many cases we can't even partly control them. Such factors include our native endowment, our upbringing and the quality of training we receive, environmental factors, and the actions of others, not to mention natural laws. An epistemology that neglects this basic fact of human life is sorely mistaken.

Call an epistemology that neglects this basic fact a *blinkered epistemology*. Blinkered epistemology tends to be "overly defensive." Overly defensive epistemologies are "intimidated" by the possibility of failure and offer misguided "guarantees" to stave off the discomforting thought of failure. Rationality can save the day. Descartes's epistemology is the most extreme example. He claimed that rationality guaranteed not only true belief, but also knowledge. Less extreme, though still blinkered, is the claim that rationality guarantees that you'll form mostly true beliefs. Less extreme still is the blinkered claim that rationality guarantees that you'll avoid massive error. Even less extreme is the blinkered claim that rationality guarantees that we are at least more likely than not to avoid massive error. Weakest of all is the blinkered claim that, at the very least, rationality does *not* make massive error likely.

In this context, a guarantee implies a necessarily true conditional: the claim *P guarantees Q* entails *necessarily, if P is true, then Q is true too*. (Alternatively and equivalently, *P guarantees Q* entails *it is impossible for P to be true, and yet Q be false*.) Applied to an example about rationality, the claim *being rational guarantees reliability* entails *necessarily, if you're rational, then you're reliable* (alternatively, it entails: *it is impossible for you to be rational and yet not be reliable*).

Foley advocates "non-defensive epistemology." A nondefensive epistemology claims that rationality offers no guarantees. There's not even a guarantee that being rational makes it more likely that you'll avoid massive error, or that being rational does not make massive error likely. It's possible that a perfectly rational thinker is wrong about virtually everything she accepts.

It is tempting to object along the following lines. Being rational is a good thing. But it wouldn't be good if it failed to provide even the weak, minimal assurance that being rational is not likely to result in massive failure. Surely, someone who fails massively exhibits some rational defect. Foley responds that "not every failure need be one of rationality." Failure might result from poor cognitive equipment, poor training, a hostile environment, sabotage, or sheer dumb luck. Those are all potential obstacles to success, and being rational doesn't guarantee that you'll overcome them, or even guarantee that you're more likely than not to overcome them. Indeed, this is one principal lesson of the extravagant demon-possibility (see §3). It's at least possible that an evil demon is watching over you, bent on deceiving you whenever you form beliefs rationally! (This is, in effect, an *intellectual curse*, analogous to the one contemplated in the aforementioned imagined tightrope scenario.)

As Foley sees it, there's no point in denying such possibilities. We must learn how to cope with them. Rather than weaving elaborate epistemological theories to obscure this vulnerability inherent to the human condition, we should accept it in a healthy way. And part of accepting it in a healthy way is to adopt a fitting conception of rationality.

Foley recommends an "egocentric" conception of rationality as a healthy response to this predicament. You are egocentrically rational to the extent that your beliefs are, or would be, "invulnerable" to "self-criticism" upon "the deepest reflection." You might still be massively wrong. But egocentric rationality requires not knowledge or true belief or even reliability. Rather, it requires only that the belief is *to your own deepest intellectual satisfaction.*

One important part of deep intellectual satisfaction is that your system of beliefs must be "self-referentially defensible," which means that by relying on those beliefs, and by using the methods you endorse, you would be able to coherently defend that system of beliefs. Such a defense would "beg the question," in the sense that, in defending the methods and beliefs, it employs those very same methods and beliefs. The defense rests on a "leap of intellectual faith" that can't be defended without taking another such leap of faith. This evinces no defect in such a defense, though, because any defense must ultimately beg the question in this way. And "some questions deserve to be begged."

It's a fair characterization to say that, on Foley's view, to be rational is to adopt procedures that, by your own lights, and to your own satisfaction, seem likely enough to succeed. What else should you do when faced with the question "How shall I proceed?" The only other option would be to proceed in a way that by your own lights, and to your own satisfaction, does *not* seem likely enough to succeed. And *that* certainly would be irrational.

It's important to stress that egocentric rationality is not the only intellectual good on Foley's view. You might be egocentrically rational even though you're massively wrong. You might have defective cognitive equipment, poor training, a dogmatic and obtuse sensibility, or an incredible run of bad luck. Those are all bad things, to be sure. But, Foley cautions us, they're not forms of irrationality.

§ 26

Reliabilism about justification (Goldman, "What Is Justified Belief?")

In "What Is Justified Belief?," Alvin Goldman offers a theory of justified belief. The theory is as brief as it has been influential: a belief is justified if and only if it is well-formed. Being well-formed is equivalent to being produced by a reliable cognitive process, Goldman thinks, so he contends that a belief is justified if and only if it is formed by a reliable cognitive process. This leads Goldman to label his view "Historical Reliabilism." It has since become better known as *process reliabilism*. Goldman's theory is designed to achieve several goals. I'll begin by explaining each of these goals. Then I'll explain Goldman's basic argument for process reliabilism.

Goldman's first goal is to reflect the "ordinary" view of justified belief. Goldman seeks to explicitly formulate the "ordinary standards"

Goldman, Alvin, "What is Justified Belief?" pp. 1–23 in G. S. Pappas (ed.), *Justification and Knowledge* (Dordrecht, Netherlands: D. Reidel, 1976). © 1976 by D. Reidel Publishing Company.

---

of justification, rather than to improve upon them or prescribe amendments to them. "Ordinary standards" are vague, so we should expect process reliabilism reflect this by being vague as well. At times, Goldman speaks as if his project were primarily psychological or sociological. For example, he says that he wants a theory that explains why we "count" or classify beliefs as justified and unjustified. If this were Goldman's project, then it would be pointless to object to his theory on the grounds that it *misclassifies* certain beliefs as justified or unjustified, so long as the "ordinary" view similarly misclassified them.[1] And sometimes Goldman responds to objections precisely along these lines: "What matters ... is what we *believe* ... not what is *true*."[2] But, by and large, process reliabilism has been treated as a philosophical theory about justification, rather than an empirical hypothesis about the psychology of epistemological judgments, even though Goldman himself is inconsistent on the matter.

Goldman's second goal is to provide a proper analysis of epistemic justification. A proper analysis provides a set of necessary and sufficient conditions that any possible belief would have to meet in order to be justified (see §18 for more on analysis). Process reliabilism is best understood as a combination of two principal theses:

(PR-N)   Necessarily, for every belief B, B is justified *only if* B is produced by a reliable cognitive process.

(PR-S)   Necessarily, for every belief B, B is justified *if* B is produced by a reliable cognitive process.

The "only if" in PR-N expresses a necessary condition (basically: reliability is a necessary condition for justification). The "if" in PR-S

---

[1]   By the same token, it would not count as evidence in favor of his view if it correctly classified beliefs as justified or not, so long as the ordinary view misclassified them.

[2]   Compare also one of Goldman's responses to an objection featuring lottery propositions: process reliabilism "is intended to capture our ordinary notion of justifiedness, and this ordinary notion has been formed without recognition of this kind of problem. The theory is not wrong *as* a theory of the ordinary (naive) conception of justifiedness" (footnote 10). (See §23 for more on lottery propositions.)

expresses a sufficient condition (basically: reliability is sufficient for justification). We can combine PR-N and PR-S by splicing together the "if" and "only if." The result is the basic, standard statement of process reliabilism:

(PR) Necessarily, for every belief B, B is justified *if and only if* B is produced by a reliable cognitive process.

PR does not reflect three features of Goldman's discussion. First, it ignores Goldman's distinction between conditionally and unconditionally reliable processes, and the related distinction between belief-dependent and belief-independent processes. These further subtleties are of secondary importance and typically don't figure into an evaluation of process reliabilism. (They're often ignored because they're irrelevant if process reliabilism is on the wrong track entirely, which most critics claim is the case.) Second, PR bypasses Goldman's talk of "base clauses," "recursive clauses," and "closure clause," since these important complexities that aren't essential to the discussion. (Goldman ends up stating his view in terms of necessary and sufficient conditions anyway.) Third, it neglects the provision that Goldman later adds to handle cases where counterevidence is ignored.

Goldman's third goal is to provide a "substantive" analysis of justification. A substantive analysis is one that analyzes justification without using any evaluative epistemic terms. Evaluative epistemic terms include "knows," "justified," "rational," "good evidence," "warranted," "plausible," "evident." By contrast, "belief," "reliable," "produced," and "cognitive process" are not evaluative epistemic terms. Process reliabilism can thus be viewed as an epistemic supervenience thesis of the highest grade: it specifies a simple and comprehensive set of nonevaluative properties that explain epistemic justification (see §13 for an explanation of supervenience).

Goldman's fourth goal – hinted at just a moment ago – is to provide an explanatory analysis, one that not only identifies the necessary and sufficient conditions of justification, but also reveals the "underlying source" of justification. By revealing the underlying source, the theory enables us to understand why justified beliefs are justified, and by the same token, why unjustified beliefs are unjustified.

Why think that process reliabilism is true? Goldman's reasoning proceeds in two steps. First, he presents numerous examples where it seems obvious that the belief in question is unjustified. In each of these cases, a "strange and unacceptable" cause produces the unjustified belief. From this he concludes that a correct theory of justification "must" place a "causal requirement" on justified belief. Second, he enumerates a variety of causal processes that correlate with justified belief, and a variety of causal processes that correlate with unjustified belief. He then notes two striking facts: the processes that correlate with justified belief are all *reliable*, and the processes that correlate with unjustified belief are all *unreliable*. A third striking fact is that not only do the *categorical* properties of justification and reliability seem to go hand in hand, so too does *the extent to which* a belief is justified seem to go along with *the extent to which* it is reliably produced: the more reliably produced, the more justified it seems, and vice versa. These striking facts can be well-explained by the hypothesis that a belief's justification is a function of how reliably it is produced, such that a belief is justified if and only if it is produced by a reliable process. In short, process reliabilism is perfectly positioned to explain these striking facts.

What sort of cognitive processes produce unjustified beliefs? Goldman lists: confused reasoning, wishful thinking, relying on emotion, relying on hunches, guessing, hasty generalization. The processes are also unreliable. What sort of cognitive processes produce justified beliefs? Goldman lists: standard perception (such as vision, touch, taste, and hearing), remembering, good reasoning, and introspection. These processes are also reliable.

By "cognitive process" Goldman means information-processing performed by the "internal equipment of the organism," which "maps" from certain inputs to doxastic outputs. The inputs are mental states of the organism, such as experiences, beliefs, or desires. The outputs are beliefs and disbeliefs. Here is an example of such a mapping. Normal humans have eyes, which pick up signals from the environment, and when this happens, the subject has a certain visual experience. Suppose it's a visual experience as of someone playing a violin. This prompts the person to believe that someone is playing a violin. In this example, the input is the visual experience, and the output is the belief. We'd say that this belief is *based on vision*, and we could characterize the overall cognitive process as *vision* or perhaps *trusting one's vision*. Here is another example. You seem to remember putting your keys on the kitchen counter, and this prompts you to occurrently believe that you put your keys on the kitchen counter. The input is the memory, and the output is the occurrent belief. The belief is *based on memory*, and the overall cognitive process is *remembering* or perhaps *trusting one's memory*.

By "reliable cognitive process" Goldman means a cognitive process that tends to produce true beliefs rather than false beliefs. How strong must the tendency be for a cognitive process to be reliable? Goldman declines to answer this question precisely, on the grounds that the correct answer is bound to be vague. But he does say that reliability doesn't require perfection: the tendency needn't be unerring to be reliable. At the same time, to have a tendency to produce true rather than false beliefs, the process must produce more true beliefs than false beliefs. So there is some vague threshold between 50% and 100% that is required for reliability. Goldman's discussion suggests that the threshold is much closer to 100% than 50%. So reliability requires succeeding at least most of the time, and perhaps the vast majority of the time, but not all the time.

A persistent criticism facing process reliabilism pertains to the *individuation* of processes. Take the earlier example involving the belief that someone is playing the violin. How broadly or narrowly should the relevant process be construed? I said that we might call it *vision*, but it's also a case of polychromatic vision, which is more specific than vision, since vision also includes monochromatic vision. It's also a case of perception, which is more general than vision. Polychromatic vision specifically might be more or less reliable than vision generally, just as vision specifically might be more or less reliable than perception generally. Suppose that these processes do differ in their reliability. The belief itself can only have one level of justification. Which level of reliability determines the level of justification? The *generality problem* for reliabilism challenges reliabilists to answer this question in a principled way. (Conee and Feldman press this objection in §24.)

It's worth noting one final feature of process reliabilism, which Goldman himself emphasizes. According to PR, in order for a belief to be justified, the believer needn't have privileged access to, or knowledge of, the fact that the belief is justified, or even any opinion at all about the factors that make the belief justified. After all, it is one thing for a belief to be reliably produced, but it is another thing for the believer to recognize or have an opinion about the way in which the belief is produced. Traditionally, epistemologists have tended to accept that if a belief is justified, then the believer must be in a position to know, or justifiedly believe, that the belief is justified. Goldman rejects this traditional view along with its access requirement. In favor of rejecting it, Goldman points to justified memory beliefs. Often times, "the original evidence" for a belief stored in memory has "long since been forgotten." If the stored belief was originally highly justified, then memory will preserve the belief and it will remain justified even if the believer has currently entirely forgotten how it was originally acquired. So long as the memory belief has an "appropriate history," Goldman thinks, it is justified.

§ 27

Reliabilism: a level assessment (Vogel, "Reliabilism Leveled")

Jonathan Vogel's paper "Reliabilism Leveled" wears its motivation on its sleeve. Its goal is to level reliabilism, to discredit it as a theory of knowledge. Note that this doesn't automatically conflict with Goldman's (§26) reliabilist theory of *justification*.

Subtleties aside, Vogel identifies reliabilism as roughly the view that knowledge "just is" reliably produced true belief. Put in the form of an analysis, the view would be:

A subject S knows that proposition P is true if and only if:

  (i)   S believes that P,
  (ii) P is true, and
  (iii) S's belief that P is reliably produced.

Vogel, Jonathan, "Reliabilism Leveled," pp. 602–23 in *The Journal of Philosophy* 97,11 (Nov. 2000). © 2000 The Journal of Philosophy, Inc.

Vogel identifies the following "principal motivation" for reliabilism. Truth is the one and only fundamental epistemic norm. And since truth is so important, we want beliefs to be "securely true."A belief is securely true to the extent that it is reliably formed, which strongly suggests that knowledge is reliably true belief. On this approach to knowledge, justification drops out of the picture entirely (unless it is supplemented with the view that justification is a function of reliability, as on Goldman's view).

Vogel distinguishes two basic versions of reliabilism. The two versions differ in their characterization of reliability. Let's begin with what Vogel calls *neighborhood reliabilism*. Intuitively, reliability comes in degrees. The apex of reliability is infallibility. A process is infallibly reliable just in case it meets the following condition: necessarily, if it produces a belief, then the belief is true. In other words, there is no possible situation in which the process produces a belief, and yet the belief is false. This amounts to an *unrestricted* guarantee that any belief produced that could possibly be produced by the process will be true. But infallibility isn't necessary for reliability. Otherwise reliabilism about knowledge would have dramatic skeptical consequences, because virtually none of our beliefs is produced by an infallible process. Neighborhood reliabilism defines a reliable process in terms of a *restricted* guarantee of truth. The mere possibility of failure doesn't preclude reliability because failure in some situations is irrelevant. The *irrelevant situations* are the "extraordinary or outlandish ones that we do not, and need not, care about."[1] (Perhaps the demon-possibility is irrelevant; see §3.) According to neighborhood reliabilism, a process is reliable just in case it meets the following condition: in all the relevant situations, if it produces a belief, then the belief is true.

Infallibility provides an unrestricted guarantee because an infallible process produces only true beliefs in *all* possible situations. Neighborhood-reliability provides a restricted guarantee because a

---

[1] This is difficult to reconcile with something Vogel says later when characterizing the "neighborhood" of worlds that the reliabilist is concerned with, namely, that the set of worlds "does not vary with ... pragmatic considerations." It is difficult to reconcile because what we do, or need to, care about *is* a pragmatic consideration.

neighborhood-reliable process produces only true beliefs in all *relevant* possible situations – in the relevant "neighborhood of possibilities," as it were.

Vogel calls the second version of reliabilism *counterfactual reliabilism*. Your belief that P is counterfactually reliably produced just in case it meets the following condition: if P weren't true, then you wouldn't believe that P. Counterfactual-reliability is equivalent to Nozick's *sensitivity condition* on knowledge. (See §21 for more on this condition, especially its truth-conditions.)

Vogel rejects both versions of reliabilism. He rejects counterfactual reliabilism because it makes it virtually impossible to have second-order knowledge. (Here Vogel's criticism of counterfactual reliabilism is virtually the same as one of Ernest Sosa's criticism of Nozick's sensitivity condition; see §22. Given the identity of counterfactual-reliability and sensitivity, this is not surprising.) To have second-order knowledge is to know that you know something. To see why counterfactual reliabilism precludes second-order knowledge, suppose you correctly believe, "I'm wearing clothes," and let "Q" abbreviate this proposition you believe. This belief of yours is counterfactually reliable because it meets the following condition:

If it weren't true that Q, then you wouldn't believe that Q.

Suppose further that you believe, "My belief that Q is true." This second-order belief is not going to be counterfactually reliable. For if it were counterfactually reliable, it would meet the following condition:

If you were to falsely believe that Q, then you wouldn't believe that your belief that Q is true.

But it is "hard to fathom" a situation where you *don't* believe that what you believe is true, when you consider the matter. So your second-order belief is counterfactually unreliable, even though your first-order belief is counterfactually reliable. And so according to counterfactual reliabilism, you know that you're wearing clothes, but you can't know that you know that you're wearing clothes. And this result will generalize to pretty much all of your first-order knowledge, making second-order knowledge virtually impossible. But, Vogel argues, it isn't that hard to gain second-order knowledge of such things. For example, it's very plausible that not only do you know that you're wearing clothes, but you know that you know that you're wearing clothes. Counterfactual reliabilism rules out too much – it places too strong of a condition on knowledge – and so it is false.

Vogel rejects neighborhood reliabilism for the opposite reason. He argues that it places too weak of a condition on knowledge, and thus incorrectly counts certain beliefs as instances of knowledge. The problem pertains to a process that Vogel calls *bootstrapping*, exemplified by the memorable example of Roxanne the gas-gauge reader. Roxanne drives her car a lot. She "implicitly" trusts that her gas gauge is reliable, although she doesn't know that it's reliable. When the gauge reads "F", Roxanne believes that the car's gas tank is full. She never uses another method to independently verify how much gas is in the tank. As it turns out, the gauge is extremely reliable at accurately representing how much gas is in the tank, so neighborhood reliabilism implies that when Roxanne believes, based on the gauge's readout, that the tank is full, she knows that the tank is full on this occasion.

Roxanne checks the gauge often. Each time she checks the gauge, she notes that it reads "F," which presumably results in her knowing that the gauge reads "F." She is, after all, highly reliable at detecting when the gauge reads "F." Moreover, each time she sees that the gauge reads "F," she forms the belief that the tank is full, which, as we already noted, is a highly reliable process and so results in her knowing that the tank is full. Additionally, each time, she puts those two pieces of knowledge together, to get the conjunction:

(R1)   On this occasion, the gauge reads "F" and the tank is full.

R1 is tantamount to:

(R2)   On this occasion, the gauge reads accurately,

so Roxanne can come to know R2. After many, many occasions on which she came to know R2, and no occasions where R2 wasn't true, Roxanne concludes:

(R3)   The gauge reads accurately all the time.

The inference from R2 to R3 is highly reliable, so Roxanne can know R3 in this way. And from here it is but a trivial inference to:

(R4)   The gauge is reliable.

Every step along the way has been highly reliable. So if neighborhood reliabilism were true, then Roxanne could come to know R4 along the lines just sketched.

But, Vogel objects, it is obvious that Roxanne can't come to know R4 in this way. She relies on the gas gauge's readings to determine whether the gas gauges's readings are accurate. From the fact that the gauge reads "F," she concludes that the tank is full, and then she relies on her (purported) knowledge that the tank is full to then conclude that the gauge reads accurately on this occasion. But surely she can't simply bootstrap her way like that into knowledge that the gauge is reliable!

There is nothing special about Roxanne's case. If neighborhood reliabilism were true, then bootstrapping would generally be a good way of coming to know that a reliable process is reliable. All you need to do is first use the process repeatedly to form the belief, "On this occasion, it's true that Q," note each time that the process indicated that Q was true, then put these facts together to deduce that the process has a great track record, and so is reliable.

§ 28

Against externalism (BonJour, "Externalist Theories of Empirical Knowledge")

BonJour argues that externalism about epistemic justification and knowledge is unacceptable and radically dissatisfying. BonJour presents his discussion as a critique of externalist foundationalist solutions to the epistemic regress problem (see §10 for more on this). But his critique is perfectly general, so I will abstract away from the details concerning foundationalism and the regress problem, and treat his discussion as a critique of externalism generally.

For present purposes, we can understand an externalist theory of knowledge as a theory of knowledge that incorporates an externalist theory of epistemic justification. Despite the fact that the title of BonJour's paper features "knowledge," justification is the primary

BonJour, Laurence, "Externalist Theories of Empirical Knowledge," pp. 53–73 in P. French, T. Uehling, Jr., and H. Wettstein (eds.), *Midwest Studies in Philosophy*, Vol. 5 (Minneapolis: University of Minnesota Press, 1980). © 1980 by *Midwest Studies in Philosophy*.

focus. So we need to first characterize externalism about epistemic justification.

Externalism contrasts with internalism. Internalism about epistemic justification says that *all* factors that help determine your belief's justification *must* be available or accessible from your first-person perspective. In short, all justifying factors must be internal to the believer's perspective. Externalism is the denial of externalism. If you're unaware of some factor and have no access to it, then that factor is *external to your perspective*. Externalism says that it's possible for some external factors to help determine justification.

Here is another way to think about the difference between internalism and externalism. Internalism and externalism agree that in order for some reason to justify your belief, you must be *appropriately related* to that reason. But what counts as being appropriately related? Internalism places a restriction on appropriate relations: you must be aware of – or, as BonJour says, have a "cognitive grasp of" – all appropriate relations: it must be "internal" to your perspective. Externalism denies that you must be aware of an appropriate relation: it allows that some could be purely "external" to your perspective.

We need to keep in mind a related but distinct issue that externalists and internalists might disagree about, namely, whether a purely external relation could *suffice* to justify a belief. This differs from the question whether an external relation could (merely) *help* justify a belief. (Compare: a financial decision might help promote a comfortable retirement, even though it doesn't suffice for a comfortable retirement.) For the most part, BonJour seems to interpret externalism as endorsing both of these claims: that an external relation could help justify a belief, and that an external relation could suffice to justify a belief.

To sharpen the issue even further, BonJour focuses on a specific version of externalism, reliabilism, which claims that a justified believer is "a reliable cognitive instrument" and that a justified belief is produced "completely reliably." For present purposes, then, let's understand the ultimate disagreement between BonJour and externalists to boil down to this question: supposing that a belief is completely reliably produced, does that suffice for the belief to be justified?

BonJour's strategy for answering this question is to produce highly specific test cases where a perfectly reliably produced belief is, intuitively, unjustified – in other words, refutation by counterexample. After several iterations and refinements to help make the case as fair as possible to the externalist, BonJour settles on this as the most probative test case:

> Norman, under certain conditions that usually obtain, is a completely reliable clairvoyant with respect to certain kinds of subject matter. He possesses no evidence or reasons of any kind for or against the general possibility of such a cognitive power, or for or against the thesis that he possesses it. One day Norman comes to believe that the President is in New York City, though he has no evidence either for or against this belief. In fact the belief is true and results from his clairvoyant power, under circumstances in which it is completely reliable (p. 369).

If externalism is true, then Norman's belief is justified. Is this the right verdict?

BonJour's claims that it is totally implausible that Norman's belief is justified. Why? Because "Norman's belief should be judged from Norman's own perspective," but from Norman's perspective it would just be "an accident that the belief" turns out to be true. And in order to be justified, it can't be, from the believer's perspective, a mere accident that it turns out true.

BonJour doesn't rest content with that line of reasoning, however, because it comes dangerously close to simply affirming "what the externalist wants to deny." Consequently, BonJour adduces two additional reasons for favoring internalism.

First, consider externalism about moral justification. Imagine an agent who is about to perform some action, but has "no belief at all about" the action's likely consequences. Suppose further that the action in question will, as a matter of fact, promote a very good outcome, indeed the best outcome of all the actions then available to the agent. The action could be anything – adopting a puppy, borrowing a library book, attending a meeting of the town council, etc. Is the action morally justified? "Surely not," BonJour says. Instead, the agent is "being highly irresponsible, from a moral standpoint, in performing the action in the absence of any evaluation of what will result from it."

Next, consider the relationship between rational action and epistemic justification. Suppose that Norman is just as described in the aforementioned case: he has a perfectly reliable clairvoyant belief that the President is in New York City, but he has no opinion or evidence about whether this belief of his is likely to be true, or any opinion or evidence about the possibility or reliability of clairvoyance, either in general or in this specific case. Now add this to the case: Norman also has a belief based on ordinary empirical and testimonial evidence that the Attorney-General is in Chicago. The evidence is good enough to make this belief fairly reasonable, though not perfectly justified, and not justified enough to meet the requirements for knowledge. Now BonJour asks an important question:

> Suppose ... that Norman finds himself in a situation where he is forced to bet a very large amount, perhaps even his life or the life of someone else, on the whereabouts of either the President or the Attorney-General. Given his epistemic situation as described, which bet is it more reasonable for him to make?

It's clear, BonJour contends, that Norman is more reasonable to bet on the Attorney-General's location. And if BonJour is correct, then the externalist is left with a "paradoxical result," namely, "that from the externalist standpoint it is more rational to act on a merely reasonable belief than to act on one that is adequately justified to qualify as knowledge (and which in fact *is* knowledge)."

This suggests the following argument against externalism about epistemic justification.

1. If externalism is true, then it can be more rational to act on a moderately justified belief than on a highly justified belief. (Premise)
2. But it can't be more rational to act on a moderately justified belief than on a highly justified belief. (Premise)
3. So externalism isn't true. (From 1 and 2)

How should an externalist respond?

§ 29

Against internalism (Goldman, "Internalism Exposed")

Why would someone be attracted to internalism about epistemic justification to begin with? What motivates internalism? Alvin Goldman proposes an answer to this question, and uses the opportunity to argue against internalism. Goldman argues that the most plausible motivation for internalism turns out to be perfectly consistent with externalism, whereas variations on that motivation that are strong enough to rule out externalism turn out to be implausible and hospitable to skepticism. Internalists thus face a dilemma: choose a motivation for your view that either is plausible but too weak, or is strong enough but implausible.

Here is a natural way to motivative internalism. The point of epistemology is to help guide our intellectual conduct by conforming to our intellectual duties. The concept of epistemic justification closely

Goldman, Alvin, "Internalism Exposed," pp. 271–93 in *The Journal of Philosophy* 96, 6 (Jun. 1999). © 1999 The Journal of Philosophy, Inc.

tracks this. We are justified in our belief if and only if we are intellectually required or permitted to believe it; and we are unjustified in
our belief if and only if we are intellectually required to not believe
it. In short, being justified is a matter of responsibility, and being
unjustified is a matter of irresponsibility. Now, given that justification is a matter of duty or responsibility, and given that the point of
epistemology is to help guide us in fulfilling our responsibilities, it is
natural to suppose that a correct theory of justification must appeal
only to factors that are readily accessible to us, or as Goldman puts it,
factors that we can "readily know to obtain or not to obtain." Call
this restriction on factors "KJ" (short for ready knowledge of justifiers). It seems natural to suppose that KJ is true because unless we
have ready access to all the facts that determine our responsibilities,
then we can't be expected to fulfill those responsibilities. And what
is left of a responsibility that we can't be expected to fulfill? Goldman
calls the set of all facts that help determine our responsibilities "justifiers." Using this terminology, then, it seems that we have come
very close to the internalist thesis, namely, that all justifiers must be
readily accessible. Internalism just is the view that all justifiers must
be accessible or available from the first-person perspective.

Goldman rejects the "guidance-deontological" conception of
epistemology and epistemic justification that underlies the natural
line of thought just sketched. He doesn't believe that the point of
epistemology is to provide a "decision guide" to intellectually
responsible conduct, nor does he accept that justification is entirely
a matter of fulfilling duties. But Goldman is willing to accept the
guidance-deontological conception for the sake of argument, and
ask whether it really does motivate internalism. He spends the bulk
of his paper arguing that it does not.

The first thing to ask is: why must the factors be *readily* accessible?
Sometimes fulfilling responsibilities is hard. For example, many of
us have a moral responsibility to care for young children, infirm
parents, or disabled relatives, but this can require an enormous
amount of patience and sacrifice. It certainly isn't readily
accomplished, and we can't always readily detect the limits of such
responsibilities. We might also have a prudential responsibility to

save for retirement, but this too can require much effort and sacrifice, isn't always readily accomplished, and we can't always readily detect this responsibility's limits. We should not expect, then, that intellectual responsibilities are any different.

It's worth pointing that this objection to KJ is consistent with the popular normative principle that "ought implies can." While there are many ways of making the content of that principle more precise, the basic idea is that if you have a duty ("ought") to accomplish something, then you must be able to ("can") accomplish it. The present objection questions only the inclusion of "readily" in KJ. Being able to accomplish something doesn't require being able to readily accomplish it. When it comes to intellectual duties, being able to know about all the justifiers doesn't require being able to readily know about them.

But suppose we grant that all justifiers must be readily accessible. The next thing to ask is: what qualifies as "readily accessible?" After all, if we interpret that phrase liberally enough, then there will be nothing left for internalists and externalists to disagree about. Prominent internalists have given us some clue about how they understand ready accessibility. One proposal is that readily accessible facts are *introspectible*. Introspection is an individual's power to detect what is occurring in his or her own conscious mind. So on this view, what Goldman calls "strong internalism," justifiers are limited to an agent's conscious mental states. Goldman identifies Roderick Chisholm as one proponent of strong internalism (see §7 for more on Chisholm's views).

Goldman rejects strong internalism because it has "drastic" skeptical consequences, as illustrated by "the problem of stored beliefs." Most of our beliefs are stored in memory. We ordinarily take many of these memorial beliefs to constitute knowledge. Indeed, most of the knowledge we ordinarily take ourselves to have is of this sort, namely, memorial knowledge. Think about all the things that we know through memory: facts about history, geography, biology, loved ones, and acquaintances, etc. But nothing in our current consciousness is even remotely relevant to justifying the vast majority of our memorial beliefs. For example, what is it about your current conscious condition that justifies you in believing that water is made of hydrogen and oxygen? That Julius Caesar was a Roman? That Japan is an archipelago? If you're like most of us, then nothing whatsoever in your current conscious condition suffices to justify these beliefs. But then strong internalism entails that all of these beliefs are unjustified, an extremely counterintuitive skeptical consequence.

The internalist might respond to this line of reasoning by increasing the scope of eligible justifiers to include both introspectible facts and facts stored in memory. Goldman calls this "weak internalism." Weak internalism is more plausible than strong internalism but it is still false due to "the problem of forgotten evidence." To appreciate this problem, notice that many memorial beliefs were acquired and justified based on information now long-forgotten. For example, if you're like most of us, you don't remember where you learned that Japan is an archipelago. But this belief of yours is still justified in virtue of the quality of its acquisition. (Or if it's unjustified, that likewise could be partly due to the poor quality of its acquisition, however long-forgotten.)

Goldman raises two other objections against internalism. The first objection begins with the observation that a correct theory of justification must acknowledge that logical and probabilistic relations are justifiers. These are relations among propositions. Logical relations include the relation of entailment. The proposition *Little Jimmy ate six cookies* entails the proposition *Little Jimmy ate at least two cookies*, since the former couldn't possibly be true unless the latter were also true. Intuitively, if you were justified in believing that Little Jimmy ate six cookies, and you recognized that this entailed that Little Jimmy ate at least two cookies, then as a result you would also be justified in believing that Little Jimmy ate at least two cookies (see §§19–23 for more on this idea). Probabilistic relations are similar to, but weaker than, entailment relations. For example, the truth of the propositions *Alfred is a Swede* and *Only 10% of Swedes live in poverty* makes it probable, though it does not guarantee that *Alfred does not live in poverty*. If you were justified in believing the first two propositions, then that would provide some provisional justification for you to believe the third one.

Returning now to Goldman's first objection, he notes that "none of these logical or probabilistic relations is itself a mental state," and concludes that internalism thus rules them out as justifiers, which is a ridiculous consequence that falsifies internalism. However, this objection clearly fails because it confuses two senses of "internal." Internalism, as Goldman characterizes it generically, is a thesis about the accessibility of justifiers, not their location. Generic internalism doesn't require that all justifiers be *in* the person, or in the person's mind, but only that they be readily accessible to the person.[1]

Goldman's second objection begins with the claim that "true epistemic principles" are justifiers. Epistemic principles are propositions which state under what conditions a belief is justified, unjustified, or the like. They are among the things that help determine whether a belief is justified, and so internalism entails that we must have ready access to them, if we are to fulfill our intellectual responsibilities and have justified beliefs. But it is notoriously difficult to discover what the true epistemic principles are. At best, a few "elite" epistemologists have learned them, but only after many years of arduous intellectual labors. Internalism thus faces a "crippling" objection, namely, that epistemic principles are not readily known by the vast majority of us, in which case they can't be among the justifiers, in which case we can't be justified in believing anything, and "wholesale skepticism follows."

[1] This confusion appears again in Section VI of Goldman's paper when he remarks, "Some readily knowable facts might be external rather than internal." As it turns out, Feldman and Conee (§31) argue that the best way to understand internalism is along the lines suggested by Goldman's slip, namely, as a thesis about where justifiers are located!

§ 30

A skeptical take on externalism (Fumerton, "Externalism and Skepticism")

Imagine that your good friend Zelda believes that astrological prediction is a reliable way of forming beliefs. You seriously doubt that she is justified in accepting this reliability claim, so you question her about the matter. "We can settle the matter easily enough," she responds, "let me just consult my astrological chart and see whether crystal ball gazing is indeed reliable." She opens a cabinet on the hutch of her desk, retrieves her astrological chart, carefully consults it, and pronounces that astrological prediction is reliable. She considers the matter settled.

Here is an important question: is it even possible that by consulting the astrological charts, Zelda could be justified in believing that astrology is reliable? More generally, could you use a certain

Fumerton, Richard, "Externalism and Skepticism," pp. 159–81 in *Metaepistemology and Skepticism* (Lanham, MD: Rowman and Littlefield, 1995). © 1995 by Richard Fumerton.

way of forming beliefs to become justified in believing that *that very way* of forming beliefs is reliable? Richard Fumerton says that, at least when it comes to any philosophically interesting sort of justification, the answer to these questions is obviously "no." Fumerton then leverages this to argue against externalism about epistemic justification.

We can represent Fumerton's argument against externalism about epistemic justification as follows:

1. If externalism is true, then it's possible for you to use a belief-forming method to justify your belief that it (the method you're using) is reliable. (Premise)
2. But it's impossible for you to use a belief forming method to justify your belief that the method you're using is reliable.
3. So externalism is false. (From 1 and 2)

Fumerton limits his conclusion to philosophically interesting conceptions of epistemic justification. He doesn't rule out that externalism might be true of some epistemically interesting properties of belief.

To see why line 1 of the argument seems true, consider the version of externalism we've been mostly concerned with, namely, reliabilism. Reliabilism says that a belief is justified if and only if it is produced by a reliable cognitive process (see §26). Reliabilism entails that "the mere reliability of a process ... is sufficient to give us justified belief," notes Fumerton, and there is no restriction on the content of a justified belief. Reliabilism entails that if a reliable cognitive process produces the belief that it itself is reliable, then the belief is justified. Reliabilists do not add the proviso, "a reliably produced belief is justified only if it isn't about the process that produced it." And if they were to suggest such a proviso, it would seem *ad hoc* and unprincipled. As Fumerton says, "There is no conceptual basis for the reliabilist to get cold feet when epistemological questions are raised" about the cognitive processes themselves, or about whether we're justified in believing that they're reliable.

What about line 2? I emphasize again that Fumerton limits his conclusion to philosophically interesting conceptions of epistemic justification. Here Fumerton explains that line 2 seems obvious to him, and invites us to carefully consider the matter and see if it seems obvious to us too. Recall the imaginary case we began this section with: your friend Zelda the astrologer. We asked whether we could use astrology to become justified in believing that astrology is reliable. Says Fumerton,

> If a philosopher starts wondering about the reliability of astrological inference, the philosopher will not allow the astrologer to read in the stars the reliability of astrology. Even if astrological inferences happen to be reliable, the astrologer is missing the point of a *philosophical* inquiry into the justifiability of astrological inference if the inquiry is answered using the techniques of astrology ... If I really am interested in knowing whether astrological inference is legitimate, if I have the kind of philosophical curiosity that leads me to raise this question in the first place, I will not for a moment suppose that further use of astrology might help me find the answer to my question (pp. 403–404).

We're left to wonder about a couple things. First, is Fumerton right about the nature of philosophical curiosity? In the quest to satisfy philosophical curiosity about the justification or reliability of certain cognitive processes, are we necessarily barred from relying on those very processes? If the answer is "yes," think about what it entails about the question "Is any cognitive process available to me reliable?" Second, supposing that Fumerton is right about the nature of curiosity, is there some other form of curiosity that an externalist epistemology could satisfy? If so, then in order to pass ultimate judgment on externalism, we would need to decide which sort of curiosity really mattered.

§ 31

A friendly take on internalism (Feldman and Conee, "Internalism Defended")

In their exceedingly clear paper, Richard Feldman and Earl Conee accomplish three things: they clarify different senses of "internalism" about epistemic justification, they present a general explanatory argument for internalism, and they respond to several objections to internalism. Their main conclusion is that since internalism is well-supported and has "plausible options" for responding to all extant objections, we should accept that internalism is true and turn our attention to working out internalism's finer details.

What is internalism? Feldman and Conee distinguish two different theses that are sometimes called "internalism" in the literature. *Accessibilism* is the view that you must have unproblematic access to all factors that help determine the epistemic justification of your beliefs. (BonJour endorses accessibilism in §28.) *Mentalism* is the

Feldman, Richard and Earl Conee, "Internalism Defended," pp. 1–18 in *American Philosophical Quarterly* 38, 1 (January 2001). © 2001 by *American Philosophical Quarterly*.

view that the epistemic justification of your beliefs is entirely determined by factors internal to your mind. Feldman and Conee contend that internalism is best understood as mentalism. In any event, they defend mentalism.

Mentalists claim that justification is entirely a function of factors internal to your mind: only mental facts can make a justificatory difference. As Feldman and Conee point out, this entails that for any two possible individuals who are exactly alike mentally, they must be "exactly alike justificationally," in that "the same beliefs are justified for them to the same extent." Mental twins are justificatory twins. For convenience, let's encapsulate this principal implication of mentalism like so: *m-twins are j-twins*.

Why accept mentalism? Feldman and Conee's main positive argument for mentalism is an explanatory argument. They consider a number of pairs of cases that have two crucial features. First, the main characters in the two cases clearly seem to differ in how well-justified they are in believing a certain proposition. For short, let's say that there is *a j-difference* between the cases. Second, the main characters are stipulated to be different mentally. For short, let's say that there is *an m-difference* between the cases. For each pair, Feldman and Conee contend that the j-difference is best explained by the m-difference. Furthermore, they consider their cases to be "representative," and so infer that it is "reasonable to generalize from them." The generalization is that every possible j-difference is entirely due to an m-difference. We never need to "appeal to anything extramental."

Notice something important. Having any particular level of justification is different from having any other particular level of justification, including *having no justification* as a limiting case. Thus, every level of justification, or lack thereof, can be understood as a j-difference. So it seems that Feldman and Conee's generalization entails mentalism. If they're right about the generalization, then they have identified a motivation for internalism importantly different from the "guidance-deontological" conception of epistemology discussed by Alvin Goldman (§29).

Here is one of Feldman and Conee's examples, followed by their commentary.

A novice bird watcher and an expert are together looking for birds. They both get a good look at a bird in a nearby tree. (In order to avoid irrelevant complexities, assume that their visual presentations are exactly alike.) Upon seeing the bird, the expert immediately knows that it is a woodpecker. The expert has fully reasonable beliefs about what woodpeckers look like. The novice has no good reason to believe that it is a woodpecker and is not justified in believing that it is.

Comment: The epistemic difference between novice and expert arises from something that differentiates the two internally. The expert knows the look of a woodpecker. The novice would gain the same justification as the expert if the novice came to share the expert's internal condition concerning the look of woodpeckers.

Now let's consider an important objection to mentalism discussed by Feldman and Conee, Goldman's "problem of forgotten evidence." Begin with one of Goldman's examples.

Last year Sally read about the health benefits of broccoli in a *New York Times* science-section story. She then justifiably formed a belief in broccoli's beneficial effects. She still retains this belief but no longer recalls her original evidential source (and has never encountered either corroborating or undermining sources). Nonetheless, her broccoli belief is still justified, and, if true, qualifies as a case of knowledge.

Feldman and Conee grant that we commonly know things despite forgetting the evidence on which it was originally based. They even grant that the original evidence is often "irretrievably lost and not part of any stored" memory or justification that we currently have. Sally's case is an example of this. But Sally's belief is clearly justified. Goldman contends that the nonmental fact about the belief's etiology helps explain why her belief is justified. How can mentalists explain it?

Feldman and Conee suggest two strategies. First, mentalists can appeal to "conscious qualities of [Sally's] recollection, such as its vivacity and her associated feeling of confidence." Second, mentalists can argue that Sally's current mental state provides a sufficient basis for her justification, including the fact that "she knows that she is generally right about this sort of thing," and other things she presumably knows, such as the fact that vegetables are good for you, along with the fact that broccoli is a vegetable. These things weren't part of her original evidence, of course, but they exist now and can explain why her belief about broccoli is justified.

Goldman now asks us to consider a revision of Sally's case. Suppose that her current mental condition is exactly as in the original description of the case, but that her belief's etiology is very different: she originally acquired the belief by reading a highly disreputable source, the *National Inquirer*. Goldman contends that this etiological fact is both "relevant" and "decisive" in rendering her belief unjustified. For the purpose of evaluating mentalism, though, Goldman need only claim that Sally's belief in the modified version is *less* justified than her belief in the original version. Is she less justified in the modified version?

Feldman and Conee say that she isn't. They agree that there is an epistemically relevant difference between the original and modified versions of the case, but they deny that it has anything to do with justification. Sally is equally well-justified in both versions of the case. And her belief is true in both versions of the case. The difference is that in the original version she knows that broccoli is healthy, but in the modified version she doesn't. This is because the modified version is a Gettier case, whereas the original isn't (see §15 for an explanation of Gettier cases). Not all epistemically relevant differences are differences in justification.

As further support for their claim that Sally is equally well-justified in both versions of the case, Feldman and Conee ask us to consider yet another variation on the case!

Suppose Sally believes both that broccoli is healthful and that peas are healthful. Suppose that her source for the former is still the *National Inquirer* but her source for the latter belief is the reliable *New York Times*. Again she has forgotten her sources, but she correctly and reasonably believes that she virtually always gets beliefs like these from trustworthy sources.

If Goldman is right, then these two beliefs are not equally well-justified, due to important differences in their respective etiologies. But, Feldman and Conee reason, this is "unacceptable," because "from Sally's present perspective, the two propositions are on a par," and she would be "unreasonable" to "give up one belief but not the other." Instead, they urge us to conclude that Sally's beliefs are equally well-justified, and the difference between them is that one is Gettiered whereas the other isn't.

§ 32

Warrant (Plantinga, "Warrant: A First Approximation")

Imagine a subject with a true belief. The overwhelming consensus among epistemologists is that although true belief is necessary for knowledge, it isn't sufficient for knowledge.[1] What else must be added in order to suffice for knowledge? Let's call that additional property, whatever it is, *warrant*. Having stipulated this meaning for "warrant," it is trivially true that knowledge is warranted true belief. But what is warrant? We've given it a name, to be sure, but epistemology begins in earnest only once we try to characterize this property more substantively.

This is the task that Alvin Plantinga sets himself in "Warrant: A First Approximation," which is the first chapter of Plantinga's *Warrant and*

---

[1] For a notable exception, see Crispin Sartwell, "Why Knowledge is Merely True Belief," *Journal of Philosophy* 89.4 (1992): 167–180.

Plantinga, Alvin, "Warrant: A First Approximation," pp. 3–20 in *Warrant and Proper Function* (Oxford and New York: Oxford University Press, 1993). © 1993 by Alvin Plantinga.

Proper Function, which is the sequel of another book of his, *Warrant: The Current Debate*. In *Warrant: The Current Debate*, Plantinga surveyed numerous contemporary theories, and considered their merits as potential accounts of warrant. He concluded that they all failed, for reasons hinted at near the beginning of the selection. Cases involving "cognitive malfunction" form "the rock on which the canvassed accounts of warrant founder."

If cognitive malfunction is the bane of extant accounts of warrant, it seems worthwhile to try to define warrant in terms of *proper cognitive function*. This way we will avoid counterexamples involving cognitive malfunction. And Plantinga proceeds precisely this way, by positing a necessary condition on warrant: your belief is warranted only if your cognitive equipment functions properly in producing the belief.

What does Plantinga mean by something *functioning properly* or *working the way it ought to*? He means that it is working the way it was designed to work. The design might be the result of intentional agency, as when a clock is designed to keep time, or the result of purely natural unintentional forces, as when a specialized organ evolves over generations because its iterations promote fitness under prevailing conditions.

Does proper functioning suffice for warrant? Plantinga denies that it does. To demonstrate this, he presents a hypothetical case in which, he intuits, the subject's belief is produced by cognitive faculties functioning as they were designed to, but the belief still isn't warranted. Imagine that you have just succeeded brilliantly on your "annual cognitive checkup." Then something strange happens: "Suddenly and without your knowledge you are transported to an environment wholly different from earth; you awake on a planet revolving around Alpha Centauri." Prevailing conditions are very different on this alien world. One important difference is that elephants are invisible to humans. Another important difference is that elephants emit radiation that causes nearby humans to believe that there is a large animal nearby. Now suppose that an elephant passes nearby. You don't see it, but you are hit by the radiation, and your cognitive faculties produce the belief that there is a large animal nearby. Your belief is true. But it isn't a good candidate for knowledge. And since warrant is that property which, when added to true belief, suffices for knowledge, it follows that your belief isn't warranted. But your cognitive faculties aren't malfunctioning: "they are working quite properly." So if proper functioning sufficed for warrant, your belief would be warranted. But, again, your belief isn't warranted. Thus, Plantinga concludes, proper functioning does not suffice for warrant.

Plantinga diagnoses the following problem with the case. Your cognitive faculties are functioning properly, but not in an environment they were designed for. Just as human lungs are designed for life on land, not in water, human cognitive faculties were designed for life on earth, not on alien planets with invisible, radiating fauna. So Plantinga proposes an additional necessary condition on warrant: your belief is warranted only if it is produced in an appropriate environment. A belief is produced in an appropriate environment if and only if the belief is produced by cognitive equipment designed for that environment.

Does proper functioning in an appropriate environment suffice for warrant? Plantinga denies that it does. To demonstrate this, he again presents a hypothetical case in which, he intuits, a subject's belief satisfies those conditions but still isn't warranted. Suppose that over-estimating one's competence promotes increased self-confidence, which in turn promotes fitness in humans. Suppose further that this selective pressure has helped shape this part of our cognitive equipment, such that it is designed to enhance self-confidence. (That is, its purpose is to enhance self-confidence.) Now consider Henrietta, a typical human in a typical earthling environment, and her falsely inflated belief about her own competence. Her belief is produced by cognitive faculties functioning properly in an appropriate environment. Is her belief warranted? No, it isn't, Plantinga says. But it would be if proper functioning in an appropriate environment sufficed for warrant. Thus, Plantinga concludes, proper functioning in an appropriate environment doesn't suffice for warrant.

Plantinga diagnoses the following problem with the case. The cognitive faculties that produce Henrietta's belief are functioning properly in an appropriate environment, but not according to a design plan *aimed at producing true belief.* Instead, the design plan is aimed, in the first place, at enhancing self-confidence. What's worse, it enhances self-confidence by producing false beliefs. So Plantinga proposes an additional necessary condition on warrant: your belief is warranted only if it is produced by cognitive faculties operating according to a design plan aimed at true belief. Whether a design plan is aimed at true belief depends on its etiology.

Does proper functioning in an appropriate environment according to a design plan aimed at truth suffice for warrant? Plantinga again denies that it does. To demonstrate this, he again presents a hypothetical case in which, he intuits, a subject's belief satisfies those conditions but still isn't warranted.

> Suppose a well-meaning but incompetent angel ... sets out to design a variety of rational persons, persons capable of thought, belief, and knowledge. As it turns out, the design is a real failure; the resulting beings hold beliefs, all right, but most of them are absurdly false. Here all three of our conditions are met: the beliefs of these beings are formed by their cognitive faculties functioning properly in the cognitive environment for which they were designed, and furthermore the relevant modules of the design plan are aimed at truth (the relevant modules of their cognitive equipment have the production of true beliefs as their purpose). But the beliefs of these pitifully deceived beings do not have warrant.

Plantinga diagnoses the following problem with the case: the design plan is not good. When it comes to cognitive design plans, being good requires being *cognitively reliable.* A cognitive design plan is cognitively reliable if and only if there is a "high objective probability" that any belief formed according to it, in the intended cognitive environment, is true. High objective probability requires more than a good actual track record of producing true beliefs and avoiding false beliefs, since a good actual track record could be established by an improbable string of good luck, rather than any merit of the design plan. It further requires a good track record in "most of the nearby possible worlds." Or, in other words, if the environment had been slightly different in any number of small but nontrivial ways, then the track record would still have been good. (See §21 for more on evaluating subjunctive conditionals.)

So, according to Plantinga, proper functioning in an appropriate environment according to a good design plan aimed at truth is necessary for warrant. Is it also sufficient? Have we finally reached a definition of warrant that Plantinga endorses? Not quite! But he is willing to endorse it as a serviceable "first approximation" of a definition, which may provide a "hint" along the road to a more satisfactory account.

Reference

Crispin Sartwell, "Why Knowledge is Merely True Belief," *Journal of Philosophy* 89.4 (1992): 167–180.

§33

Intellectual virtues (Zagzebski, *Virtues of the Mind*)

Moral philosophy and epistemology share at least two important features. First, they both deal with value. A central concern of moral philosophy is goodness; a central concern of epistemology is knowledge. Second, they both deal with agency. A central concern of moral philosophy is moral agency; a central concern of epistemology is intellectual agency. Linda Zagzebski exploits these commonalities to offer a unified approach to moral philosophy and epistemology. She does this by putting virtues at the center of her approach.

Let's begin by locating what a virtue is. At the broadest level, it is a quality or attribute. More specifically, it is a good quality, or an excellence. For a person to have a virtue is for that person to have an

Zagzebski, Linda, Selections from *Virtues of the Mind*, pp. 134–7, 166–84 in L. Zagzebski, *Virtues of the Mind* (Cambridge: Cambridge University Press, 1996). © 1996 by Cambridge University Press.

Epistemology: A Guide, First Edition. John Turri.

excellence. (Persons aren't the only things that can have virtues – e.g. one virtue of an excellent knife is its sharpness – but Zagzebski focuses on virtues of persons, so we will too.) More specifically, it is an *acquired* excellence. And it must have been acquired in a specific way. In order for an excellence to be a virtue, on Zagzebski's approach, the person must have cultivated it through hard work over time. A further feature of virtue is that it is an entrenched part of the person's character, partly "defining who the person is." So virtues are excellences of a person, acquired through hard work, partly definitive of the person's character.

Now let's consider a virtue's structure. A virtue has two components: motivation and reliability. Zagzebski defines a motivation as "a disposition to have a certain motive," and she defines a motive in turn as "an emotion that initiates and directs action to produce" a desired end or goal. Due to the motivational component, a virtue orients you "toward the world," emotionally disposes you to strive for a certain goal. For example, a beneficent person is motivated to perform good deeds. Reliability is the other component of virtue. A virtuous person has a reliable ability to bring about or promote the goal that is the object of the component motivation. For example, a beneficent person is not only motivated to perform good deeds, but in appropriate circumstances reliably performs good deeds. Someone who consistently fails to do good isn't beneficent, even if they consistently intend and try their best to do good.

The difference between the moral and intellectual virtues is that the motivational component of a moral virtue is ultimately love of the good, whereas the motivational component of an intellectual virtue is ultimately love of knowledge (or, perhaps more broadly, love of "cognitive contact with reality"). Zagzebski speculates that each of these motivations might ultimately derive from a more fundamental motivation, the love of being in general, but she doesn't commit to it.

Zagzebski thus views intellectual virtues as entrenched excellences of a person, acquired through hard work, partly definitive of the person's character, and rooted in a love for knowledge, which dispose the person to seek, and enable the person to reliably obtain, knowledge. They also dispose the person to cultivate subsidiary motivations that will enable her to more effectively pursue knowledge and other cognitive goods that enhance knowledge, such as intellectual skills, habits, understanding, and experience. Zagzebski's theory of intellectual virtue is thus hospitable to reliabilism (see §§26–27), since she considers the intellectual virtues to be a special "subset of truth-conducive traits." Some examples are intellectual honesty, conscientiousness, and open-mindedness.

Zagzebski makes allowance for some intellectual virtues that don't fit this general profile. Consider the virtue of creativity. Being creative might not generate a "high percentage" of true beliefs, but over time it does lead to the discovery of new truths and methods for discovering yet further truths. It is through creativity that some of humanity's greatest intellectual advancements have been made. Consider how creative Albert Einstein had to be to imagine that light sets the cosmic speed limit, and how creative Rosalind Franklin had to be to develop x-ray diffraction techniques for photographing DNA molecules. Creativity thus counts as truth-conducive in a more indirect but no less important way: "If only 5 per cent of a creative thinker's original ideas turn out to be true, her creativity is certainly truth conducive because the stock of knowledge of the human race has increased through her creativity."

§ 34

Virtue epistemology (Greco, "Virtues and Vices of Virtue Epistemology")

In the last section, we encountered a theory of intellectual virtue. Virtue epistemology is an approach to epistemology that not only develops a theory of intellectual virtue, but puts virtue to work in explaining epistemic justification, value, and knowledge. John Greco's goal is to explain some of virtue epistemology's main strengths, and to articulate an even better version of it.

Recall that Linda Zagzebski classifies an intellectual virtue as a type of excellent character trait acquired through hard work, rooted in a love of knowledge, and which enables the person to reliably get knowledge (§33). Greco classifies an intellectual (or "cognitive") virtue as an ability to reliably acquire true beliefs and avoid false beliefs. These are importantly different views. Greco's view doesn't require that the ability be a character trait acquired through hard

Greco, John, "Virtues and Vices of Virtue Epistemology," pp. 413–32 in *Canadian Journal of Philosophy* 23, 3 (1993). © 1993 by *Canadian Journal of Philosophy*.

Epistemology: A Guide, First Edition. John Turri.
© 2014 John Wiley & Sons, Ltd. Published 2014 by John Wiley & Sons, Ltd.

work or that it be rooted in a love of knowledge. Both views agree that intellectual virtues are reliable, though we have seen that Zagzebski allows for exceptions.

According to Greco, a principal thesis of what we can call *austere virtue epistemology* is that your belief has positive epistemic status if and only if it results from your cognitive virtue. *Positive epistemic status* is that which "turns true belief into knowledge," and so is roughly equivalent to what Alvin Plantinga calls "warrant" (§32). Given the similarities between Greco's characterization of cognitive virtue and Plantinga's definition of proper function, it's fair to count Plantinga's "proper functionalism" as a version of austere virtue epistemology.

Austere virtue epistemology has at least two noteworthy strengths. First, it explains why perceptual and memory beliefs have positive epistemic status, whereas superstitious and wishful beliefs don't: perception and memory are cognitive virtues, whereas superstition and wishful thinking aren't. (Compare Alvin Goldman's defense of process reliabilism as an account of epistemic justification, §26.) Second, it provides a direct response to skepticism about the external world: we can know that the external word exists because we have cognitive virtues, which distinguishes us from our victimized counterparts in dream-worlds and demon-worlds.

But austere virtue epistemology faces two serious objections. The first objection is that it is too strong – it requires too much – since it rules out certain beliefs that have positive epistemic status. The example of a perfectly deceived victim of a Cartesian demon illustrates the objection (§§3, 21). Such victims could have positive epistemic status, even though they lack cognitive virtue. Indeed, there is a sense in which the victims are as justified as we are in holding our beliefs. But they lack cognitive virtue because their belief-forming methods are almost perfectly *unreliable* in the environment they inhabit. So positive epistemic status doesn't seem to require cognitive virtue.

The second objection to austere virtue epistemology is that it is too weak because it falsely classifies certain beliefs as having positive epistemic status. The following example of Greco's illustrates the objection.

173

Consider the case of Mary, who is in most respects a normal human being. The relevant difference is that Mary's cognitive faculties produce the belief in her that there is a tiger nearby whenever there is a tiger nearby, and even in cases where Mary does not see, hear or otherwise perceive a nearby tiger. Mary's brain is designed so as to be sensitive to an electromagnetic field emitted only by tigers, thus causing her to form the relevant belief in the appropriate situation, and without any corresponding experience, sensory or otherwise. We can imagine that this cognitive feature was designed by natural processes of evolution, or that it was literally designed by a beneficent creator, one who realizes that tigers are dangerous to beings like Mary and who therefore wishes to equip her with a reliable warning device. Now suppose that a tiger is walking nearby, and that Mary forms the appropriate belief. Add that Mary has no evidence that there is a tiger in the area, nor any evidence that she has such a faculty. Rather, she has considerable evidence *against* her belief that there are tigers in the area.

Does Mary's belief that there is a tiger nearby have positive epistemic status? Greco answers that it "clearly ... does not," even though austere virtue epistemology rules that it does. For Mary's belief results from cognitive virtues ("properly functioning faculties in an appropriate environment"). Greco says that Mary's belief lacks positive epistemic status because it is "epistemically irresponsible" from Mary's own point of view.

To overcome these objections, Greco proposes wedding virtue epistemology to "norm internalism." Norm internalism says that your belief is justified if and only if it is formed "in conformance with" the rules of belief-formation that you "countenance." Rules of belief-formation are epistemic norms, which is why it's called *norm* internalism. Rules that you countenance are rules that you follow when reasoning "conscientiously," which means that they are, in an important sense, endorsed from your perspective and operate internal to your mind, which is why it's called norm *internalism*.

This brings us to Greco's positive proposal, which we can represent as follows.

> Your belief has positive epistemic status if and only if (a) it results from some cognitive virtue of yours, and (b) you have this cognitive virtue because you conform to epistemic norms that you countenance.

Clause (a) is the austere virtue-theoretic account of positive epistemic status, and it ensures that a belief with positive epistemic status is "objectively" virtuous, or reliable. Clause (b) adds something distinctive beyond standard virtue epistemology. It adds an element of "subjective" virtue, or responsibility. In light of this, call it a form of *responsibilist virtue epistemology*.

On Greco's responsibilist view, knowledge requires that you have the relevant cognitive virtue because you are firmly disposed to follow the epistemic norms that you endorse when you reason conscientiously. The "subjective" element of virtue explains why you have the "objective" element: *you are reliable because you are responsible*. Greco neatly encapsulates the view, "Knowledge is true belief which results from a cognitive virtue, where this virtue has its basis in S's conforming to epistemic norms which S countenances."

How does responsibilist virtue epistemology handle the objections to austere virtue epistemology? On the one hand, in the case of Cartesian victims, we can say that their beliefs are subjectively virtuous, because they are formed by conforming to rules that the victims countenance. This remains true even though the victims lack objective virtue. On the other hand, in the case of Mary's belief that a tiger is nearby, we can say that even though her belief is objectively virtuous, it isn't subjectively virtuous. It isn't subjectively virtuous because Mary is stipulated to be a normal human except for her unique electromagnetic sensitivity, normal humans don't countenance believing that a tiger is nearby when there is no perceptual or testimonial evidence that a tiger is nearby, and there is no such evidence in Mary's case.

In short, Greco argues that responsibilist virtue epistemology isn't too strong because it allows that subjective virtue underwrites a sort of justification, even in the absence of objective virtue; and it isn't too weak because it requires subjective virtue to explain objective virtue in cases of knowledge.

175

§ 35

Knowledge, luck and virtue (Pritchard, "Cognitive Responsibility and the Epistemic Virtues")

A chicken sexer is someone who sorts chicken hatchlings according to their sex. This is a common practice in the gruesome business of factory farming. Male chicks aren't profitable to the egg industry, so they are identified early after hatching and then either ground up alive in a meat grinder, and maybe turned into chicken feed for their sisters, or tossed into a trash bin where they slowly suffocate to death under the weight of the other male chicks that quickly accumulate on top of them. Female chicks are highly lucrative, so they are identified early too and spared an early death, though this is hardly a blessing, since the life of laying hens is filled with intense misery from beginning to end.

Chicken sexers are interesting to epistemologists because they are extremely reliable at identifying a chick's sex, often at a glance, but they typically can't explain how they do it. They can't articulate the basis for their highly reliable and efficient judgment. They have a

Pritchard, Duncan, "Cognitive Responsibility and the Epistemic Virtues," pp. 181–201 in *Epistemic Luck* (Oxford: Oxford University Press, 2005). © 2005 by Duncan Pritchard.

reliable ability that is, from their own perspective, inexplicable. Indeed, some of them even have *false* beliefs about how they do it. But this doesn't rob them of their ability.

Duncan Pritchard uses an example of a chicken sexer along with a distinction between two forms of epistemic luck, "veritic epistemic luck" and "reflective epistemic luck," to argue against virtue epistemology. Let's first consider the distinction, and then consider the argument.

A true belief is *veritically lucky* if and only if: it could easily have been false, given the way it was actually formed. For example, suppose I own one ticket in a fair, single-winner lottery that sold one million tickets. I have a one-in-a-million chance of winning. Suppose further that I have a hunch that today is my lucky day. And suppose further that on this basis I believe that I will win, and that my belief is true. My belief is true but veritically lucky because it could very easily have been false, given the way it was actually formed. In most "nearby possible worlds" where I form my belief in the way that I actually do – based on my hunch that I'll get lucky – my belief turns out false.

Reflective epistemic luck is different. Sometimes believers are wrong about how their beliefs are actually formed. As we just saw, veritic luck is a function of the way a belief is actually formed. By contrast, reflective luck is a function of *how a believer thinks* her belief was actually formed. A true belief is *reflectively lucky* if and only if: if it were formed in the way the believer thinks it was formed, then it could easily have been false. For example, suppose that Sungmi is a highly reliable chicken sexer who has false beliefs about how her ability works.[1] Sungmi is unaware of her reliable chicken-sexing track record, and she falsely thinks that she judges based on how the chicks smell. (She actually judges based on how they look.) Now consider her true belief, based on her highly reliable visual ability, that this particular chick is male. Sungmi's belief isn't veritically lucky because it couldn't easily have been false, given that it

---

[1] The example is modeled after one Pritchard uses in *Epistemic Luck* (Oxford University Press: 2005, p. 174), which isn't reprinted in the anthology. The example is importantly similar to Greco's example of Mary, who has a peculiar ability to detect nearby tigers via special magnetic fields (§34).

was formed through her highly reliable visual chicken-sexing ability. But that's not relevant to whether her belief is reflectively lucky. To determine whether it's reflectively lucky, we ask: could it have easily been false, if it were formed in *the way she thinks it was formed*? Yes, it could have, because (we may stipulate) Sungmi is highly unreliable at judging a chick's sex based on how it smells.

Having distinguished between veritic and reflective luck, Pritchard proceeds to argue against virtue epistemology, on two main grounds. On the one hand, he argues that neither main versions of virtue epistemology – austere virtue epistemology and responsibilist virtue epistemology – can properly define knowledge, due to a problem with veritic luck. On the other hand, he argues that both versions of virtue epistemology have a problem with reflective luck. We'll begin with the problem of veritic luck.

Does Sungmi know that this particular chick is male? Austere virtue epistemology defines knowledge roughly as true belief produced by cognitive virtue, where a cognitive virtue is understood as an ability to reliably acquire true beliefs and avoid false beliefs (see §34). Sungmi's belief is true and produced by a cognitive virtue. So austere virtue epistemology rules that her belief counts as knowledge. Is this the right result? Pritchard tends to agree that it is the right result, but not because he agrees with austere virtue epistemology.

One obvious lesson of the Gettier problem (see §15), Pritchard notes, is that veritic luck is inconsistent with knowledge. One possible explanation for this is that knowledge requires safety, and safety is inconsistent with veritic luck. (See §22 for more on safety.) This is the explanation that Pritchard prefers. He contends that the possibility of a safety-based treatment of Gettier cases shows that we don't need austere virtue epistemology to handle the Gettier problem.

Moreover, Pritchard continues, austere virtue epistemology can't handle certain Gettier cases, such as this one:

> Mary has highly reliable eyesight. She enters her living room, sees the man sitting in the chair, and on that basis believes, "My husband is in the living room." Unknown to Mary, the man she sees is her husband's twin brother, who recently and unexpectedly returned from Australia

after a twenty year absence. But as luck would have it, Mary's husband is in the living room. He is dozing behind the couch, unnoticed by Mary.[2]

Mary has a true belief produced by cognitive virtue, but she still doesn't know.

Does responsibilist virtue epistemology handle this case any better than austere virtue epistemology? Recall that responsibilist virtue epistemology adds an additional necessary condition on knowledge, namely, that the believer has the relevant cognitive virtue because she is responsible (see §34). Pritchard argues that this additional condition fails to properly handle Mary's case. Mary's relevant cognitive virtue is her good visual judgment. We can simply add to the case that she has good visual judgment because she responsibly collects and evaluates visual evidence. So she satisfies the responsibilist definition of knowledge. But she still doesn't know.

Returning now to Sungmi's knowledge, rather than invoke Sungmi's cognitive virtue to explain her knowledge, Pritchard contends, we can instead invoke the *safety* of her belief. A belief is safe if and only if it isn't veritically lucky – that is, it wouldn't easily have been false, given the way it was actually formed. Sungmi has a safe true belief; and her belief counts as knowledge; so we can explain why she knows by supposing that knowledge requires safe belief, rather than virtuous belief.

So both main versions of virtue epistemology face a problem with veritic luck, and are seemingly outperformed by a simple safety-based theory of knowledge. That is Pritchard's first main criticism of virtue epistemology. His second main criticism is that neither version of virtue epistemology offers a plausible account of reflective luck, to which we now turn.

Consider again Sungmi's belief that this particular chick is male. Although Pritchard tends to agree that Sungmi's belief counts as knowledge, he nevertheless claims that there is "certainly *something* epistemically deficient" about her belief. Pritchard says that this

---

[2] Modeled after a case by Linda Zagzebski, *Virtues of the Mind* (Cambridge University Press, 1996, pp. 285–287).

deficiency is due to the fact that Sungmi can't "take cognitive responsibility for the truth" of her belief, and so can't "properly *claim*" that she knows that this chick is male. In short, although her belief counts as knowledge, it isn't "cognitively responsible," and she can't claim to have this knowledge. But to be able to claim to know something is "a very desirable epistemic" state, in part because it enables her to be "a reliable informant" about what she knows.

Austere virtue epistemology has nothing to say about cognitive responsibility. Its story begins and ends with cognitive virtues, understood merely as reliable abilities, without mentioning the value of being able to claim that you "know," or being a good informant. And despite its name, responsibilist virtue epistemology doesn't speak to the sort of cognitive responsibility involved in being able to claim that you "know," or being a good informant. To see why, notice that we can add that Sungmi's ability is due to her careful evaluation of the visual evidence, even though she falsely thinks that it's due to a responsible evaluation of olfactory evidence. Sungmi thus lives up to everything that responsibilist virtue epistemology demands of her, even though her belief is clearly importantly deficient.

Pritchard's view is that a belief is cognitively responsible in the relevant way only if it isn't reflectively lucky. And what explains why a belief isn't reflectively lucky is that the believer has good, reflectively accessible evidence about how her belief was formed and that it was formed safely. This is an *internalist* anti-reflective-luck condition (see esp. §§28–31 for more on internalism). Moreover, Pritchard contends, when we combine this internalist condition with a safety condition, we get everything we want in our evaluation of Sungmi's belief. In light of this, Pritchard concludes that this combination of views is preferable to virtue epistemology.

References

Duncan Pritchard, *Epistemic Luck* (Oxford University Press, 2005, p. 174).
Linda Zagzebski, *Virtues of the Mind* (Cambridge University Press, 1996, pp. 285–287).

§ 36

Epistemic value and cognitive achievement (Sosa, "The Place of Truth in Epistemology")

Consider two excellent cups of coffee. Each is hot, aromatic, rich, and distinctive. Not even the greatest coffee connoisseur could find grounds for judging one better than the other. Is one of these cups of coffee better, *qua* cup of coffee, than the other? Certainly not, we're apt to think. They're equally good cups of coffee.

Now suppose it turns out that one of the cups, cup A, was produced by a highly reliable, state-of-the-art, new coffee machine, whereas cup B was produced by an unreliable, beaten up, old coffee machine. Does this further etiological fact make cup A a better cup of coffee than cup B? Again, certainly not. Once the machines have done their work in producing the two cups, the machines' comparative quality makes no difference to the cups' intrinsic properties.

Sosa, Ernest, "The Place of Truth in Epistemology," pp. 155–79 in M. DePaul and L. Zagzebski (eds.), *Intellectual Virtue: Perspectives From Ethics and Epistemology* (Oxford and New York: Oxford University Press, 2003). © 2003 by Ernest Sosa.

Epistemology: A Guide, First Edition. John Turri.
© 2014 John Wiley & Sons, Ltd. Published 2014 by John Wiley & Sons, Ltd.

The fact that cup A was produced by a better machine doesn't make it any more aromatic, rich, or distinctive.

We might value the reliable machine over the unreliable machine. But that's because it reliably produces good cups of coffee. We value coffee machines only instrumentally, as a means to the desired end: good coffee.

In this book, we have spent considerable time asking what distinguishes knowledge from true belief. But we haven't asked why it even matters. What makes knowledge so special? Is it worth the trouble to attain knowledge instead of mere true belief? Is knowledge even any better than true belief? Most epistemologists take it for granted that knowledge is obviously better than true belief. More specifically, *knowing P* is obviously epistemically better *in itself* than is *merely truly believing P*. But what could this additional value consist in? In "The Place of Truth in Epistemology," Ernest Sosa identifies three sorts of epistemic value that a broadly reliabilist, truth-centered epistemology can invoke to answer these questions.

Truth-centered epistemology accepts that true belief is the sole fundamental intellectual value. Broadly, reliabilist approaches to knowledge distinguish knowledge from mere true belief by reference to the reliability of the belief-forming processes involved. Call the combination of a broadly reliabilist approach and truth-centered epistemology *truth-centered reliabilism.*

For much the same reason that the reliable etiology of cup A doesn't make it better than cup B, it can easily seem that truth-centered reliabilism can't explain why knowledge is better than true belief. For suppose that true belief is the only epistemic value. The reliability of a belief-producing process attains its value through its tendency to produce what is valuable, namely true belief. That is, reliability of cognitive processes is only instrumentally valuable, as was the case earlier with the reliability of coffee machines. Now consider an occasion on which we have the epistemically valuable thing: a true belief that P. Adding that this true belief was reliably produced adds no further epistemic value, just as adding that cup A was reliably produced added no further gustatory value. So if truth-centered reliabilism is true, then knowledge is no better epistemically than true belief. Many epistemologists take this to be refutation of truth-centered reliabilism.

Sosa resists this line of reasoning against truth-centered reliabilism by carefully distinguishing among different sorts of value. First, there is intrinsic value, which is value a thing has in itself. For example, the pleasantness of a pleasant experience is an intrinsic value of the experience, and the beauty of a painting is an intrinsic value of the painting. Second, there is instrumental value, which is value a thing has in virtue of producing something that has intrinsic value. For example, an aspirin has instrumental value because it causes relief from a throbbing headache, which relief is intrinsically valuable; a coffee machine has instrumental value because it produces coffee that people take pleasure in drinking, which pleasure is intrinsically valuable. The instrumental value of something "derives from the intrinsic value found in" its "causal progeny."

Instrumental value is parasitic on intrinsic value, via the causal relation. Does this imply that instrumental value doesn't *really* matter? Does it imply that instrumental value is evaluatively epiphenomenal – a mere shadow of true value? Sosa thinks not. To see why, compare two worlds, W1 and W2. In each world, three events occur.

W1: X1, Y1, Z1
W2: X2, Y2, Z2

Let's stipulate that each of these events is intrinsically valuable. Let's further stipulate that X1's intrinsic value equals that of X2, Y1's intrinsic value equals that of Y2, and Z1's intrinsic value equals that of Z2's. Both worlds have the same amount of intrinsic value. Does it follow that they are equally good worlds? Well, by stipulation they have the same overall intrinsic value. But is that all that matters?

Let's stipulate a couple more details about W1 and W2. In W1, the three events are causally isolated: none of the three events causes either of the others. In W2, the three events are causally connected: X2 causes Y2, and Y2 causes Z2. To reflect these added details, let's alter our visual representation of the worlds,

W1: X1, Y1, Z1
W2: X2 $\rightarrow$ Y2 $\rightarrow$ Z2

where the arrows represent causal relations. In light of this further information, it seems that X2 is better than X1, and Y2 is better than Y1. This is because of the difference in instrumental value. Sosa considers this to be a "special sort of instrumental value," and labels it *praxical value*, which is the value of "bringing about something valuable." If Sosa is right about praxical value, then it provides an additional resource for truth-centered reliabilists to explain why knowledge is better than true belief.

Beyond praxical value, Sosa identifies three other resources for truth-centered reliabilism. The resources are inspired by Aristotle's virtue theory. By exploiting them, truth-centered reliabilism arguably becomes a version of virtue epistemology.

First, there is a difference between succeeding by luck and achieving success. Consider a bull's-eye in archery. A rank beginner could close his eyes, let an arrow fly, and hit a bull's-eye. He succeeds, but it was just luck. Compare that success to the bull's-eye of a master archer, whose skill is on full display as she nocks the arrow, aims, releases the arrow with precision, and hits a bull's-eye. She succeeded, and did so through a skillful performance. There is more to admire in a skillful success than a lucky success. A skillful success is more valuable.

Compare now two master archers, both of whom are incredibly reliable shots, and both of whom hit a bull's-eye on this occasion. Are these shots equally admirable? That all depends. Suppose that our first master archer performs just as she did in the earlier example, whereas our second archer, despite his reliability, performs poorly on this occasion, but is helped up by a fortuitous gust of wind that guides his shot back on target. Both of our archers succeed, but only the first succeeds through skill. Despite the fact that both archers are equally reliable, the first archer's shot is better than the second archer's shot. Call this additional value *achievement value*.

Truth-centered reliabilism might define knowledge as true belief produced by a reliable cognitive process. Or it might define knowledge as true belief *achieved* through a reliable process (what Sosa calls a "deed of true believing"). The additional value of achieving true belief would make knowledge better than mere true belief.

Second, human flourishing – what Aristotle and the ancient Greeks called *eudaimonia* – involves not only success, but achievement as well, succeeding through skillful rational activity. Achievement is partly constitutive of flourishing, and since flourishing is intrinsically valuable, achievement thereby gains some measure of value too. Call this *constitutive value*. In intellectual matters, true belief counts as a success. Achieving true belief is thus partly constitutive of intellectual flourishing, and thereby gains some measure of constitutive value. So if truth-centered reliabilism defines knowledge as true belief achieved through a reliable process, it could explain the value of knowledge over mere true belief.

In calling our attention to praxical value, achievement value, and constitutive value, Sosa highlights several ways that truth-centered reliabilism could potentially explain the added value of knowledge over mere true belief. But, Sosa contends, this is not all that needs explaining.

Third, consider again the ubiquitous Cartesian demon (§§3, 21), and two of its victims.

> The first victim takes in quite fully and flawlessly the import of her sense experience and other states of consciousness, to an extent rarely matched by any human, and then reasons therefrom with equal prowess to conclusions beyond the reach of most people, and retains her results in memory well beyond the normal. The other victim is on the contrary extensively handicapped in her cognitive faculties and performs with singular ineptness. Clearly one of these victims is better off than the other; you would prefer to be and perform like the first and unlike the second. However, neither one attains truth at all.

Neither victim achieves a true belief, nor succeeds in getting a true belief by luck, nor even succeeds in forming beliefs that cause further true beliefs. So none of their beliefs has any of the values identified earlier: they don't have the intrinsic epistemic value of truth, from which it follows that they lack achievement value, from which it follows that they lack constitutive value; and they don't cause any further true beliefs, so they lack praxical or other relevant instrumental value. But the first victim obviously performs better than the second victim, and this must be so in virtue of her performance's greater epistemic value. What sort of epistemic value?

Sosa proposes a new category, *performance value*, which is a measure of the value that an agent or performance would bring if "properly installed." An uninstalled thermostat could be such that *if* it were properly installed in your home, it would perfectly regulate your home's temperature, thereby causing you enhanced comfort. The thermostat thus has performance value. Similarly, if the first demon victim were properly "installed" in a normal human environment, a wealth of true beliefs and knowledge would ensue. The first demon victim thus has considerable epistemic performance value. By comparison, the second demon victim would perform poorly even if properly installed in a normal human environment, and so has considerably less performance value. Sosa proposes that this is how truth-centered reliabilism can explain the obvious value differential between the two demon victims.

§ 37

Giving up on knowledge (Kvanvig, "Why Should Inquiring Minds Want to Know?")

Jonathan Kvanvig thinks that knowledge doesn't really matter and philosophers should stop studying it. Coming from an epistemologist, this is a bold and surprising pair of claims, indeed! What leads him to make them?

We engage in cognition constantly. We evaluate cognition regularly. What place does knowledge have in understanding the nature and evaluation of cognition? Why should we think that knowledge has a special role to play here?

Perhaps knowledge is the ideal cognitive state. If it were the ideal cognitive state, then it would have an important role to play in understanding the nature and evaluation of cognition. But knowledge isn't the ideal cognitive state, Kvanvig notes. Or, at least, knowledge isn't the

Kvanvig, Jonathan L, "Why Should Enquiring Minds Want to Know?: Meno Problems and Epistemological Axiology,") pp. 426–52 in *The Monist* 81, 3 (1998). © 1998, THE MONIST, La Salle, Illinois 61301, USA.

Epistemology: A Guide, First Edition. John Turri.
© 2014 John Wiley & Sons, Ltd. Published 2014 by John Wiley & Sons, Ltd.

ideal cognitive state if ideal cognition is something that we humans could possibly have or sensibly strive for. The ideal cognitive state is not only true but also infallible, incorrigible, permanent, and utterly indubitable. No human belief is infallible, incorrigible, permanent, and utterly indubitable.

Perhaps knowledge is the cognitive state that we humans want, or ought to want, to achieve. If it were, then it would play an important role in understanding the nature of human cognition and its evaluation. But it doesn't seem like knowledge is the cognitive state that we want, or ought to want, to achieve. Kvanvig reports, "I want to be able to tell immediately and directly, without any special effort, the truth value of any claim that has or will have any effect on my life. I want cognitive excellence of a certain sort with minimal effort. I don't think I'm idiosyncratic in this regard." If that sounds too sophisticated, then let's stick with this: "I want to get to the truth, and I want to be sure I have. I'm sure you're roughly the same in this regard." If either of these is a fair characterization of our cognitive aspirations, then knowledge isn't part of the picture. For "no mention of the concept of knowledge ... need be made to understand such desires."

Nearly every philosopher nowadays rejects the traditional view that knowledge is justified true belief (§15). Philosophers reject the traditional view because they are convinced that having a justified true belief doesn't suffice for knowledge. In other words, it's possible to have a justified true belief that P, even though you don't know that P. This is possible in cases where your justified belief is only *accidentally* true. (Gettier cases are like this.) With that point in mind, Kvanvig asks, if all your beliefs were justified and true, what difference would it make if they were only accidentally true and so failed to count as knowledge? "So what? Why should you care?" Any difference is trivial, at best.

Kvanvig considers an objection to this last claim. The objection resembles a suggestion made by virtue epistemologists, such as John Greco and Ernest Sosa (§§34, 36), which is that to know is to achieve true belief, to believe the truth "in virtue of our powers," not by accident. Don't we want to believe the truth in virtue of our powers, rather than by accident? Kvanvig concedes that there is something to this suggestion, but denies that it shows that knowledge is valuable or worthy of serious philosophical attention. One of Kvanvig's main reasons for denying this is that there are counter-examples to the claim that to know is to achieve true belief, so even if our goal is to achieve true belief, it doesn't show that our goal is knowledge. (See Pritchard's discussion of Gettier cases in §35 for an idea of how such a counterexample might go.)

Finally, Kvanvig considers a completely different suggestion for why knowledge might be valuable and so worth serious philosophical attention. Perhaps knowledge is the norm of assertion. That is, perhaps knowledge is what licenses us to claim that something is true: we may assert P *only if* we know P. Assertion is very important for us. So if knowledge is the norm of assertion, that would make it valuable, and provide ample motivation for studying it.

There is some linguistic evidence for the hypothesis that knowledge is the norm of assertion.[1] First, consider how we challenge assertions: we challenge them by questioning whether the speaker believes what they said, or whether they have evidence for what they said, or whether what they said is true, and even whether they know what they said. The following are all typical challenges to an assertion:

- That's not true.
- You don't believe that.
- You don't have any evidence for that.
- You don't know that.

Here is one explanation for why these are typical challenges to assertion: knowledge is the norm of assertion, and all these challenges deny that the speaker satisfies a necessary condition of knowledge. Second, consider that we typically feel compelled to retract an asser-

---

[1] For a state-of-the-art review of all the linguistic data, along with an explanatory argument for the view that knowledge is the norm of assertion, see John Turri, "The Express Knowledge Account of Assertion," *Australasian Journal of Philosophy* 89.1 (2011): 37–45.

tion if it turns out that we didn't know whereof we spoke. That is, we feel pressure to retract *ignorant assertions*. One explanation for this pattern of retraction is that knowledge is the norm of assertion, and we implicitly recognize this, so we feel pressure to retract ignorant assertions.

Kvanvig rejects the proposal that knowledge is the norm of assertion. He has at least two lines of reasoning against the view. First, we normally feel pressure to retract ignorant assertions, and claiming that a speaker doesn't know whereof he speaks is normally a way of challenging the legitimacy of his assertion. But *normally* doesn't mean *always*, and in this case, Kvanvig argues, the exceptions disprove the rule. Consider avowals of religious faith.

> Consider someone who takes Pascal's advice of going to Mass and hoping for the best; in line with such advice, a person may sincerely avow that God exists even though that person does not (yet) believe it. Furthermore, no one in such a condition need be moved to retract the assertion upon complaint that the assertion is not backed by belief; at most, what you would get is an excuse for saying it, suggesting that the speaker understands that he or she has violated a condition on assertion that *normally* holds, but does not hold in this case.

Second, there is an important difference between *retracting the content of an assertion* and *retracting the act of asserting it*. Otherwise put, there is a difference between "taking back only *what is said*" and "taking back *the saying of it*." We'll retract the content of an assertion if it's proven false, or if we're presented with new evidence for thinking that it's false. But if, at the time of our original assertion, we believed what we said on the basis of good evidence, then we won't retract the act of asserting. In such a situation, Kvanvig reports, "I'll retract my statement," but I won't say that my act of asserting it "was out of order." Compare that to a case where we either don't believe what we assert, or believe it based on poor evidence. Even if our assertion turns out to be true, we will acknowledge that our act of asserting was out of line, and we might even be willing to apologize for it. Moreover, Kvanvig argues, to glean the norm of assertion, we should be guided by the conditions under which the act of asserting is out of line, not the conditions under which it is appropriate to retract the content of an assertion. This suggests that justified belief is the norm of assertion, not knowledge.

Having surveyed many ways of shoring up the purported value of knowledge and its centrality to philosophical inquiry, Kvanvig is ultimately unpersuaded. He recommends that we should quit focusing so much on knowledge, and instead pay attention to "the nature of exemplary cognition" and the intellectual virtues that enable it.

Reference

John Turri, "The Express Knowledge Account of Assertion," *Australasian Journal of Philosophy* 89.1 (2011): 37–45.

§ 38

Giving up on (exact) truth (Elgin, "True Enough")

Epistemologists are fixated on truth. Belief aims at truth. Justification is an indication of, or a means to, truth. Evidence is evidence of the truth. Reliability is reliability in getting at the truth. Intellectual duties are duties to learn the truth. Knowledge requires truth. Truth, truth, truth. If cognition is the solar system, then truth is the sun.

But is truth really the superstar of cognition? Catherine Elgin argues that it is not. Truth is, at best, one costar among many on cognition's stage. She focuses on one of truth's costars: understanding. Let's first consider her case against "truth-centered epistemology," and then consider her alternative approach to epistemology, which features understanding.

For present purposes, let *truth-centered epistemology* (what Elgin calls "veritism") be the view that truth is the only fundamental

Elgin, Catherine Z., "True Enough," pp. 113–131 in *Philosophical Issues* 14, Epistemology (2004). © 2004 by *Philosophical Issues*.

cognitive goal or value. What matters epistemically is truth, and what we ought to do is figure out what is true.

The main argument against truth-centered epistemology goes as follows.

1. If truth-centered epistemology is true, then our best science is epistemologically illegitimate. (Premise)
2. Our best science isn't epistemologically illegitimate. (Premise)
3. So truth-centered epistemology isn't true. (From 1 and 2)

Elgin assumes that line 2 of the argument is uncontroversial, and she certainly seems to be on safe ground here. Unless we're willing to embrace a fairly radical form of skepticism, we should be willing to grant line 2. Science is "cognitively good."

What about line 1? Elgin introduces several facts in support of it. First, science involves generalizing from data. But data gets compiled and handled in ways that everyone acknowledges doesn't fully accord with "independently ascertained truth." We discard outliers or ignore the fact that the data points don't exactly fit, say, a lovely parabolic curve. Second, science involves applying idealized formulas and models that don't accurately describe the phenomena under investigation. For example, we use the ideal gas law to explain the behavior of gasses. This "law" depicts "gas molecules as perfectly elastic spheres that occupy negligible space and exhibit mutual attraction." But no such molecule exists. To take another example, the model used to explain a pendulum's motion assumes a frictionless pivot and a rigid though massless rod. But no such pendulum exists.

If we abandon truth-centered epistemology, does chaos ensue? Can we accept wild falsehoods in the name of scientific progress? No, there are still standards of epistemic acceptability. In the examples Elgin offers to support line 1, even though scientific practice countenances deviation from the truth, it relies on claims that are "good approximations" of the truth. If an astronomer treats planets as "point masses," it's only because "given the size and distribution of planets in the solar system, what holds for properly characterized point masses also holds for planets." The ideal gas law misdescribes molecules, but its "divergence from the truth" is "negligible." It is "true enough" for our cognitive purposes.

But what is the relevant cognitive purpose? It is to understand, says Elgin. Understanding has a different object and different requirements than belief does. The object of belief is an individual proposition, which is a discrete meaningful unit of thought. Propositions are either true or false. Elgin agrees that truth is a norm of belief, that a false belief is epistemically bad and ought not be held. The object of understanding is a *domain of phenomena*, such as physics or hominid evolution. Domains are much broader than individual propositions. They are neither true nor false, although they do have a structure. Understanding can be expressed propositionally, but it can be expressed in other forms too, such as graphs or pictures. Importantly, you can understand something even if your understanding is based essentially on a falsehood. But how could you base your understanding on some falsehood without *believing* that falsehood, thereby violating the truth requirement on belief that Elgin herself endorses? Because belief isn't the only cognitive attitude you can have toward a proposition. Even if you don't believe P, you can still "cognitively accept" P. To believe P is to take it that P is true. To cognitively accept P "is to take it that P's divergence from truth, if any, does not matter cognitively." Its divergence does not matter cognitively just in case it doesn't prevent us from understanding the phenomenon in question.

To understand a domain is in part to "see affinities between" what might otherwise seem to be "disparate occurrences" within that domain, to recognize deep and important patterns and relationships. We understand a domain when we can "construe seemingly divergent phenomena as variants of a common scheme, or as perturbations of a regular pattern, or as deviations from a simple norm."

Felicitous falsehoods are false propositions that we accept and which promote our understanding of a domain. They "afford epistemic access" to patterns that would otherwise elude us. For example, if it turns out that gravity isn't accurately described by an inverse *square* law,

$$F = G\frac{m_1 m_2}{r^2}$$

but instead,

$$F = G\frac{m_1 m_2}{r^{1.9998639}}$$

we might nonetheless properly accept that it is an inverse square. We might properly accept this if its divergence from the truth promotes a greater understanding of physical phenomena. And it could promote a greater understanding of physical phenomena because, say, it helps us see patterns in how basic physical forces work. Consider Coulomb's Law, which describes the electrical force exerted by one charged particle on another similarly charged particle,

$$F = k\frac{q_1 q_2}{r^2}$$

It has the same exact form as Newton's gravitational law. But even if the actual law was slightly different, say,

$$F = k\frac{q_1 q_2}{r^{2.000652}}$$

that would not obscure an extraordinary resemblance between the two forces. We could see the two laws as "variations on a common theme," thus "configuring" physical phenomena in a way conducive to understanding. This enhanced understanding would be "the justification for the falsehoods."

§ 39

Naturalized epistemology advertised (Quine, "Epistemology Naturalized")

W.V. Quine's "Epistemology Naturalized" is a partisan comparison of two radically different visions of epistemology. The competing visions disagree on a number of points, including the goal and method of epistemology. One competitor is the "old epistemology" inspired by philosophers from the seventeenth through early twentieth centuries. Quine rejects old epistemology and instead favors a new approach that he calls *naturalized epistemology*.

Old epistemology traces back to Descartes. At the very outset of his *Meditations on First Philosophy*, Descartes explains that he is motivated to establish something "firm and lasting in the sciences."[1] That is why he engaged in his meditations. An arduous reconstruction of his cognitive

---

[1] All Descartes quotations are from Donald Cress's translation of *Meditations on First Philosophy*, 3edn (Hackett, 1993).

Quine, W. V., "Epistemology Naturalized," pp. 68–90 in *Ontological Relativity and Other Essays* (Columbia University Press, 1969). © 1969 by Columbia University Press.

Epistemology: A Guide, First Edition. John Turri.
© 2014 John Wiley & Sons, Ltd. Published 2014 by John Wiley & Sons, Ltd.

habits and attitudes is required prior to doing science. He must begin by doubting anything that isn't entirely certain or reliable, beginning most conspicuously with his senses. His senses might be badly malfunctioning, or he might be merely dreaming, in which case his sensory experiences would be no better than a mirage. So severely and efficiently does Descartes doubt that by only the seventh – seventh! – paragraph of Meditation One, he reasons, "Thus it is not improper to conclude from this that physics, astronomy, medicine, and all the other disciplines" concerned with the material and social world are suspect. And to begin Meditation Two, he reminds himself,

> I suppose that everything I see is false. I believe that none of what my deceitful memory represents ever existed. I have no senses whatever. Body, shape, extension, movement, and place are all chimeras.

Descartes then tries to recover all that has been lost to doubt. He may appeal only to that which he is absolutely certain of: his own conscious thoughts. The contents of Descartes's conscious mind are the only props allowed on stage for the opening soliloquy in his epistemological drama. And each inference he makes along the way must be as indubitable as his starting points.

By the end of his meditations, Descartes convinced himself that he "should not doubt" that he has a body, that "various other bodies exist around" him, that his memory and senses are generally reliable guides to the world, and that he can even distinguish dreaming from waking, so long as he's careful. Now he can get on to the business of doing science!

Notice two features of Descartes's approach that help characterize old epistemology. First, epistemology *precedes* and *justifies* empirical science. It is the foundation of science. Proper science begins only after we've properly regimented our cognitive habits through the most rigorous epistemological scrutiny. Second, certainty is the standard of success. Epistemologically proper starting points must be absolutely certain, and so must every inference along the road to recovering the external world and commencing with empirical science.

Another important theme in old epistemology, according to Quine, is the urge to "[identify] objects with impressions." By this Quine means that traditionalists, such as David Hume, accepted a *metaphysical* thesis about the nature of "physical" objects, such as apples and tables and mountains: they are nothing but sensory experiences, or collections thereof.[2] An apple *is nothing more than* the redness we see and the sweetness we taste. A rock is *nothing more than* the grayness we see and the roughness and hardness we feel. If this metaphysical thesis is true, then it simplifies greatly the quest for certainty about some aspects of the "physical" world: we can be certain that observed physical objects exist because they *just are* sensory experiences, and we can be certain that our sensory experiences exist. Sensory experiences are among the contents of the conscious mind. Metaphysical reduction brings epistemological payoff.

A related theme in old epistemology is a *semantic* thesis about the meaning of sentences about the physical world. George Berkeley is the most famous proponent of this semantic thesis. Berkeley claimed that "the table exists" is equivalent in meaning to "I see and feel the table"; "there was a figure" is equivalent to "a figure was perceived"; "there was an odor" is equivalent to "an odor was smelled"; "there was a color" is equivalent to "a color was perceived"; "there was a sound" is equivalent to "a sound was heard"; and so on. This semantic thesis complements the metaphysical thesis discussed earlier. If *all we mean* when we say things about ordinary objects is that we undergo (or perhaps would undergo) certain patterns of sensory experiences, then surely ordinary objects, should any exist, *must be* collections of sensory experience. (Compare: if "mother" just means "female parent," then of course if a mother exists, then she must be a female parent – nothing more, and nothing less.) This aspect of the traditional vision culminated in Rudolf Carnap's attempt to, as Quine puts it, "account for the external world as a logical construct of sense data." Semantic equivalence enables metaphysical reduction.

---

[2] Quine singles out Hume in connection with this thesis, but here Hume follows George Berkeley; see Berkeley's *Treatise Concerning the Principles of Human Knowledge*.

Another plank of old epistemology is fear of circularity. Recall that, according to the tradition, epistemology precedes and justifies empirical science. This applies especially to the epistemology of perception and empirical beliefs. Science aims to provide generalizations that allow us to predict the course of experience, and explanations that help us to understand why things happen. But scientists need proper data in order to responsibly generalize; scientists need to know that the event happened in order to responsibly explain why it happened. Thus, it would be objectionably circular, and obviously so, to appeal to the results of empirical science when doing the epistemology of perception and empirical beliefs.

The fear of circularity manifests itself in another way too: the problem of induction. Science presupposes that nature at least tends toward uniformity, even if it isn't perfectly uniform: consistent patterns observed in the past are at least likely to persist in to the future; if all observed quantities of copper conduct electricity, then it is at least likely that unobserved quantities of copper conduct electricity too. But what justifies us in accepting that nature at least tends toward uniformity? It doesn't seem that we can be justified by a priori reflection that nature tends toward uniformity, because it's not contradictory to claim that nature doesn't tend toward uniformity. Can we properly reason our way to the conclusion that nature does so?

Hume argued that we couldn't possibly do so. For all reasoning is either deductive or inductive. In proper deductive reasoning, the truth of the premises guarantees the conclusion. But none of the premises we're justified in accepting about the natural world *guarantees* that nature tends toward uniformity. So deductive reasoning won't help. In proper inductive reasoning, the truth of premises makes it likely that the conclusion is true. But none of the premises we're justified in accepting about the natural world *makes it likely* that nature tends toward uniformity, *unless* the argument implicitly assumes that nature does tend toward uniformity! To see why, suppose we have as a premise that in the past every observed unsupported object has fallen. Does this premise make it likely that *the next* observed unsupported object will fall too? Not unless the behavior of observed unsupported objects tends toward uniformity. Does the premise in question make it likely that *unobserved* unsupported objects fall? Again, not unless the behavior of unsupported objects tends toward uniformity. Any such inductive reasoning therefore "must be evidently going in a circle, and taking for granted" that which it attempts to prove.[3] And such circularity is clearly vicious (or so Hume and others assume, without argumentation). So inductive reasoning won't help either. Overall, then, the infamous problem of induction presupposes that circularity is unacceptable.

To sum up, we can identify at least seven commitments of old epistemology:

- *Superiority of epistemology*: epistemology precedes and justifies empirical science.
- *Enabling goal*: the goal of epistemology is to enable empirical science and "rationally reconstruct" its findings.
- *Certainty and infallibility*: certainty attained by infallible means is necessary for epistemic success.
- *Subjectivism*: private episodes (conscious sensory experiences) are the basis of both certainty and meaning.
- *Semantic equivalence*: sentences about physical things mean the same thing as sentences about sensory experience.
- *Metaphysical reduction*: physical things just are (sets of) sensory experiences.
- *Anti-circularity*: Circularity is epistemologically unacceptable.

Quine's alternative vision for epistemology, his "naturalized epistemology," differs from the old approach on all counts. The old vision begins to unravel with its misguided emphasis on certainty and the completely implausible claim of semantic equivalence. The "Cartesian quest for certainty," which "had been the remote motivation" of traditional epistemology, is "a lost cause." Descartes failed, and for good reason – there simply is no way to validly (deductively) infer the existence of external objects, let alone all or even most of empirical science, from our sensory experiences. We also "must despair" of the semantic program that equates "physical" and "sensory" vocabulary, and we

---

[3] David Hume, *Enquiry Concerning Human Understanding* 4.2.

must despair more generally of any attempt to "translate science" into the language of sensory experience. That's just obviously *not what we mean* when we speak of apples, rocks, tables, plants, animals, galaxies, or any other category of sensible objects.

Once we've given up on those planks of the old approach, the others quickly follow. Semantic equivalence was really the only hope for motivating the astonishing claim that physical objects are nothing more than collections of sensory experiences. So metaphysical reduction falls by the wayside too. The quixotic quest for certainty motivated the retreat to the subjective as a basis for justification and meaning, so we can give up subjectivism too. Besides, it's acutely "ironic" that a project intended to validate science – an enterprise whose gold standard is "intersubjective agreement" and public scrutiny of hypotheses – would nominate private, subjective sensory experiences as the basis of all meaning and justification. After all, empirical science is a public, communal enterprise. What's more, empirical science seems to be *by far our best way* of discovering how the world works, having delivered centuries of significant, tangible, and often fantastic results. Science has done all this without epistemology "rationally reconstructing" its deliverances or providing it with a foundation of certainty. Epistemology is not prior to science; epistemology is not superior. But, then, if we're not trying to ground science on epistemology, and if science is our best way of learning about the world, and science is an activity that happens in the world, then it makes sense to *do science* to better understand how science actually proceeds. Worries about circularity at this point are not so much punctilious as fatuous. And if we like, we can use the label "epistemology" for that branch of science which studies how cognition and theorizing actually proceeds – that is, how "input," in the form of "stimulation of sensory receptors," relates to "output," in the form of beliefs and theories.

To sum up, we can identify at least six main principles of Quine's new, naturalized epistemology:

- *Subordination of epistemology*: Epistemology is a branch of empirical science, in particular of psychology.

- *Explanatory goal*: The goal of epistemology is to understand science as a social institution, including how cognition and theorization actually work.
- *Modesty*: Incrementally enhanced confidence and understanding attained by fallible means is sufficient for epistemic success.
- *Intersubjectivism*: Public episodes are the basis of meaning and justification.
- *Semantic verificationism*: The meaning of an empirical sentence consists in what would count as evidence that it is true.[4]
- *Nonreduction*: Physical things are not (sets of) sensory experiences; it is "likelier than not" that they are public and "corporeal."
- *Circularity*: Circularity is acceptable and unavoidable, at least in some forms.

It would be a mistake, I think, to scour Quine's paper for a sustained argument in favor of naturalized epistemology. Better to think of it as a reminder of why the old approach is hopeless, along with a detailed advertisement for a new approach. "Epistemology Naturalized" paints a picture of stark contrasts and invites you to consider the potential benefits of its namesake.

References

David Hume, *Enquiry Concerning Human Understanding*.
Rene Descartes, *Meditations on First Philosophy*, 3rd edn.
George Berkeley, *Treatise Concerning the Principles of Human Knowledge*.

[4] This vastly oversimplifies the claims Quine makes, or gestures toward, about meaning in "Epistemology Naturalized." In addition to verificationism, he also advocates semantic *holism* and a socialized form of *behaviorism*. (As a corollary, he also advocates the *indeterminacy of translation* for theoretical sentences, as opposed to "observation sentences.") But these issues are far too challenging and remote from our primary concerns to dwell upon here.

§ 40

Naturalized epistemology criticized (Kim, "What is 'Naturalized Epistemology'?")

Jaegwon Kim agrees with W.V. Quine (§39) that the old episte-mology, which traces from Descartes through Hume up to the Logical Positivists of the early twentieth century, is a "lost cause." The central aim of the old epistemology – to justify empirical science by deducing its findings with certainty from indubitable founda-tions concerning the character of sensory experience – is simply impossible to achieve. Kim takes this to be uncontroversial. But Kim rejects Quine's recommendation to epistemologists in light of old epistemology's failure.

Quine recommends that we "naturalize epistemology." Epistemology, on Quine's vision, is just a "chapter of psychology." We conduct empirical scientific investigation to see how cognition

Kim, Jaegwon, "What is 'Naturalized Epistemology'?" in J. Tomberlin (ed.), *Philosophical Perspectives* 2. Epistemology (Atascadero, CA: Ridgeview Publishing Co., 1988), pp. 381–405. © 1998 by *Philosophical Perspectives*.

Epistemology: A Guide, First Edition. John Turri.
© 2014 John Wiley & Sons, Ltd. Published 2014 by John Wiley & Sons, Ltd.

"really proceeds." We use science to study science as a social institution. We use science to learn how experience prompts belief in humans, how humans formulate theories in light of our observations, and how humans choose among them. We conceive of evidence as "the stimulation of ... sensory receptors." We decide which sentences serve as the ultimate test of scientific theories – that is, which sentences are "observation sentences" – by discovering which sentences all competent language users would assent to "under uniform stimulation" of their sensory receptors.

Quine even mentions a couple more specific projects as examples of naturalized epistemology. On the one hand, he suggests investigating "perceptual norms," which are perceptual analogues of phonemes. Phonemes are the minimal perceptually distinct units of speech. Humans tend to group phonemes into about thirty different types. Of course, the actual diversity of units of speech is much greater than this. But we habitually tend to "rectify" them all and treat them as one of thirty basic kinds. We might call these *phonemic habits* or *norms*. Similarly, Quine suggests that there might be *perceptual norms*, a limited range of basic elements of sensory experience toward which we "rectify all perceptions." The set of these constitute, as it were, a set of "epistemological building blocks" in humans. Science could reveal them. On the other hand, Quine suggests investigating "evolutionary epistemology," or the study of the evolution of cognitive traits such as color vision and inductive reasoning.[1]

Notice one thing that doesn't show up in Quine's sketch of naturalized epistemology: *justification*. This omission motivates Kim's opposition to Quine's recommendation. Kim takes it as "uncontroversial" that epistemology is "a normative inquiry whose principal aim is a systematic study of the conditions of justified belief." But nothing in Quine's approach counts as either normative or concerned with justification. According to Kim, Quine "is asking us to set aside the entire framework of justification-centered epistemology," and to replace it with "a purely descriptive ... science of human cognition." The contrast between normative and descriptive is crucial here.

---

[1] All quotations in this paragraph are from Quine, §39.

A *normative discipline* concerns itself with how things *ought* to be, how it would be *good* for things to be, and why. For example, epistemology studies what doxastic attitudes we ought to form, what doxastic attitudes are good to form, and why. In short, epistemology is concerned with justified belief. By contrast, a *descriptive discipline* concerns itself simply with how things are. For example, modern physics seeks to describe the way the physical world works, and hopefully produce general theories that help us to explain and predict the course of events. Modern physics doesn't concern itself with how the world *ought* to work, or how it would be *good* for the world to work. Similarly, cognitive science seeks to describe the way cognition proceeds, and, in its more ambitious moments, how science itself works as a social institution. Cognitive science doesn't tell us, for example, how chemical receptors in the brain ought to work, or distinguish between good and bad ways to set up scientific institutions. Of course, the findings of physics or cognitive science are often highly relevant to learning how we ought to proceed, or what would be good to do, but these are evaluative conclusions based on descriptive scientific findings, not scientific findings themselves.

Kim does not impugn the value of psychology or of descriptive science more generally; on the contrary, he respects these disciplines and thinks that they are important and ought to be pursued. Rather, Kim rejects Quine's naturalized epistemology as a "lame" substitute for traditional epistemology, unworthy of the label "epistemology." It has a completely different subject matter and purpose from traditional epistemology. Investigating how human sensory receptors are irradiated is no substitute for investigating how sensory experience provides good evidence for beliefs or theories. Investigating how humans actually draw inferences is no substitute for investigating what makes an inference appropriate.

If normativity disappears from our inquiry, then so does justification. And if justification disappears, then so does knowledge. In light of this, Kim concludes, Quine's recommendation is spurious.

Kim takes his critique a step further. If normativity disappears, then so does belief. Belief is a normative category. In order to recognize something as a belief, you have to recognize it as a state of a believer, and so recognize a believer. But in order to recognize someone as a believer, with this particular belief, you must assume that she has a coherent and mostly rational set of beliefs, along with other propositional attitudes, such as desires (see §11 for more on this Davidsonian approach to belief). And this in turn requires evaluating the believer, and the specific belief in question, as measuring up to some overall standard of "evidence and justification." But Quine's recommended project is a purely descriptive enterprise, so it can't even be concerned with beliefs and believers! Belief and believers disappear along with knowledge and justification. Surely this is an absurd result, Kim thinks, one that exposes the Quinean project as a mere pretender to the title of "epistemology."

Nevertheless, Kim still accepts that descriptive facts are relevant, indeed essential, to epistemology. For he accepts that epistemic properties "supervene" on, or are explained by, "factual descriptive properties." In other words, Kim accepts what we earlier called *the epistemic supervenience thesis* (see §13). Supervenience is "fundamental" to our understanding of epistemic properties. Normative epistemology is thus enriched by the factual descriptions uncovered by empirical science, even though empirical science can't replace normative epistemology.

§ 41

Naturalized epistemology radicalized (Antony, "Quine as Feminist")

Is modern Western epistemology ("mainstream" epistemology) inherently oppressive and subservient to elite interests? Or does it contain radical potential to redress widespread injustices suffered by weak, marginalized, and downtrodden social groups? Can it help promote a "more just, human, and nurturing world?" Louise Antony confronts these questions and concludes that, notwithstanding popular misconceptions to the contrary among feminists, mainstream epistemology does have potential to contribute to radical and beneficial social change.[1]

---

[1] It's worth noting that even posing these questions probably suggests that epistemologists have far more power than they actually do.

Antony, Louise M., "Quine as Feminist: the Radical Import of Naturalized Epistemology," pp. 185–225 in L. Antony and C. Witt (eds.), *A Mind of One's Own* (Boulder, CO: Westview, 1993). © 1993 by Westview Press, a member of the Perseus Books Group.

Epistemology: A Guide, First Edition. John Turri.
© 2014 John Wiley & Sons, Ltd. Published 2014 by John Wiley & Sons, Ltd.

Antony spends considerable time exploring ways that feminist philosophers have interpreted the history of modern Western epistemology, including contemporary analytic epistemology. Antony argues that they seriously misinterpret some important aspects of this tradition, which undermines their critique of it. Antony goes so far as to say that the critique involves "gross distortion," "oversimplification," and "cartoonish" portrayals. The details of all this misinterpretation needn't concern us here. Instead, we'll focus on an issue that Antony thinks is absolutely crucial for epistemologists to come terms with – objectivity and the evaluation of bias – and how she thinks naturalized epistemology can handle it.

Academic pursuits and disciplines are thoroughly social. Their heavy intellectual component doesn't lessen their social character. We should expect these social institutions to be influenced by political power. And we shouldn't be surprised if such influence shapes academic disciplines in a way that benefits those who wield power. And since patriarchy and capitalism are two of the most powerful forces shaping our society, we shouldn't be surprised if predominant forms of scholarship end up reinforcing patriarchy and capitalism. Many feminists, including Antony, accept that this is true of the most successful and respected form of scholarship in contemporary society: empirical science. In modern industrialized Western societies, science "is very much an instrument of oppression."

How could science be held in such high esteem if it is an instrument of oppression? One important ideological component is the notion of *objectivity*. A popular notion is that proper scientific inquiry is objective. Competent scientists completely divest themselves of any preconceptions, theoretical commitments, moral values, emotional attachments, and personal goals. They dispassionately record observations, analyze the data, and draw warranted conclusions. The process is "mechanical," "passive," and "value neutral." Its results are subject to intense scrutiny and must be reproducible to pass muster. If the public could be persuaded that science was thus objective, then ruling elites could leverage that fact to imbue their agenda with an aura of legitimacy. After all, it's hard to take issue with policies bearing the imprint of scientific objectivity: they are supported by an impartial, automatic, and reproducible process bound to deliver, or at least approximate, the truth. An epistemology that reinforced such a notion of scientific objectivity might thus be complicit in political oppression.

Some feminist philosophers deny that science is objective, on the grounds that scientific inquiry is a human endeavor, and no human endeavor is objective. Every inquiry is thoroughly situated or "embedded." It begins from a specific place, specific time, and specific assumptions; it is conducted by a specific group of persons with specific characteristics, including goals and values, which inevitably influence the questions they ask, the data they gather, their interpretation of the data, and the conclusions they draw. Value-neutral, impartial, mechanical inquiry is a pernicious myth: bias infects the process from beginning to end. If correct and widely acknowledged, this might well quash any aura of legitimacy lent by science to oppressive policies.

But now we face a puzzle. If every intellectual project is inevitably biased, then so is the feminist critique of objectivity! It too advances an agenda. Bias is "ubiquitous and ineliminable." So should we exchange our trust in biased science for trust in biased feminism? What do we gain as a result? Antony puts the question pointedly to feminists: "What are we complaining about? Is it just that we want [inquiry] to be distorted in *our* favor, rather than in" favor of current elite interests? This is *the puzzle of bias* for feminist critiques of scientific objectivity.

Antony proposes a solution: embrace bias but distinguish between good and bad biases. Distinguishing good from bad biases is an epistemological project. And, Antony contends, naturalized epistemology prescribes the best method to execute the project. For, as we saw earlier (§39), according to naturalized epistemologists, epistemological questions are empirical questions. We make careful observations in order to assess which biases tend to produce knowledge and which ones don't. Indeed, we must make careful observations to even assess which biases are actually operative in our intellectual lives. Empirical psychology is the best way to learn how we actually form our beliefs, which assumptions we take for [...] granted, and which alternative hypotheses we simply ignore.

209

What sort of bias is good, you might wonder. Isn't bias by definition *bad*? No, it isn't, and it is a testament to the myth of objectivity that we're even tempted to think so. Consider our tendency to expect the future to resemble the past, or more generally to expect nature to tend toward uniformity. Unless we were instinctively biased to expect the future to resemble the past, we would be at an utter loss to learn from experience. Bias makes experience our greatest teacher. We couldn't survive without bias, much less succeed in organized scientific inquiry. More mundane examples of good bias are readily identified. We are biased to interpret a human smile as signifying a pleasant disposition, to interpret a large cat's silhouette or a snake's form as signifying danger, and to interpret that distinctive abdominal twinge as a sign that nourishment is needed.

Of course, just as it's incorrect to assume that all biases are bad, it would be disastrous to conclude that all biases are good. Suppose we're socialized to simply assume that, say, women have less mathematical ability than men, or to assume that indigenous cultures are violent. Those biases are morally objectionable and intellectually harmful, individually and socially, because they promote the acquisition of false beliefs and function to exclude potentially valuable contributors from common scientific pursuits.

In light of all this, Antony contends that objectivity is neither possible nor desirable. We should be deeply suspicious of any approach that tries to convince us otherwise. Rather than indulge in potentially harmful fantasies about perfectly impartial science, we should instead, following the lead of naturalized epistemologists, pursue "an empirical theory of biases." If intellectual practices unfairly discriminate based on gender, class, ethnicity, or otherwise, then it is *an empirical fact* that such discrimination takes place. Empirical investigation will reveal it. Uncovering such facts and telling the truth about them has "radical" potential. In this way, Antony points out, naturalized epistemology can promote "radical epistemological action."

§ 42

A apriori justification and unrevisability (Putnam, "There is at Least One A Priori Truth")

On one interpretation, W.V. Quine denied that there is any a priori truth. Hilary Putnam disagrees with Quine on this point. The dispute is crystallized in a simple question: is any statement such that it "would never be *rational* to give up?" And by "never" Putnam means "absolutely, unconditionally, truly" under no circumstances. He isn't satisfied with examples involving statements that wouldn't be rational to give up merely relative to a certain body of knowledge (so-called contextual apriority), even if that body of knowledge is vast and substantial. So we might reasonably replace the "would" in Putnam's question with "could."

Putnam unfortunately multiplies terms beyond necessity. For example, he switches between "truth" and "statement." He claims

Putnam, Hilary, "There is a Least One A Priori Truth," pp. 153–170 in *Erkenntnis* 13 (Dordrecht, Netherlands: D. Reidel Publishing Co., 1978). © 1978 by D. Reidel Publishing Company.

Epistemology: A Guide, First Edition. John Turri.
© 2014 John Wiley & Sons, Ltd. Published 2014 by John Wiley & Sons, Ltd.

that, for Quine, questions about what is a priori amount to questions about what is "analytic" or "unrevisable," and then Putnam distinguishes between different senses of "unrevisable." Putnam introduces the "epistemic interpretation" of unrevisability, and then goes on to refer to it as "the moderate doctrine" on "a priori truth." For present purposes, we'll simply bypass all this terminological variety and focus on the simple question posed in the previous paragraph.

As already mentioned, Putnam answers our question affirmatively. To support his position, Putnam rightly notes, "one [successful example] is all we need." Putnam's candidate is "the Minimal Principle of Contradiction" (MPC), which says: not every statement is both true and false. Putnam equates its being rational to give up MPC with its being rational to accept its denial. Its denial is, "every statement is both true and false." Putnam probably moves too quickly here, though, because to give up some claim isn't the same as accepting its denial. For instance, you might go from accepting it to suspending judgment on it. But to suspend judgment on a claim isn't to accept its denial.

Previously, people have mistakenly thought that certain statements couldn't be rationally given up. Developments in mathematics and science proved them wrong. For example, people used to think that it couldn't be rational to give up on the claim that Euclidean geometry accurately described physical space. But not only could it be rationally given up, it has actually been rationally given up. People used to think that it couldn't be rational to give up on the statement that space and time are completely separate physical quantities. But again, not only could it be rationally given up, it has been. And Putnam himself accepts that developments in quantum mechanics make it rational to give up on certain logical principles that were thought to be unrevisable. So why is Putnam confident that MPC won't suffer a similar fate? Why think that no further developments in mathematics or science will one day make it rational to give up MPC?

To answer that question, we first need to understand what is going on in those other cases where people rationally gave up on a statement that was previously thought to be rationally unrevisable. In those cases, a sophisticated physical theory inconsistent with the relevant statement made specific, surprising, testable predictions that turned out to be true. The best explanation for why the predictions turned out to be true is that the physical theory itself is true. But then since the physical theory is inconsistent with the statement, the statement must be false. This is how it becomes rational to give up the statement. For example, Einstein's General Theory of Relativity made novel predictions about the passage of time and the behavior of light. Observations confirmed the predictions, and this counts greatly in favor of the theory. Einstein's theory is inconsistent with a Euclidean treatment of physical space. So it is now rational to give up on the claim that Euclidean geometry accurately describes physical space.

Can this happen to MPC? No, Putnam says, and this is why he is confident that MPC won't suffer a similar fate. In order for a physical theory to be inconsistent with MPC, the theory would have to consist of "every statement and its negation." But it's hard to understand what it could mean for such a theory to make specific, surprising, testable predictions. Indeed, it's hard to view it as making predictions at all, or even to understand what such a "theory" amounts to. At this point it certainly seems that the burden falls on Putnam's opponents. They must either explain how such a theory makes relevant predictions, or develop another approach to undermine MPC.

Putnam is still attracted to the idea that there is a sense in which every statement, including MPC, is potentially revisable. He distinguishes between two senses of "revise": *negation* and *accusation*. (Putnam uses the label "negation," but not "accusation.") To revise a statement P *by negation* is to accept its contradictory, not-P. To revise P *by accusation* is to charge that it is conceptually defective, that some concept it contains is somehow illegitimate or inapplicable to relevant cases. Putnam thinks that every statement is potentially rationally revisable by accusation, though the same isn't true of revision by negation – MPC, at least, is an exception to the latter sort.

213

Logical principles even weaker than MPC might serve Putnam's purpose too. For example, consider the *Modal Minimal Principle of Contradiction* (MMPC): not every statement is both *necessarily* true and *necessarily* false. Even if it turned out that MPC was rationally revisable by negation, it wouldn't follow that MMPC was rationally revisable by negation too. By contrast, it's hard to imagine that MMPC might turn out to be rationally revisable even though MPC does not.

§ 43

A priori justification and revisability (Casullo, "Revisability, Reliabilism, and A Priori Knowledge")

What is a priori knowledge? There is no completely uncontroversial answer to this question, but perhaps the least controversial answer is that a priori knowledge is knowledge justified independently of experience. Putative examples of such knowledge include our knowledge of simple mathematical and logical truths. But as we saw from Putnam's discussion (§42), some have thought that a priori knowledge also must be *rationally unrevisable*. That is, if you have a priori knowledge that P, then your justification for P couldn't be rationally undermined or defeated. In "Revisability, Reliabilism, and A Priori Knowledge," Albert Casullo's primary goal is to sever the supposed link between apriority[1] and rational unrevisability.

[1] "Apriority" is an abstract noun derived from the adjective "a priori."

Casullo, Albert, "Revisability, Reliabilism, and A Priori Knowledge," pp. 187–213 in *Philosophy and Phenomenology Research* 49, 2 (Dec. 1988). © 1988 by *Philosophy and Phenomenology Research*.

Let's follow Casullo and call the view that future evidence can't rationally deprive you of a priori justification *the unrevisability thesis* ("UT" for short). There is a strong and a weak version of UT. (From this point on, by "deprive" I shall mean "rationally deprive.") The strong version of UT ("SUT" for short) says that no future evidence *of any kind* can deprive you of a priori justification. The weak version of UT ("WUT") says that no future *experiential* evidence can deprive you of a priori justification. Given the plausible assumption that not all evidence is experiential, if SUT is true, then WUT must be true too. In other words, SUT entails WUT. But WUT does not entail SUT. For even if we suppose that no experiential evidence could deprive you of a priori justification, it doesn't follow that no nonexperiential evidence could similarly deprive you.

Given that SUT entails WUT, it follows that if WUT is false, then SUT is false too. So let's look at Casullo's argument against WUT. The heart of Casullo's argument is the case of Phil. Phil is an expert logician. He is extremely reliable at proving interesting theorems. His evidence that a certain proof is valid is not experiential. Rather, upon reflection it just seems obvious to him that it is valid. And he almost invariably gets it right. But Phil is not infallible. He sometimes, albeit very rarely, makes mistakes. The mere fact that his logical powers are fallible doesn't stop him from being justified in believing that a particular proof is valid. Nor does his fallibility stop him from gaining knowledge in many cases that this proof is valid. On the rare occasion when he does make an error, but the proof nevertheless seems valid to him, he doesn't know that it is valid, but he is still justified in believing that it is valid. And this is a paradigmatic case of a priori justification. Now, in order to generate a case to test WUT, let's see whether, in this paradigm case, further experience could deprive Phil of this a priori justification.

Casullo says that experience could do this, in the following way. Suppose that Phil commissions a brilliant cognitive neuroscientist, Maria, to study his logical powers. Phil wants to decrease his error rate. Through painstaking neurological observation, measurement, and analysis, Maria isolates the malfunction that causes Phil's errors. Phil makes a logical error when and only when a specific pattern of neural activity takes place. Now suppose that Phil believes that the particular proof he just constructed is valid. Upon reflection it seems obvious to him that it is valid, so his belief is a priori justified. Now suppose that soon thereafter Mary analyzes the neurological data and informs Phil that the offending pattern of neural activity just took place as he formed his opinion. Phil trusts Mary and has no reason to suspect that she is trying to deceive him or has erred in gathering or analyzing her data. Based on her testimony and past experience, he accepts that the offending pattern is responsible for his belief.

Here is the key question: at the end the story, has Phil lost *at least some* of the a priori justification he had for believing that the proof is valid? Casullo submits that the answer is "yes." Phil's a priori justification has been revised in light of subsequent experience. Thus, WUT is false.

Casullo imagines the following objection on behalf of WUT. If subsequent experience deprived Phil of justification, then Phil's earlier justification was partly based, at least implicitly, on the fact that he had not had undermining experience. But his not having such experience is itself an experiential matter. Thus, Phil's earlier justification was not independent of experience and so was not a priori. And if Phil's justification isn't a priori, then Phil's case can't be a counterexample to WUT, which pertains specifically to a priori justification.

Casullo replies by denying the initial conditional premise of the objection. From the fact that subsequent experience deprives Phil of justification, it does not follow that his earlier justification was implicitly based on the fact that he hadn't had an undermining experience. As an analogy, Casullo asks us to consider the introspective justification we have for thinking that we are, say, in pain or anxious or some other mental condition. It could turn out that neuroscience uncovers strong correlations between neural states and mental states. And it could turn out that neuroscientific observation leads you to revise your opinion about whether you're in pain. (Perhaps it's just a very serious itch or some other intensely annoying sensation that leads you to mistakenly believe that you're in pain.)

From this it doesn't follow that your earlier belief that you're in pain was based on the assumption that neuroscience hadn't provided you with contrary evidence. Similarly, in Phil's case, his earlier belief that the proof was valid wasn't based on the assumption that neuroscience hadn't provided him with contrary evidence.

§ 44

Philosophical method and empirical science (Bealer, "A Priori Knowledge and the Scope of Philosophy")

George Bealer argues for a pair of bold claims about philosophy's relationship to empirical science. He argues that philosophy is *Autonomous*, meaning that philosophers can answer most central philosophical questions without "relying substantively" on empirical science. He also argues that philosophy is *Authoritative*, meaning that when philosophy and empirical science offer conflicting answers to the same central philosophical question, the philosophical answer is better supported. Bealer's argument for the Autonomy and Authority of philosophy spring from theses about the epistemology of intuitions, or a priori knowledge and evidence.

Bealer, George, "A Priori Knowledge and the Scope of Philosophy," pp. 121–42 in *Philosophical Studies* 81 (Kluwer Academic Publishers, 1996). © 1996 Kluwer Academic Publishers.

Bealer states his central argument admirably briefly in the opening passages of his paper. But its terseness threatens to make the argument less lucid than a novice might hope for. With the goal of making the argument's logic absolutely clear, we can represent it like so:

1. Intuitions are evidence. (Premise)
2. If intuitions are evidence, then modal reliabilism about evidence is true. (Premise)
3. So modal reliabilism about evidence is true. (From 1 and 2)
4. If modal reliabilism about evidence is true, then if scientific essentialism is no barrier, then philosophy is Autonomous and Authoritative. (Premise)
5. So if scientific essentialism is no barrier, then philosophy is Autonomous and Authoritative. (From 3 and 4)
6. Scientific essentialism is no barrier. (Premise)
7. So philosophy is Autonomous and Authoritative. (From 5 and 6)

The argument is valid (if its premises are true, then its conclusion must be true too). So let's see what Bealer says on behalf of the premises, starting with 1.

Before explaining why intuitions are evidence, let's first clarify what an intuition is. It won't hurt to think of intuition as the intellectual or rational analogue of perceptual experience. In virtue of having a perceptual experience – say, of a pine tree – things visually seem a certain way to you, namely, that there is a pine true. In virtue of having an intuition – say, of two being the only even prime number – things intellectually seem a certain way to you, namely, that two is the only even prime number. A visual appearance usually leads you to believe that things are the way they appear, but the seeming is distinct from the belief. Likewise, an intellectual appearance (i.e. an intuition) usually leads you to believe things are the way they appear, but the seeming is distinct from the belief.

We standardly treat intuitions as evidence. We routinely employ or rely on them when critically evaluating and justifying our beliefs, which is precisely the role that evidence plays in our cognitive economy. For example, recall JTB, the view that knowledge is justified true belief. Gettier argued that JTB is false, on the grounds that in certain possible cases, it seems that someone has a justified true belief that P, even though she doesn't know that P (§15). Gettier appeals to our *intuitions* about such cases to refute JTB. This is standard procedure, and not just in philosophy. In the course of everyday life, in the courtroom, in the lab, and elsewhere, the fact that something seems just obviously false is taken as a strike against it. Of course, our intuitions are fallible: sometimes the ways things obviously seem is subtly misleading or even completely wrong. But notice that when we do end up concluding that a previous intuition was wrong, we do so by relying on *other* intuitions. In all these ways, intuitions fit the profile of evidence just as well as perceptual experience does. On Bealer's view, intuition and perception are basic sources of evidence.

Suppose someone objects that only experience is evidence, and that relying on intuition is disreputable. Bealer calls this position *radical empiricism* about evidence. Radical empiricism disagrees with our routine procedure, which, as noted earlier, does treat intuition as a source of evidence. Bealer argues that radical empiricism is dialectically impotent. Radical empiricists can't support their view by appealing to our ordinary procedure for supporting a theory, because they are seeking to overturn a central feature of that procedure. The alternative is to proceed by relying only on the evidence of the senses and showing how we could construct a comprehensive theory of the world on that basis alone. If radical empiricists could do that, then intuition would be discredited, or at least rendered superfluous, as a source of evidence. But, Bealer argues, there is a serious problem with this. For it seems that if intuition conflicted with comprehensive empiricist theory of the world, then that would count against the empiricist theory. For example, suppose that the empiricist theory didn't include some version of the principle of noncontradiction: if a proposition P is true, then P isn't also false. Given the obviousness of this principle, we would conclude that the empiricist theory wasn't comprehensive after all. We wouldn't conclude that the empiricist theory was correct and that intuition was wrong. That is because such intuitions "are evidentially as basic as evidence gets." The radical empiricist challenge to line 1 of the argument fails.

What about line 2? Basic sources of evidence must be reliable. A reliable truth-connection is partly constitutive of basic evidence, part of what makes something a source of basic evidence. And, as we already mentioned, Bealer takes intuition to be a basic source of evidence. So intuition is reliable. Bealer then asks about the nature of the connection between evidence and truth. Is evidence only *contingently* reliable, or is it *necessarily* reliable? If it were only contingently reliable, Bealer claims, then absurd results would follow. For example, in weird circumstances, "reliable telepathically generated guesses" could count as evidence. So evidence must be necessarily reliable, though not necessarily infallible. Bealer hypothesizes that something like this characterizes the relevant modal connection for intuition:

> In suitably good cognitive conditions, it is necessary that if a subject proceeds carefully and systematically, then most of the claims she accepts based on intuition will be true.

Suitably good cognitive conditions include having adequate traits of "attentiveness and intelligence." Careful and systematic a priori procedure involves:

> (1) canvassing intuitions; (2) subjecting those intuitions to dialectical critique; (3) constructing theories that systematize the surviving intuitions; (4) testing those theories against further intuitions; (5) repeating the process until equilibrium is approached.

Bealer calls this a procedure of a priori justification. One question about its a priori status comes from the second component, dialectical critique. The natural interpretation is that dialectic is interpersonal. So it involves testimony from others. But testimony from others is typically considered to be a paradigm case of *empirical* (as opposed to a priori) justification: it depends on experiencing and evaluating messages from others. Doubt concerning its a priori status is amplified by the fact that, in the end, Bealer views significant, genuine philosophical progress as a long-term, socialized enterprise. He writes, "collectively, over historical time, undertaking philosophy as a civilization-wide project, we can [achieve sufficiently good cognitive conditions] to obtain authoritative answers" on core philosophical questions. Although this remark concerns cognitive conditions specifically, the emphasis on dialectic in characterizing the procedure, along with viewing real progress as a "civilization-wide" project, strongly suggests that testimony and inherited culture play a central role in achieving the philosophical justification we're aiming for, and also that the equilibrium in the fifth component will be social rather than individual. It's not entirely clear why all this should count as a priori, or what we gain from sharply contrasting it to the empirical justification characteristic of experimental science.

This brings us to line 4 of the argument. Setting aside scientific essentialism for the moment, why think that modal reliabilism about evidence would make philosophy Autonomous and Authoritative? Beginning with Authority, the simple reason is that whereas intuition is necessarily reliable, "no such necessity ever holds for science." Even under optimal cognitive conditions, it's possible that our best scientific theories are "largely mistaken." So since philosophy proceeds by intuition, and intuition alone, there's a clear sense in which it enjoys an advantage over science when the two disagree, which is just to say that philosophy is Authoritative. Turning now to Autonomy, Bealer's reasoning is more complicated, but it appears to come down to this. In order for philosophy to be Authoritative, our cognitive condition must be very good: our philosophical intelligence and attentiveness must be "very high." But if it it's very high, then it is plausible that it is high enough to make significant progress on central philosophical questions. In other words, it's plausible that philosophy is Autonomous. And even if it isn't high enough yet, it is plausible that further collective efforts can improve it sufficiently to make it high enough. So even if philosophy isn't Autonomous yet, it is Quasi-autonomous, with the hope of becoming fully so.

223

We now come to line 5. Scientific essentialism is the view that "there are necessities ... that are knowable only with the aid of empirical science," or what we might call *empirical necessities* for short. No amount of a priori reflection and intuition could reveal these. For example, it is widely accepted that it is an empirical necessity that water is composed of hydrogen and oxygen. But certainly this can't be known nonempirically. We need to conduct experiments and make observations to discover this, which makes our knowledge empirical, not a priori. (Alternatively, we might get it on testimony from someone who has done these things. But as already mentioned, testimonial knowledge is also empirical.) Empirical necessities involve things whose natures can be hidden beneath all superficial appearances. Water is composed of hydrogen and oxygen, but another liquid, identical to water in all superficial ways, might have a very different underlying chemistry. For all our ancestors knew based on the smell, taste, and feel of water, it might have been a chemical element, not a compound.

If all or most of the central philosophical questions involved empirical necessities, then philosophy would be neither Autonomous nor Authoritative. But, Bealer argues, "most, if not all," central philosophical questions do not involve empirical necessities. Call a world *qualitatively identical* to ours if it is inhabited by beings whose experiences are qualitatively identical to ours. We can imagine a qualitatively identical world where the inhabitants never drink water because the clear, odorless, tasteless, and nutritive liquid that fills the lakes and streams is a chemical element rather than water. But we can't imagine a qualitatively identical world where the inhabitants never experience pain, but some other unpleasant mental state indistinguishable from pain. Similarly, Bealer continues, we can't imagine a qualitatively identical world where the inhabitants don't understand a language, or experience pleasure, or decide to do things, or know things. While Bealer leaves open that some central philosophical questions pertain to empirical necessities, he concludes that most do not, and so scientific essentialism undermines neither the Autonomy nor the Authority of philosophy.

Before closing this section, it's worth asking whether Bealer is right to include *knowledge* on his list of central philosophical concerns that don't involve empirical necessities. Throughout this book, we have repeatedly encountered radical scenarios that are inconsistent with knowledge, but which are said to be qualitatively indistinguishable from our actual situation. Such scenarios involve demons, dreams, hallucinations, and brains-in-vats. Suppose that we do have some knowledge. And suppose further that such radical, knowledge-precluding scenarios are imaginable and genuinely possible. It would then follow that *knowledge* patterns with *water* instead of *pain*. And if *knowledge* patterns with *water* instead of *pain*, then Bealer is wrong to include it on his list, and Quine was at least on the right track when he claimed that proper epistemology is just a chapter of empirical science. At least one central branch of philosophy – the one we're concerned with in this book – would be neither Authoritative nor Autonomous. How might Bealer respond?

§ 45

Experimental epistemology (Weinberg, Nichols and Stich, "Normativity and Epistemic Intuitions")

Appealing to what seems obvious is a common theme in epistemology and philosophy more generally. Following Bealer's usage (§44), let's call such seemings *intuitions*. Intuitions are afforded deep respect when adjudicating among competing philosophical theories, including theories about the nature of knowledge and allied epistemological categories. To a first approximation, intuitions in philosophy are the analog of observations in empirical science. Other things being equal, a philosophical theory that unifies and explains a greater range of intuitions is to be preferred, and one that flouts powerful intuitions is to be avoided, just as a scientific theory that unifies and explains a greater range of observations is to be preferred, and one that apparently contradicts what we observe is to be avoided. We prize a philosophical

Weinberg, Jonathan M., Shaun Nichols, and Stephen Stich, "Normativity and Epistemic Intuitions," pp. 429–60 in *Philosophical Topics* 29, 1 & 2 (2001). © 2001 by *Philosophical Topics*. Used with permission of the authors and University of Arkansas Press, www. uapress.com theory that enables us to achieve "reflective equilibrium" among the widest range of our intuitions, to harmonize our judgments about specific cases and general principles.

When is a belief rational, reasonable, justified, or the like? Epistemologists rely pervasively on intuitions when answering these important normative questions. Epistemologists thus commit themselves to the assumption that our intuitions help us to at least approximate the truth on such matters. Jonathan Weinberg, Shaun Nichols, and Stephen Stich critically evaluate the presuppositions of this methodology, what they call "Intuition Driven Romanticism."[1] If the method is used to generate normative conclusions about how you ought to form beliefs, then it presupposes that relying on our intuitions is a way of generating credible normative conclusions. To the extent that this crucial presupposition is dubious, intuition-driven normative epistemology is discredited.

Weinberg, Stich, and Nichols argue that the crucial presupposition is dubious, and thus that intuition-driven normative epistemology is discredited. And it might be somewhat surprising to learn that their method for casting doubt on the presupposition is *empirical*. They make their case by utilizing the methods of experimental psychology.

Consider a couple interesting facts. Most of the main figures that we have discussed in this book, and nearly all of the revered figures in the historical canon of epistemology, are relatively affluent adult white Western males. Suppose they achieve reflective equilibrium among their intuitions. Their intuitions are taken as "inputs" to the

---

[1] Weinberg, Nichols, and Stich officially characterize an intuition as a "spontaneous judgment." A judgment is a species of belief, or perhaps belief-formation, so this characterization officially conflicts with Bealer's explicit view, which is to sharply distinguish intuition from belief. Bealer himself claims that experimental work in cognitive and social science, which serves as a model for Weinberg, Nichols, and Stich, isn't concerned with intuition in the sense relevant to philosophical methodology. I don't think that anything important necessarily turns on this because Weinberg, Nichols, and Stich could simply interpret the judgments they're studying as being based on, or expressive of, intuitions. Whether the two sides are simply talking past one another is worth bearing in mind.

philosophical engine, appropriate trade-offs and adjustments are made, equilibrium is achieved, and normative conclusions about how you ought to form beliefs are generated as "outputs." But what if we started with a different set of intuitions? And what if, by starting with a different set of intuitions, we ended up with different outputs? Would it be better to trust the conclusions of the relatively affluent adult white Western males, or the alternative conclusions?

Surely it's possible to start with different intuitions. And surely it's possible that doing so could lead to different outputs. But not only is a different intuitive starting point possible, it seems to be actual. Weinberg, Nichols, and Stich devised a series of experiments to gauge the epistemic intuitions among a variety of demographics. The results were surprising.

When presented with a standard Gettier case (see §15), Westerners are overwhelmingly likely, at an approximate rate of 3 out of 4, to intuit that the Gettier subject does not know. By contrast, people from East Asian cultures are slightly more likely than not to intuit that the Gettier subject *does* know. And people from Indian subcontinental cultures are likely, at an approximate rate of 3 out of 5, to intuit that the Gettier subject does know. These are significant differences. If we start with the intuition that the Gettier subject does know, it can have dramatic effects on our theory of knowledge. Similarly, when presented with a version of Dretske's zebra/mule case (see §19), Westerners are very likely, at an approximate rate of 7 out of 10, to intuit that the subject does not know. By contrast, people from Indian subcontinental cultures are equally likely to intuit that the subject does know as they are to intuit that the subject does not know. Again, if we don't take it as a defeasible starting point that the subject in Dretske's case does not know, it could have significant effects on what reflective equilibrium will look like.

Socioeconomic status also seems to influence epistemic intuitions. Weinberg, Nichols, and Stich compared the relation between socioeconomic status, salient error possibilities, and intuitions about knowledge. When presented with a case involving a specific, salient error possibility that the person in question hadn't considered, people of low socioeconomic status were approximately three times

228

more likely than people of high socioeconomic status to intuit that the person does know. Similarly, people of low socioeconomic status were three times more likely to intuit that the subject in Dretske's zebra/mule case does know.

The upshot of all this is that many "normal, flourishing people" have intuitions that diverge fundamentally from the "standard" intuitions of contemporary epistemologists. This is enough to make us reconsider the significance of intuition-driven epistemology, as it's currently practiced. As Weinberg, Nichols, and Stich put it, given the diversity of intuitions, "What reason is there to think that the output of one or another of these" reflective equilibria "has real (as opposed to putative) normative force?" Why should we even "take any of [it] seriously?"

We can sum up Weinberg, Nichols, and Stich's argument as follows:

1. If there is significant diversity of intuition among normal, flourishing people, then intuition-driven epistemology is discredited. (Premise)
2. There is significant diversity of intuition among normal, flourishing people. (Premise)
3. So intuition-driven epistemology is discredited. (From 1 and 2)

Line 1 is a normative claim about the significance of such diversity. Line 2 is an empirical claim about the actual distribution of intuitions. Line 1 might be contested on the grounds that some intuitions are more trustworthy than others, even among normal, flourishing people. Weinberg, Nichols, and Stich are skeptical of this response. But even if we grant that certain people's intuitions are privileged, it would still be an empirical question whether there was intuitional diversity among the privileged. Line 2 might be contested on the grounds that the surveys conducted thus far were flawed, or by doing further surveys which generated different results. But again, this is an empirical question. Either way, epistemologists who want to defend intuition-driven epistemology as it's currently practiced might well need to get up "from the philosopher's armchair" and "go get some *data!*"

§ 46

Natural kinds, intuitions and method in epistemology (Kornblith, "Investigating Knowledge Itself")

Hilary Kornblith sets two related goals in the selection "Investigating Knowledge Itself." He aims, on the one hand, to emphasize two previously underappreciated aspects of a "thoroughly empirical" and "fully naturalized" epistemology, and on the other, to overcome outstanding challenges to naturalized epistemology. The main such challenge is to explain the legitimate role of intuitions within a naturalized framework.

Quine began the modern movement of naturalized epistemology, famously claiming that epistemology is just a chapter of empirical science, namely, psychology (§39). But Quine's discussion was to a large extent programatic and hortatory. The tasks of filling in the details and putting naturalized epistemology into practice fell to

Kornblith, Hilary, "Investigating Knowledge Itself," pp. 1–27 in H. Kornblith, *Knowledge and its Place in Nature* (Oxford: Clarendon, 2002). © 2002 by Hilary Kornblith.

Epistemology: A Guide, First Edition. John Turri.
© 2014 John Wiley & Sons, Ltd. Published 2014 by John Wiley & Sons, Ltd.

others. Relevant work on these tasks began in earnest in the 1960s with the advent of causal theories of knowledge, and then in the 1970s and 80s with the advent of reliabilism (§26) and tracking theories (§§21, 19). For example, Robert Nozick said that knowing is a special "way of being connected to the world," a "real factual relation, subjunctively specifiable," which he called *tracking* (§21). Discovering and explaining such real factual relationships sounds like a task best left to empirical science. Even if epistemology wasn't going to be wholly absorbed by empirical science, as Quine urged, it looked poised to cede large swaths of important territory.

As a committed naturalist himself, Kornblith claims that two crucial features of naturalized epistemology haven't been properly emphasized. First, if epistemology is to be naturalized, then knowledge must be a natural kind. Phenomena aren't fit objects of scientific inquiry if they resemble each other only superficially or in virtue of arbitrary conventions. Thus there is no science of green things, or of Tuesdays: green things are united as a group only by their superficial appearance, and Tuesdays are united as a group by an utterly arbitrary convention. (See §6 for related discussion.) By contrast there is a "robust phenomenon" of animal cognition and knowledge, of which human varieties are particularly interesting. Although it's not included in the selection for the anthology, it's worth noting Kornblith's positive account of knowledge's status as natural kind. He calls knowledge an "ecological kind." Knowledge is true belief produced by reliable cognitive capacities. Such beliefs are

> instrumental in the production of behavior successful in meeting biological needs and thereby implicated in the Darwinian explanation of the selective retention of traits. The various information-processing capacities and information-gathering abilities that animals possess are attuned to the animals' environment by natural selection, and it is thus that the category of beliefs that manifest such attunement – cases of knowledge – are rightly seen as a natural category, a natural kind.[1]

---

[1] Hilary Kornblith, *Knowledge and Its Place in Nature* (Oxford University Press, 2002); quotes from pages 62, 65.

Second, just as the primary object of astrophysics is stars, real natural objects in our galactic environment, the primary object of naturalized epistemology should be knowledge itself, a real natural relation that animals bear to facts. Accordingly, the primary object of epistemology should not be our concept of knowledge or the terms we use to ascribe knowledge, any more than the primary object of astrophysics should be our concept of stars or the terms we use to refer to them. Instead of analyzing concepts or vocabulary, Kornblith urges, epistemologists should investigate worldly cognitive relations and activities.

Preoccupation with conceptual analysis has long been associated with the appeal to intuitions in philosophy. (To *have an intuition* is just for something to *seem obviously true* to you; see §44 for more details.) If I'm investigating my concept of knowledge, then it's tempting to think that I don't have to leave my armchair to make important discoveries. After all, I possess the concept; it's "in my mind" and available for inspection by reflection. Having reflected carefully enough, it might just seem obviously true to me that knowledge requires true belief. And this intuition, born of careful reflection and mastery of the concept, is good evidence that my concept of knowledge applies only to true beliefs. However, if I'm investigating a real, natural relation in the world, then it's not the least bit tempting to think that I can make important discoveries from my armchair. This brings us to the main challenge to naturalized epistemology that Kornblith seeks to overcome.

Appealing to intuitions is not only *standard* procedure, it is epistemologists' *main* procedure, and often their *only* procedure. Even naturalized epistemologists employ the procedure. But intuitions are a source of nonempirical – that is, a priori – justification. This seems hard to reconcile with Kornblith's view that knowledge is a natural kind to be studied empirically. So are naturalists committed to saying that epistemologists' procedures are mostly unjustified and irrelevant to understanding knowledge?

Kornblith denies that this is a commitment of naturalism. He argues that a fully naturalized epistemology is perfectly consistent with armchair methodology, because armchair methodology is empirical. It is empirical for at least two reasons. First, epistemologists don't consider individual, idiosyncratic intuitions to be probative. They consider widely shared intuitions to be probative. The more widely shared, robust, and less controversial the intuition, the more probative. They seek to achieve reflective equilibrium among these intuitions. But it's an empirical matter which intuitions fit this profile. Second, our intuitions are influenced by our background beliefs, and our background beliefs are shaped by experience, which in turn is heavily influenced by social and historical processes. What seems obviously true in one culture or epoch can seem obviously false in another. Intuitions might be "phenomenologically basic," in the sense that we don't engage in conscious reasoning to affect which intuitions we have. But still they have an "inferential heritage." This heritage is introspectively inaccessible, hidden from conscious reflection, and recoverable only through extensive historical and psychological investigation. In light of all this, there's very little to recommend the idea that armchair methodology provides nonempirical justification.

To substantiate this with a specific example, Kornblith points to our intuition that knowledge doesn't require certainty. Descartes had the intuition that knowledge requires certainty. He was wrong; we are right. But what gives us the right to say that? Because we have the benefit of several hundred years of hindsight into the progress of modern science, which informs our intuition. The justifying force of our intuition is not – at least, not primarily – due to "a priori insight into the nature of knowledge." It is instead due to the well-confirmed observation that science has produced enormous amounts of knowledge unaccompanied by certainty.

Kornblith compares the use of intuitions in epistemology to the initial spadework of gathering a sufficient set of specimens for inductive inference and generalization in empirical science. Suppose we're aspiring mineralogists. Having recently arrived in a new land, we might take an interest in the local rocks. We gather a bunch of samples of similar looking rocks, ones that are good enough candidates to belong to the same mineralogical kind. We then put them under a microscope to estimate their microstructure; we put some into a furnace to determine their melting point; we submerge some to see how much water they displace and determine their density, etc. The rocks might turn out to be a motley crew, displaying great diversity at a more fundamental level. Or they might form a genuine kind of rock, so that our initial shared superficial impressions were correct. Intuitions in epistemology are like those initial shared superficial impressions of the rocks. They help us identify a promising enough set of specimens for further investigation. But epistemologist's intuitions are no more a priori than the mineralogist's. And this is why armchair methodology is fully consistent with naturalism's empirical commitments.

Despite reconciling naturalism and armchair methodology, Kornblith emphasizes that methdology's limitations. Even if our empirically informed intuitions provide a defensible *starting point* for epistemology, they certainly aren't a respectable *end point*. It's a poor mineralogist who insists on classifying rocks based on how they appear to the naked eye, despite the microstructural diversity revealed by subsequent observation and experimentation. Similarly, it's a poor epistemologist who insists on classifying beliefs based on intuition, despite the psychological diversity revealed by cognitive science. The understandable "appeal to intuition early on" in our inquiry "should give way to more straightforwardly empirical investigations." The more progress we make in understanding how cognition actually proceeds, the less we should rely on intuition to sort cases.

Reference

Hilary Kornblith, *Knowledge and Its Place in Nature* (Oxford University Press, 2002).

§ 47

Contextualism and skeptical puzzles (DeRose, "Solving the Skeptical Problem")

In the previous section, we saw that Hilary Kornblith views knowledge as a natural kind that ought to be studied empirically. Kornblith recommends this approach over armchair analysis of our concept of knowledge, or the vocabulary we use to ascribe knowledge. We focused on Kornblith's opposition to conceptual analysis, and also noted the alignment between Kornblith's view and Robert Nozick's (§21) claim that knowledge is a "real factual relation, subjectively specifiable," between a fact and an agent. In this section, we'll look at another approach in contemporary epistemology that draws inspiration from Nozick, but which focuses intensely on our epistemic terminology and inclinations to apply words such as "knows."

DeRose, Keith, "Solving the Skeptical Problem," pp. 1–7,17–52 in *The Philosophical Review* 104, 1 (1995). © 1995 by *The Philosophical Review*.

As we've noted before, it seems possible that I am nothing more than brain in a vat, floating serenely in a nourishing amber liquid, hooked up to electrodes feeding me a constant flow of radically misleading sensory stimuli, the unwitting subject of an elaborate cognitive scientific experiment by an advanced species of extraterrestrials. If I were in such a situation, I wouldn't have hands. I would be a handless brain in a vat (a "BIV" for short). BIVs are mere brains without appendages, perfectly deceived by their captors. Call this the BIV-possibility.

The following trio of claims is inconsistent.

1. I know that I have hands.
2. If I know that I have hands, then I know that I'm not a handless BIV.
3. I don't know that I'm not a handless BIV.

At least one of these three claims is false. But which? The skeptic argues that since 3 and 2 are both true, 1 is false. Moore argues that since 1 and 2 are true, 3 is false (§4). Who is right?

Perhaps the most satisfying solution would be to find some merit in each position, and to explain how each can seem so plausible on its own. Part of the appeal of *epistemic contextualism* is that it doesn't force us to say, once and for all, whether Moore or the skeptic speaks truthfully. Rather, they each speak truthfully in their own way. Let's consider how the contextualist tries to accomplish this. This will require some background explanation about language use.

We use sentences to ask questions, issue imperatives, and make assertions. For simplicity, let's focus on the use of declarative sentences to make assertions. Consider the sentence "Eva writes poetry." The sentence is made up of three expressions: "Eva," "writes," and "poetry." The term "poetry" has a single, fixed meaning. It means the same thing on Monday morning when I use it in the course of uttering "Eva writes poetry," and on Thursday evening when you say "A good society values poetry." You and I assert different propositions, but our respective uses of "poetry" contribute exactly the same thing to the propositions we express, namely, it picks out poetry so that we can say something about it.

Some ordinary expressions are context-sensitive. A context-sensitive expression can contribute different things on different occasions of use to the proposition expressed. If I say "I like poetry" and you say "I like poetry," we're uttering exactly similar sentences, but we express different propositions. That's because the personal pronoun "I" is a context-sensitive expression. It picks out the speaker on its occasion of use. When I use it, it refers to me; when you use it, it refers to you. Similarly, if someone in London says "It is raining here" and someone in Canberra says "It is raining here," then even though they utter exactly similar sentences, they express different propositions. That's because "here" is a context-sensitive expression. It refers to a contextually salient location. In the one case, it refers to London; in the other, it refers to Canberra.

Context-sensitive expressions create a special sort of possibility for mere verbal disagreement. Suppose I tell you that Izzy said, "It is raining here," and Nottingham responded, "It is not raining here." Judging from my description, they appear to disagree. But then I tell you that Nottingham is in England, Izzy is in Australian, and they're talking via videoconference. The appearance of disagreement dissolves.

Keith DeRose proposes that "knows" is a context-sensitive expression too, and that this proposal promises to dissolve a venerable skeptical challenge. The basic idea is simple. In order for a knowledge ascription of the form "S knows that Q" to express a true proposition, S must be in a strong enough epistemic position with respect to the proposition Q. But *how strong* is strong enough? This varies, and is determined by the conversational context in which the knowledge ascription is made. In an ordinary context, we speak truthfully when we say things like, "I know that I have hands," or, "I know that the presidential election will be held in early November." We meet the standard of epistemic strength that is ordinarily operative and required for the knowledge ascription to be true. But then the skeptic enters, and starts asking things like, "How do you know that you're not just a handless BIV, who is being perfectly deceived into thinking that it has hands?," or, "How do you know that a natural disaster won't strike and force the election to be postponed until the end of November?" Somehow, DeRose claims, this "manipulates the … standards for knowledge, thereby creating a context in which [the skeptic] can *truthfully* say that we" do not know that we have hands, or that the election will be held in early November. As competent language-users, we sense that the skeptic says something true, given the context; but we also implicitly sense that "as soon as we find ourselves" back in an "ordinary" conversational context, it will again be true to say, "I know that I have hands," and, "I know that the election will be held in early November."

This is the general contextualist explanation of why the trio of claims, 1–3, puzzles us. We sense that there is something right about Moore's response (deny 3) and the skeptic's response (deny 1). But we sense this only implicitly. It's hard to explicitly identify or articulate the fact that the introduction of a potent skeptical hypothesis amounts to a semantic sleight-of-hand. The skeptic herself might not even explicitly recognize that this is, in fact, what she is doing.

But what is the specific mechanism by which the skeptic accomplishes this? DeRose identifies a "conversational rule" that assists the skeptic, *The Rule of Sensitivity*, which says: when someone says that you know P, the standards for how good an epistemic position you must be in to count as knowing tend to rise so as to require your belief that P to be *sensitive*. Recall that for your belief that P to be sensitive means that if P were false, you wouldn't believe P. When P is the proposition *you are not a BIV*, your belief is guaranteed to be insensitive. For if you were a (perfectly deceived) BIV, then you would still believe that you weren't. Thus, the Rule of Sensitivity prevents you from truthfully claiming that you know that you're not a BIV. And when the skeptic says that you don't know that you're not a BIV, the very invocation of the BIV possibility alters the context so that what the skeptic says is true. Moreover, DeRose claims, no matter what the conversational context is, 2 from the puzzling triad remains true: if you know that you have hands, then you know that you're not a handless BIV. Thus, the skeptic seemingly carries the day against Moore ... until things return to normal, and we once again speak truthfully when we claim knowledge!

And it is precisely this variation in standards and truth-values that generates the puzzlement we feel when faced with the puzzling triad.

§ 48

Contextualism and infallibilist intuitions (Lewis, "Elusive Knowledge")

David Lewis defends epistemic contextualism. Although Lewis's defense shares some features in common with Keith DeRose's defense (§47), it also differs in important respects. Here we'll focus on what's distinctive in Lewis's view.

Lewis's starting point is that it "sounds contradictory" to speak of "fallible knowledge." To fallibly know P is to know P without being able to eliminate all the possibilities inconsistent with P. According to Lewis, if you claim that S knows P, but you also grant that S can't "eliminate a certain possibility" which is inconsistent with the truth of P, then "it certainly seems as if you have granted that S does not after all know that P." The presumptive explanation for why this sounds contradictory is that it *is* contradictory. So knowledge can't

Lewis, David, "Elusive Knowledge," pp. 549–67 in *Australasian Journal of Philosophy* 74, 4 (1996). © 1996 by *Australasian Journal of Philosophy*.

Epistemology: A Guide, First Edition. John Turri.
© 2014 John Wiley & Sons, Ltd. Published 2014 by John Wiley & Sons, Ltd.

be fallible; it must be infallible. However, for just about every claim we ordinarily take ourselves to know, there are possibilities that we can't eliminate: "we never have infallible knowledge." So, since knowledge must be infallible knowledge, it follows that we never have knowledge. But this conclusion is "absurd."

How do we reconcile the intuition that infallibilism is correct with the denial of rampant skepticism? It might initially seem that we can't. We'll need to choose to be fallibilists and avoid skepticism, or embrace skepticism in order to retain infallibilism. But, Lewis argues, we can "dodge the choice" by embracing epistemic contextualism.

After some stops and starts, Lewis ultimately defines knowledge as follows: you know P if and only if every possibility in which P is false is either (a) eliminated by your evidence, or (b) being properly ignored. Taken on its own, this definition is not yet a form of contextualism, because a hallmark of contextualism is *contextual variability*. The contextual variability enters when we add that your evidence never eliminates all possibilities in which P is false, and which possibilities are properly ignored varies from context to context. Your evidence eliminates a possibility just in case the possibility is inconsistent with your "entire perceptual experience and memory" – that is, you *could not* have had all of your memories and experiences if that possibility were true (compare the discussion of impossible combinations from §4). Lewis proposes a series of rules which are intended to explain what it is to properly ignore a possibility. Sometimes he uses the convenient and pithy phrase "relevant alternatives" to name the class of possibilities that aren't properly ignored (see §19). Let's consider Lewis's list of rules.

The Rule of Actuality: what is actual is always relevant. If it is actually the case that not-P, then it is relevant that not-P, which of course conflicts with P, thereby preventing you from knowing that P. This is why knowledge is factive.

The Rule of Belief: a possibility is relevant if the subject is, or should be, sufficiently confident that it is actually true. What counts as *sufficiently confident* depends on how much is at stake. How much is at stake varies according to context.

The Rule of Resemblance: if an alternative is relevant, then any possibility that saliently resembles it is also relevant. Salient resemblance varies according to context. Lewis claims that this rule explains why you can't know that you'll lose a fair lottery: the possibility that any given ticket will win is salient and it saliently resembles the possibility that any other given ticket will win; so either *all or none* of those possibilities can be ignored; but they can't all be ignored; so none of them can be ignored.

The Rule of Reliability: we have a defeasible entitlement to ignore the possibility that our basic channels of information are unreliable. Our basic channels of information include perception, testimony, and memory. For example, most of the time we may properly ignore the possibility that we're the subject of massive hallucination or undetectable deception. For an entitlement to be defeasible means that it can be undercut or overridden by other considerations. So if I ingest a known hallucinogen, then that subsequently defeats my entitlement to ignore the possibility that I'm hallucinating.

The Rule of Method: we have a defeasible entitlement to presuppose that samples we collect are representative, and that the best explanation of a data set is the true explanation. In other words, we may (defeasibly) ignore the possibilities that sampling is unrepresentative, and that the best explanations lead us astray.

The Rule of Conservatism: if it is a known convention that people in the community ignore certain possibilities, then we have a defeasible entitlement to ignore those possibilities too. What counts as the community can vary according to context.

The Rule of Attention: attending to an alternative makes it relevant. In other words, if you don't ignore a possibility, then it is not properly ignored. It is typically this rule that the skeptic exploits in order to manipulate the context so that he can truly say, for example, "You do not know that you have hands." For once the skeptic introduces the possibility that you are a handless BIV, you attend to that possibility. It is no longer ignored, and so no longer properly ignored. And all your evidence and memories are consistent with the possibility that you're a handless brain-in-a-vat. So you no longer know that you have hands.

This is why knowledge is "elusive." Once we start asking serious questions, or doing serious epistemology, the context is altered so that formerly irrelevant alternatives become relevant. And our evidence is often incapable of eliminating these now-relevant alternatives.

There are a few other noteworthy features of Lewis's view. First, Lewis denies that justification is necessary for knowledge. He asks, "What (non-circular) argument supports our reliance on perception, on memory, and on testimony?" And he notes that we often "don't even know how we know" things. From this he seems to conclude that we have knowledge that is not based on "reasons," and furthermore that we have knowledge that isn't justified. Second, Lewis also denies that knowledge requires belief. Lewis seems to reason as follows: knowledge doesn't require confidence, but belief does require confidence, so knowledge doesn't require belief. Third, Lewis allows that some knowledge is "unclaimable," meaning that it is so fragile and elusive that merely giving voice to it suffices to make ineliminable alternatives relevant. Fourth, Lewis allows that you can know that some alternative is possible just by ignoring it in a context where it is proper to do so.

Lewis also ventures a "guess" about why our concept of knowledge would work this way. The basic idea is simple: humans are stupid and incompetent. We are too stupid to keep precise track of which possibilities our evidence eliminates, and we are too inarticulate to be able to precisely and conveniently enough explain to others which possibilities our evidence eliminates. But we are smart enough to be able to keep track of, and articulate, which *relevant* possibilities our evidence eliminates. Knowledge ascriptions are thus "a very sloppy way of" communicating "incomplete" but potentially useful information. They are "handy but humble approximations" of what we would ideally like to be keep track of and communicate.

§ 49

Contextualism and intuitional instability (Cohen, "Contextualist Solutions to Epistemological Problems")

Stewart Cohen's paper provides an excellent example of how two philosophers can agree on the big picture despite disagreeing about important details. Cohen agrees with David Lewis (§48) that epistemic contextualism is true, but Cohen disagrees with the specific way that Lewis applies contextualism to solve important problems in epistemology.

As noted over the past couple sections, epistemic contextualists claim that the content of a knowledge ascription – statements of the form "S knows that P" – varies depending on the ascriber's context. Contextualists disagree about why this happens. Cohen favors a form of contextualism which says that the content varies because knowledge requires justification, and the amount of justification required varies

Cohen, Stewart, "Contextualist Solutions to Epistemological Problems: Scepticism, Gettier, and the Lottery," pp. 289–306 in *Australasian Journal of Philosophy* 76, 2 (1998). © 1998 by *Australasian Journal of Philosophy*.

Epistemology: A Guide, First Edition. John Turri.
© 2014 John Wiley & Sons, Ltd. Published 2014 by John Wiley & Sons, Ltd.

across contexts. That is, in order for an ascriber to truthfully say "S knows that P," S's justification must be strong enough, but what counts as strong enough depends on a variable feature of the ascriber's context. Lewis rejects Cohen's version of contextualism because Lewis rejects the claim that knowledge requires justification. Lewis proposes instead that knowledge requires ruling out all relevant alternatives, where relevance is a context-dependent matter determined by a set of conversational rules.

Lewis argues that his view can solve three significant epistemological problems all at once: the problem of skepticism, the lottery problem, and the Gettier problem. In one form or another, we've covered these problems repeatedly throughout this book. It would certainly count significantly in favor of Lewis's view if it could provide a unified solution to these three problems.

Cohen agrees with Lewis that contextualism offers an attractive solution to the problems of skepticism and the lottery, but disagrees that it can solve the Gettier problem. To motivate his position, Cohen establishes a criterion to identify problems amenable to contextualist resolution. The criterion is *intuitional instability*. When a problem is amenable to contextualist resolution, "we are of two minds" about how to answer the key question. For example, in ordinary contexts, we find it intuitively plausible that we know lots of things about the physical world around us. But when the skeptic shows up and introduces clever skeptical hypotheses, our intuitions begin vacillating. We sense that if we were to ascribe knowledge, we would be saying something false. And yet we still have the sense that in a different context the knowledge ascription would be true. Thus, our intuitions about the truth value of knowledge ascriptions are unstable. This is intuitional instability.

Similarly, Cohen and Lewis agree that we suffer from intuitional instability when it comes to lottery propositions – that is, propositions such as *My lottery ticket is a loser* or *You will lose the lottery*. The key case here is that of Poor Bill, first introduced by Lewis. "Pity poor Bill!" writes Lewis, "He squanders all his spare cash on the pokies, the races, and the lottery. He will be a wage slave all his days. We know he will never be rich." Cohen writes of Poor Bill,

It seems intuitive to say we know he will never get rich. Yet we also find it intuitive that we do not know he will lose the lottery. But these intuitions take us in opposing directions. We know he'll never get rich only if we know he'll lose the lottery. Thus we find ourselves vacillating between thinking we know he'll never get rich and so that he'll lose the lottery, and thinking we know neither of these things.

When the possibility that Bill will win the lottery isn't salient, we can truly say that we know he won't be rich. But if it is salient, then we can't truly say that we know. It's easy enough to slide between such contexts, and when we're in a context where the possibility is salient, we can easily imagine ourselves being in a context where it isn't. So we vacillate. We suffer intuitional instability.

Now the key question is whether we also suffer intuitional instability when it comes to Gettier cases. Cohen argues that we don't and that this undermines a contextualist treatment of the Gettier problem. Cohen focuses on a specific Gettier case to make the point. Sam looks out across the field and sees what clearly appears to be a sheep on the hill. So Sam believes that there is a sheep on the hill, and his belief is justified. But Sam is actually looking at a rock chiseled and painted to look exactly like a sheep. Coincidentally, unseen by Sam, there is a sheep right behind the rock. So Sam has a justified true belief that there is a sheep on the hill. But, Cohen claims, Sam obviously does not know that there is a sheep on the hill. Moreover, this is not a peculiar feature of the context in which Cohen wrote his paper, or the context in which we are evaluating what he wrote. There is no context, Cohen contends, in which it would seem true to say "Sam knows that there is a sheep on the hill." "Intuitively," writes Cohen, this knowledge ascription is false regardless of what context the speaker is in, and regardless of which features of Sam's case are salient in the speaker's context. Our intuition that Sam doesn't know is "strong and stable." So is our intuition that ascribing knowledge to Sam is and would be false. We don't vacillate. Thus, we lack a basis to favor a contextualist treatment of the Gettier problem.

§ 50

Knowledge and action (Stanley, "*Knowledge and Practical Interests*, Selections")

We have seen a strong push for epistemic contextualism over the last three sections. But many epistemologists reject epistemic contextualism. Jason Stanley is one of them. In the selections from his book, Stanley does two main things. On the one hand, he argues against epistemic contextualism. On the other hand, he advocates an alternative approach to epistemology. The alternative, Stanley claims, captures the illusory appeal of contextualism.

Let's begin with Stanley's argument against contextualism. We can understand the basic argument as follows: if epistemic contextualism is true, then knowledge ascriptions will behave like other context-sensitive expressions; but knowledge ascriptions don't behave like other context-sensitive expressions;

Stanley, Jason, "Introduction" and "Knowledge Ascriptions and Context-Sensitivity," pp. 1–15, 47–73 in *Knowledge and Practical Interests* (New York: Oxford University Press, 2005). © 2005 by Jason Stanley.

Epistemology: A Guide, First Edition. John Turri.
© 2014 John Wiley & Sons, Ltd. Published 2014 by John Wiley & Sons, Ltd.

so epistemic contextualism isn't true. Context-sensitive expressions tend to have certain distinctive features. For example, consider gradable adjectives, such as "flat" or "tall." It is acceptable to say, "Michigan is flat, but not really flat," or, "Amanda is tall, but not very tall." In general, when we have a gradable adjective that describes being a certain way, we can pry apart *being that way*, on the one hand, from *very much being that way*, on the other. But it is not acceptable to say, "Keith knows that the bank is open on Saturdays, but he doesn't really know that the bank is open on Saturdays."[1]

Consider also an important feature of personal pronouns and demonstratives, which are also central classes of context-sensitive expressions. The referent of a demonstrative or personal pronoun can shift in discourse. To coin a phrase, they are *transparently referentially dynamic*. They uncontroversially change their referent in readily detectable ways. For example, suppose I say, "It is now three seconds before five o'clock." After a few moments you ask me, "Is it past five o'clock?," and I say, "Yes, it is now past five o'clock." Now suppose you continue the conversation by saying, "Oh, so you admit that your previous statement was false." It is sensible for me to reply, "I admit no such thing. What I said before was true when I spoke." This is because "now" changes its referent as the discourse progresses. Or to take another example, suppose that Amanda and Keith are discussing candidates for the male lead in a play. "What about Sam?" Keith asks. "He's too tall," answers Amanda. "Okay, what about Brad?" Keith asks. "He's not too tall," answers Amanda. Keith can't sensibly object that Amanda has contradicted herself, because "he" changed its referent as their conversation unfolded.

But "knows" doesn't seem to work this way. To make this point, Stanley asks us to imagine a conversation taking place

---

[1] This comparison between gradable adjectives and knowledge attributions isn't included in the excerpts from Stanley's book reprinted in the anthology. But it's important and relates to our earlier discussion of contextualism, so I include it here.

within Dretske's zebra/mule case (§19). The conversation might go like this:

A: {looking at a zebra in a normal zoo} I know that is a zebra.
B: But can you rule out that it's a cleverly painted mule?
A: No, I can't rule that out.
B: So you admit that you don't know that it's a zebra, and what you said earlier is false?
A: I admit no such thing. What I said earlier was true, because the possibility that it was a cleverly painted mule wasn't relevant then.

If "knows" is context-sensitive in the way that demonstratives or personal pronouns are, then we should expect A's final statement to seem perfectly acceptable. But it isn't perfectly acceptable. Instead, Stanley claims, "it is extremely difficult to make sense of A's denial except as a lie."

Of course, contextualists might claim that "knows" has an utterly unique profile among context-sensitive expressions. Nothing Stanley says rules this out. But such a maneuver runs the risk of appearing ad hoc. Better for the contextualist would be to identify an uncontroversial class of context-sensitive expressions, which "know" behaves like. Given the lack of success up till this point, Stanley thinks, it seems unlikely that the contextualist will succeed.

Now let's turn to the other half of Stanley's project: his alternative approach to epistemology. Contextualists have gotten a lot of mileage out of pairs of cases. The pairs feature a protagonist who self-ascribes knowledge. The main difference between the two cases is what is at stake. In one of the cases, very little is at stake, but in the other case, very much is at stake. For example, suppose that the line at the bank is very long on a Friday afternoon, and Hannah is deciding whether to wait in line now to deposit her paycheck, or to come back on Saturday morning when any line would be much shorter. Not much turns on whether Hannah gets her paycheck deposited before Monday. Moreover, she was at the bank last week on Saturday morning, and it was open. So she says to herself, "I don't want to waste time waiting in line. I know that the bank will be open tomorrow morning, so I'll come back then." And she's right: the bank is open this Saturday. Intuitively, contextualists claim, Hannah speaks correctly when she self-ascribes knowledge. Call this the *low-stakes bank case*.

Now let's change one detail of the case: Hannah has just written a check to pay her mortgage, and if she doesn't deposit her paycheck *before* Monday, the check will bounce, the bank will foreclose on her home, she'll lose tens of thousands of dollars of equity, all of which will ruin her life for the foreseeable future. With this much at stake, it no longer seems correct for Hannah to say, "I know that the bank will be open tomorrow morning," even if it's true that the bank will be open. Call this the *high-stakes bank case*.

There is an intuitive difference between Hannah's knowledge-ascription in the low-stakes case versus the high-stakes case. It seems correct for her to say "I know" in the low case but not in the high case, even if we hold constant the quality of Hannah's evidence, her confidence, and the truth of her belief. Contextualists say that this is evidence for their view that knowledge ascriptions are context-sensitive: the apparent truth of a knowledge ascription varies depending on the context.

Stanley rejects the contextualist explanation of this variability. The contextualist gives a semantic explanation in terms of the supposed context-sensitivity of the verb "knows." But, as we've already seen, Stanley argues that there is independent reason to doubt that "knows" is context-sensitive. So he explains the variability another way: he connects knowledge to action. Stanley agrees that Hannah speaks truthfully in both the low-stakes case and the high-stakes case, and he agrees that her evidence is equally good in the two cases, and is willing to grant that her confidence is equally high in the two cases. So how can it turn out that she truthfully ascribes knowledge to herself in the one case, but not in the other? Because, Stanley claims, whether you know depends partly on what's at stake for you. Purely *"practical facts"* about "the costs of being right or wrong" can directly affect whether you know. Given two subjects with the same level of evidence, and the same confidently held true belief, it could turn out that one of them knows whereas the other doesn't *merely because one has more at stake.*

Intellectualism is the view that practical facts can't directly affect whether you know. Stanley rejects intellectualism. Instead of explaining the variability of knowledge ascriptions by positing context-sensitivity of "knows," Stanley explains it by positing a direct "conceptual connection" between knowledge *itself* and the wisdom or propriety of acting based on certain beliefs.[2]

Reference

John Turri, "Linguistic Intuitions in Context: A Defense of Pure Nonskeptical Invariantism," in *Intuitions*. Edited by Anthony Booth and Darrell Rowbottom (Oxford University Press, Forthcoming).

---

[2] For an explanation of the variability that neither embraces contextualism nor rejects intellectualism, see John Turri, "Linguistic Intuitions in Context: A Defense of Pure Nonskeptical Invariantism," in *Intuitions*. Edited by Anthony Booth and Darrell Rowbottom (Oxford University Press, Forthcoming).

§ 51

Rationality and action (Fantl and McGrath, "Evidence, Pragmatics, and Justification")

Earlier, we saw Richard Feldman and Earl Conee defend the view that whether you're justified in believing a proposition is determined entirely by the evidence you have (§24). More generally, for any two agents, if they have the exact same evidence, then they are equally justified in believing all and only the same propositions. They call this view *evidentialism*. Jeremy Fantl and Matthew McGrath argue that evidentialism is false.

Fantl and McGrath's argument against evidentialism can easily seem very complicated. It begins with observations about knowledge, leading to an argument, a "conversion" of the "argument pattern into a principle," then various strengthenings of the principle, including analogous observations about epistemic justification,

Epistemology: A Guide, First Edition. John Turri.
© 2014 John Wiley & Sons, Ltd. Published 2014 by John Wiley & Sons, Ltd.

an argument about epistemic justification, followed by some corollaries – all supplemented by appendices containing dozens of lines of formal proofs. Although the complications are important for some purposes, they're inessential to appreciating the basic idea behind it all. So we'll focus on the intuitive basis, and set the complications aside. (Once you understand the basic idea behind their view, you might think that you've identified a serious objection. Before jumping to conclusions, you'll want to investigate whether the complications can handle the objection.)

Before getting into the details, it's worth making a methodological note. Fantl and McGrath emphasize that their central argument "does not appeal to intuitions about particular cases," but instead is "a theoretical argument for a condition on justification." As far as the explicit statement of the argument – the various 1–3's, primed and unprimed – this is technically correct. But the premises of their argument are motivated initially by appealing to intuitions about (very) abstractly described cases – cases involving you, the proposition P, and a decision to do A or B – and they further support the plausibility of their conclusion by showing how it helps us explain intuitions about some very detailed cases – the Train Cases. In the present case at least, there's no bright line between a theoretical argument and intuitions about cases. So it probably isn't worth dwelling too much on whether Fantl and McGrath have succeeded in providing a "theoretical," as opposed to case-based, argument against evidentialism.

Here is a key passage:

> If you know that p, then it shouldn't be a problem to act as if p. If it is a problem to act as if p, you can explain why by saying that you don't know that p. Suppose you are faced with some decision – do A or do B – where which of these is better depends on whether p. You know that if p [is true], A is the thing to do, but that if not-p [is true], B is. To say in one breath, "I know that P" and in the next breath, "But I'd better do B anyway, even though I know that A is the thing to do if p [is true]" seems incoherent. If you really know that p, and you know that if p, A is the thing to do, then it's hard to see how you could fail to know that A is the thing to do in fact. But then you ought to do A.

Fantl and McGrath take these observations to suggest that the following argument is valid, where "P" names a proposition, and "A" names a type of action.

1. You know that P is true. (Premise)
2. You know that if P is true, then you ought to A (or: then it's rational for you to A). (Premise)
3. So you ought to A (or: So it's rational for you to A.) (From 1 and 2)

It can be useful to see the reasoning formalized that way. It also can be useful to encapsulate the essential idea as briefly as possible. And, in fact, Fantl and McGrath do precisely that for us in the first sentence of the passage quoted earlier: "if you know that p, then it shouldn't be a problem to act as if p." This formulation might raise questions about what it means to *act as if* a proposition is true. But it shouldn't. When you know P, it's because you believe P in such a way that the belief constitutes knowledge. So another way of putting the essential idea might be: if your belief that P constitutes knowledge, then it's rational for you to act based on that belief. (It's rational put knowledge to work.) The idea of acting based on a belief or knowledge is perfectly clear.

Another key claim in Fantl and McGrath's discussion is that stakes matter for the rationality of action. More precisely, how much is at stake can affect whether it's rational for you to perform a certain action (or whether you ought to perform that action). This is where the Train Cases are relevant: they make the general point vivid and concrete. In Train Case 1, you have a ticket on the train to Providence, and you're wondering whether the train makes a stop in Foxboro. You mildly prefer that the train not stop in Foxboro, because then you'll have to spend a few less minutes in transit. So you ask one of the other passengers waiting for the train, "Does this train stop in Foxboro?" The man answers, "Yes, it stops in Foxboro. They told me when I bought the ticket." You believe him, and it is in fact true. "Intuitively," Fantl and McGrath say, you know that the train stops in Foxboro based on the man's testimony, and you are justified in believing that it does. It's rational for you to get on the train without further checking into whether the train stops in Foxboro. It's rational for you to board without further inquiry.

Compare that with Train Case 2, which is similar to Train Case 1, except for the following difference: instead of having a mild preference that the train not stop in Foxboro, "you absolutely need to be in Foxboro" before long because "your career depends on it." If you get on a train that does not stop in Foxboro, you will be ruined. One of the other passengers waiting for the train says, "This train stops in Foxboro. They told me when I bought the ticket." And this man is in fact right. "Intuitively," Fantl and McGrath say, you do not know that the train stops in Foxboro based on the man's testimony, and you are not justified in believing that it does. It is *not* rational for you to get on the train without further checking into whether the train stops in Foxboro. It is *not* rational for you to board without further inquiry.

As reflected in the previous paragraph, according to Fantl and McGrath, what is true of knowledge in these cases is also true of justification: "whatever it is rational for a knower to [do], is also rational for an otherwise identical subject who is merely justified in believing to [do]." Fantl and McGrath's usage of "justified" makes this more plausible. They define justification like so: you are justified in believing P if and only if you have evidence that is good enough to know. This makes all of their observations about knowledge directly relevant to evidentialism, which, recall, is a thesis about the relationship between justification and evidence, not knowledge and evidence.

Now consider what the earlier claim about the relationship between knowledge and rationality can tell us about the two Train Cases. In Train Case 1, you know that the train stops in Foxboro, and it is rational for you to board without further checking. In Train Case 2, it is not rational for you to board without further checking, and you do not know that the train stops in Foxboro. Both of these judgments are easily explained by the general principle that if you know that P, then it is rational for you to act based on your knowledge – that is, it's rational to put knowledge to work. In the

Train Cases, "P" is "the train stops in Foxboro," and the relevant action is "board without further checking." So, when applied to the Train Cases, the principle yields:

> If you know that the train stops in Foxboro, then it is rational for you to board without further checking.

In Train Case 1, you know that the train stops in Foxboro, so it follows that it's rational for you to board without further checking. But in Train Case 2, it is not rational for you to board without further checking, so it follows that you don't know that the train stops in Foxboro. Moreover, Fantl and McGrath endorse a similar explanation for our intuitions about what you are, or are not, justified in believing in the Train Cases. The relevant principle here would be:

> If you're justified in believing that the train stops in Foxboro, then it's rational for you to board without further checking.

Only one more piece is needed to clinch the argument against evidentialism: how much is at stake doesn't affect how much evidence you have. In each of the Train Cases, you have the same evidence for thinking that the train stops in Foxboro, namely, a fellow passenger's testimony. The fact that more is at stake in Train Case 2 doesn't augment or diminish the evidence you have for the proposition that the train stops in Foxboro. Despite the sameness of evidence, the protagonists in the Train Cases differ in whether they are justified in believing that the train stops in Foxboro. Thus, we have a pair of cases where justification is *not* determined entirely by the evidence. So evidentialism is false.

Evidentialists might respond that we're being too lenient with the protagonist in Train Case 1. That person doesn't know, and isn't justified in believing, that the train stops in Foxboro. If evidentialists are right about that, then we can treat both Train Cases similarly, and we no longer have a counterexample to evidentialism.

In response, Fantl and McGrath point out that although this strategy might seem promising as far as it goes, it ultimately has highly counterintuitive skeptical consequences. For, suppose we change Train Case 1 so that you double-check at the ticket counter and are told that the train will stop in Foxboro. Surely, it would seem, this gives you the justification and knowledge that the train will stop in Foxboro. Yet we can contrast that to a very high-stakes case where you have the testimony from the ticket counter, but where your entire family will be tortured and killed if you're not on the next train that stops in Foxboro. Is it rational for you to board the train without, say, double-checking with the conductor herself? Probably not. So in order to avoid the counterexample, the evidentialist must say that the protagonist in *neither* case has knowledge or justification. More generally, in order to avoid all such potential counterexamples, the evidentialist will have to endorse the following principle:

> S is justified in believing that p only if anyone with S's evidence for p, *no matter what the stakes*, would be rational to act based on their belief that P.

But, as Fantl and McGrath point out, this principle rules out many intuitive "cases of justification based on induction, testimony, memory, rational intuition, and perhaps even direct perception." Thus, evidentialism requires us to embrace grim skeptical consequences. Better, Fantl and McGrath think, to avoid skepticism by rejecting evidentialism.

Fantl and McGrath conclude that the rationality of acting based on your belief that P helps set the standard for how much evidence you need in order to know, or be justified in believing, that P is true. In this way, the practical encroaches on the epistemic.

§ 52

One invariantist's scorecard (Hawthorne, "Sensitive Moderate Invariantism")

It's useful to think of John Hawthorne's discussion as an invitation. Hawthorne invites us to judge a competition between two views, contextualism and a form of invariantism, *sensitive moderate invariantism* ("SSI" for short). The views are rival attempts to provide a "unified semantic perspective on knowledge claims." In other words, Hawthorne invites us to decide which view gives a better account of the meaning of knowledge ascriptions. As already noted (§§47–51), contextualism is the view that "knows" is a context-sensitive expression and that the content, and hence the truth-value, of a knowledge ascription varies according to the features of the ascriber's conversational context. Sensitive moderate invariantism denies that "knows" is context-sensitive and claims instead that

Hawthorne, John, "Sensitive Moderate Invariantism," pp. 157–91 in *Knowledge and Lotteries* (Oxford: Clarendon, 2004). © 2004 by John Hawthorne.

Epistemology: A Guide, First Edition. John Turri.
© 2014 John Wiley & Sons, Ltd. Published 2014 by John Wiley & Sons, Ltd.

knowledge itself depends on "the kinds of factors that in the contextualist's hands make for ascriber-dependence." In a word, one principal difference between contextualism and SSI is that contextualism is a *semantic thesis* about the meaning of "knows" and knowledge ascriptions, whereas SSI is a *metaphysical thesis* about the nature of knowledge itself.

To help us decide between contextualism and SSI, Hawthorne provides us with a scorecard populated by several "constraints" that a satisfactory view must satisfy.[1] Here I'll focus on three that Hawthorne thinks favor SSI. A full comparison of the "scorecards" for the two views is far beyond the scope of the present discussion.

1. *The Practical Reasoning Constraint*: knowledge is the norm of practical reasoning.
2. *The Assertion Constraint*: knowledge is the norm of assertion.
3. *Disquotational Schema for "Know"*: If a competent speaker sincerely utters "A knows that P," then that person believes that A knows that P.

The Practical Reasoning Constraint says that knowledge is the norm of practical reasoning – that is, knowledge sets the standard for whether you should rely on a certain belief when deciding what to do. In any case where what you should do depends on whether P is true, you should act based on P if and only if you know that P is true. SSI satisfies the Practical Reasoning Constraint because SSI is directly inspired by it. Hawthorne explains the most promising version of SSI in terms of the effect that the "practical environment" has on knowledge. "The basic idea is clear enough," he writes, "insofar as it is unacceptable ... to use a belief that p as a premise in practical reasoning on a certain occasion, the belief is not a piece of knowledge at that time." By contrast, contextualism runs into the following trouble. Suppose that an agent is reasoning about what

---

[1] The wording for the constraints provided in the following mainly comes from Chapter 2 of John Hawthorne's *Knowledge and Lotteries* (Oxford University Press, 2004). The selection in the anthology doesn't offer clear definitions.

to do, and in the course of her reasoning she relies on the claim that her train leaves at 6 p.m. And further suppose that given the standards operative in her conversational context, she can truly say, "I know that the train leaves at 6 p.m." But further suppose that given the standards operative in the agent's father's conversational context, he can truly say, "She does not know that the train leaves at 6 p.m." If knowledge is the norm of practical reasoning, then he may infer, "She should not act based on her belief that the train leaves at 6 p.m." But this is a peculiar result, given that the agent herself can truly say that she knows. SSI, being a form of invariantism, doesn't allow that the daughter and the father both speak truthfully, and so doesn't encounter this problem.

Similar remarks apply to the Assertion Constraint. The Assertion constraint says that knowledge is the norm of assertion – that is, in terms of the epistemic or evidential standards that speakers or informants are expected to meet, you may assert P if and only if you know that P is true. Now suppose that our agent is in a high-stakes context and can truthfully say, "I don't know that my train leaves at 6 p.m." And suppose that our agent's father is in a low-stakes context and can truthfully say, "She knows that her train leaves at 6 p.m." If knowledge is the norm of assertion, then the father may infer, "So she may assert that her train leaves at 6 p.m." But this is a peculiar result, given that she herself can truthfully say that she doesn't know that her train leaves at 6 p.m. SSI, being a form of invariantism, doesn't allow that the daughter and the father both speak truthfully, and so doesn't encounter this problem.

A principal advantage of SSI, according to Hawthorne, is that "it offers the best hope yet for respecting the intuitive links between knowledge, assertion, and practical reasoning." Hawthorne mentions several other constraints which do not clearly favor SSI over contextualism.

4. *The Moorean Constraint*: very many ordinary knowledge ascriptions are true.
5. *Single-Premise Closure Constraint*: necessarily, IF you (a) know that P, (b) know that P entails Q, (c) competently deduce Q

from P, (d) thereby come to believe Q, and (e) throughout retain knowledge of P and of the fact that P entails Q, THEN you know Q.

6. *Multi-Premise Closure Constraint*: necessarily, IF you (a) know each of the propositions P1 … P*n*, (b) know that P1 … P*n* entails Q, (c) competently deduce Q from P1 … P*n*, (d) thereby come to believe Q, and (e) throughout retain knowledge of P1 … P*n* and of the fact that P1 … P*n* entails Q, THEN you know Q.

7. *Epistemic Possibility Constraint*: if you know that P, then for you the epistemic probability of not-P is zero.

8. *Objective Chance Principle*: If you know that there is a nonzero objective chance that an event E will occur, then for you the epistemic probability that E will occur is nonzero.

Contextualism and SSI both equally well satisfy the Moorean Constraint because each view is appropriately non-skeptical. Of course, the two views give different explanations for why many ordinary knowledge ascriptions are true. The contextualist explanation proceeds in terms of the strength of epistemic position required in ordinary contexts in order for knowledge ascriptions to turn out true. The SSI explanation proceeds in terms of the sorts of practical reasoning that would be appropriate in ordinary contexts. Here we leave aside a detailed explanation of how SSI and contextualism respectively satisfy the remaining four constraints.

Hawthorne flags at least two noteworthy objections to SSI. On the one hand, SSI seems "unfair to thinking people." Consider the "thinking person" who reflects on the fallibility of his memory and thus worries that he didn't turn off the stove before leaving home. He suffers from "self-induced anxiety" and it is arguably not appropriate for him to practically reason from his belief that he turned the stove off. According to SSI, the thinking person doesn't know that he turned off the stove. Compare him to "the dullard" who doesn't consider the fallibility of her memory and thus doesn't worry that she failed to turn off the stove. She suffers from no anxiety and it is arguably appropriate for her to practically reason from her belief that she turned it off. Hawthorne acknowledges that SSI might imply that thinking persons are at an epistemic disadvantage, but he doesn't concede that this is clearly the wrong verdict.

On the other hand, SSI implicates us in some fairly systematic errors. Suppose that we're in a situation where it is vitally important that the plane flies directly to Detroit. We're organ couriers assigned to deliver a liver to a patient in Detroit. To do so, we must take a plane. But there is a catch: we should get on the plane only if it is a *direct* flight to Detroit. If it isn't direct to Detroit, then the liver will spoil and we should instead deliver the liver to a local patient who is lower on the transplant list. We're in the airport at the gate. It says right there on the board that the plane is direct to Detroit. But given what's at stake – given our practical environment – we're not willing to base our decision solely on that. Not only are we unwilling to flat-out base our decision on the claim that the flight is direct to Detroit, we don't take ourselves to know that the flight is direct to Detroit either.

But what about the casual traveler waiting next to us at the gate, returning home from a pleasant vacation? She says to her partner, "It's a good thing that the flight is direct to Detroit. Layovers are so annoying." Very little is at stake for her. Yet we, the organ couriers, are inclined to think that *she doesn't know either*. But why? It seems that we're apt to "over-project" our own ignorance onto her. Related to our tendency to over-project ignorance onto others, neither do we find ourselves thinking, "If only less was at stake, we would know that the flight is direct to Detroit," or, "Perhaps the only thing stopping us from knowing that the flight is direct to Detroit is that we're worrying too much." If SSI is the correct theory and respects the Moorean Constraint, then these tendencies are all errors. SSI's proponents owe us some explanation for why we're prone to such errors. Hawthorne proposes that results from experimental psychology provide the outlines of an acceptable explanation.

In the final analysis, Hawthorne is not confident that SSI outperforms contextualism. And it's unclear, according to Hawthorne, whether we'll be able to come up with arguments or evidence that would allow us to confidently decide which view is preferable. For Hawthorne is skeptical that we can provide "a relatively manageable theory of the detailed semantic workings of our language." The correct view might be "cognitively unavailable to us."

Reference

John Hawthorne, *Knowledge and Lotteries* (Oxford University Press, 2004).

§ 53

A relativist theory of knowledge attributions (MacFarlane, "The Assessment Sensitivity of Knowledge Attributions")

John MacFarlane's paper is an exceedingly clear and elegant attempt to provide what John Hawthorne called a "unified semantic perspective on knowledge claims" (§52). MacFarlane introduces three basic "facts about our use of knowledge attributions." He then argues that each of the three standard views about the semantics of knowledge attributions in the literature – strict invariantism, sensitive invariantism, and contextualism – fails to satisfactorily explain one of the three basic facts about knowledge attributions. Then he argues that a fourth view, relativism, well explains all three basic facts. MacFarlane concludes that relativism is the best semantic theory of knowledge attributions.

MacFarlane, John, "The Assessment Sensitivity of Knowledge Attributions," pp. 197–233 in Tamar Szabó Gendler and John O'Leary Hawthorne (eds.), *Oxford Studies in Epistemology*, Vol. 1 (Oxford: Clarendon, 2005). © 2005 by Oxford University Press.

Let's use a simple example along with a simple question to illustrate the four different views. *The example*: Angelo looks at the information on the side of the bottle and forms the belief that the medication doesn't contain penicillin; Sarah says, "Angelo knows that the medication doesn't contain penicillin"; later Geno is asked to evaluate the truth-value of Sarah's claim. Overall, the example involves three separable contexts: (1) Angelo's original context of belief-formation, (2) Sarah's context of utterance, and (3) Geno's context of evaluation. *The question*: what determines the true answer for Geno to give?

Strict invariantism says that the true answer for Geno to give is determined *entirely* by Angelo's original context of belief-formation. In particular, according to strict invariantism, the true answer is determined by whether it was, at the time of belief-formation, true that the medication didn't contain penicillin, whether Angelo's evidence and reasoning were appropriately connected to the truth of the matter (see §§15–17), and whether Angelo's evidence met the one invariant standard required for knowledge. The one invariant standard is the same in Angelo's original context of belief-formation, Sarah's context of utterance, and Geno's context of evaluation.

Sensitive invariantism also says that the true answer for Geno to give is determined entirely by Angelo's original context of belief-formation *but with a twist*. In particular, according to sensitive invariantism, the true answer is determined by whether it was, at the time of belief-formation, true that the medication didn't contain penicillin, whether Angelo's evidence and reasoning were appropriately connected to the truth of the matter, and whether Angelo's evidence met the one *variant* standard required for knowledge. The variant standard requires, roughly, that Angelo's evidence is *good enough for him to properly act based on his belief* that the medication doesn't contain penicillin. In short, the one variant standard is keyed to Angelo's "practical environment" (see §52). Angelo's practical environment determines whether his true belief counts as knowledge, whether Sarah's knowledge attribution is true, and what the true answer is for Geno to give.

The difference between strict invariantism and sensitive invariantism is best illustrated by considering what they imply about two slightly different versions of the example. In one version, Angelo inspects the bottle in order to determine which of his two friends had won a $1 bet about the medication's contents; in the other version, Angelo inspects the bottle in order to determine whether he can administer the medication to an ill loved one with a fatal allergy to penicillin. Strict invariantism entails that the true answer for Geno is the same in each version of the example. By contrast, sensitive invariantism can treat the two versions differently. For example, sensitive invariantism can say that the true answer for Geno is affirmative in the case of the $1 bet but negative in the case of the fatal penicillin allergy.

Contextualism says that the true answer for Geno to give is determined partly by Angelo's original context of belief-formation and partly by Sarah's context of utterance. In particular, according to contextualism, the true answer is determined by whether it was, at the time of belief-formation, true that the medication didn't contain penicillin, whether Angelo's evidence and reasoning were appropriately connected to the truth of the matter, and whether Angelo's evidence met the variable epistemic standard required for true knowledge attributions in Sarah's context of utterance. Suppose that Angelo's belief was true and based on evidence appropriately connected to the truth of the matter. If Sarah was in a normal, low-stakes context when she said, "Angelo knows that the medication doesn't contain penicillin," then probably she said something true and the true answer for Geno is affirmative. But if Sarah was in a skeptical or high-stakes context when she made her statement, then she probably said something false and the true answer for Geno is negative.

Relativism says that the true answer for Geno to give is determined partly by Angelo's original context of belief-formation and partly by Geno's context of evaluation. In particular, according to relativism, the true answer is determined by whether it was, at the time of belief-formation, true that the medication didn't contain penicillin, whether Angelo's evidence and reasoning were appropriately connected to the truth of the matter, and whether Angelo's evidence met the variable epistemic standard required for true knowledge attributions in Geno's context of evaluation. Suppose that Angelo's belief was true and based on evidence appropriately connected to the truth of the matter. If Geno is in a normal, low-stakes context when he evaluates Sarah's claim, then probably the true answer for Geno is affirmative. But if Geno is in a skeptical or high-stakes context when he evaluates Sarah's claim, then probably the true answer for Geno is negative.

To summarize, invariantists claim that the true answer for Geno is determined entirely by facts about Angelo's original context of belief-formation. Contextualists claim that it is determined by a combination of facts about Angelo's original context of belief-formation and facts about Sarah's context of utterance. Relativists claim that it is determined by a combination of facts about Angelo's original context of belief-formation and facts about Geno's context of evaluation.

Now that we've explained the four different theories, we can state MacFarlane's main argument.

1. There are four competing semantic theories of knowledge attributions: strict invariantism, sensitive invariantism, contextualism, and relativism. (Premise)
2. The correct semantic theory must well explain all of the following facts about our practicing of making and assessing knowledge attributions: (a) the variability of our standards for making knowledge attributions, (b) our unwillingness to mix standards at a single context of use, (c) our habits of retracting knowledge attributions. (Premise)
3. Strict invariantism doesn't well explain (a) the apparent variability of our standards for making knowledge attributions. (Premise)
4. Sensitive invariantism doesn't well explain (b) our unwillingness to mix standards at a single context of use. (Premise)
5. Contextualism doesn't well explain (c) our habits of retracting knowledge attributions. (Premise)

6. Relativism well explains all three of the facts about our practice of making and assessing knowledge attributions. (Premise)
7. So relativism is the best of the four semantic theories of knowledge attributions. (From 1–6)

What we've said thus far should clarify premise 1 of the argument. Premise 2 is based primarily on MacFarlane's own introspective reports and social observations about how knowledge attributions work.

Consider 2(a). Our habits of attributing knowledge vary depending on the circumstance. MacFarlane normally takes himself to know that his car is in the driveway where he parked it, and he will attribute such knowledge to himself. But if someone asks him, "How do you know a thief hasn't stolen and driven away since you last saw it?," he will change his tune and deny that he knows that it's still in the driveway. According to MacFarlane, when this happens, "It doesn't seem right to describe me as having learned something, or as correcting a mistake," or to say that I was speaking nonliterally either before or after the thief-possibility was mentioned. This perfectly ordinary "shift from claiming to know to denying that I know" makes trouble for strict invariantism, which makes no allowance for variable or "shifty" standards. If the standards for knowledge don't vary, then why do we shift from claiming to know to denying to know? MacFarlane doubts that strict invariantists can satisfactorily answer this question, so he accepts premise 3.

Consider 2(b). Suppose that we're considering two different people in very different practical environments who happen to be considering the same proposition. For example, let's consider what we'd want to say about cognizers in the two versions of our earlier example. Each considers whether a certain medication contains penicillin and concludes that it does not. Angelo Low does this in order to decide which of his two friends won a $1 bet about the medication's contents; Angelo High does this in order to decide whether he can administer the medication to an ill loved one with a fatal allergy to penicillin. Does Angelo Low know? Does Angelo High know? We're strongly inclined to answer these questions the same way. We don't say that Angelo Low knows whereas Angelo High doesn't. But if sensitive invariantism were true, we should expect *mixed verdicts* of precisely this sort to be correct. MacFarlane doubts that sensitive invariantists can satisfactorily explain our disinclination toward mixed verdicts, so he accepts premise 4.

Consider 2(c). Consider again whether MacFarlane knows where his car is parked. MacFarlane normally takes himself to know that his car is in the driveway where he parked it, and he will attribute such knowledge to himself. But if someone asks him, "How do you know a thief hasn't stolen and driven away since you last saw it?," he will change his tune and deny that he knows that it's still in the driveway. Moreover, suppose we ask him, "Well you say that now, but earlier you said that you did know it. Do you still stand by your earlier statement?" MacFarlane will respond by *retracting* his earlier statement because he considers it to be *false*. He does *not* respond by saying, "Actually, what I said earlier was true because my belief satisfied the epistemic standards in place at that earlier context of utterance." But if contextualism were true, we shouldn't expect retraction of this sort. Rather, we should expect the metalinguistic retort "But it was true by the standards operative at the time … " to be appropriate. MacFarlane doubts that contextualists can satisfactorily handle this problem, so he accepts premise 5.

Regarding premise 6, it's no surprise that relativism can explain all three facts because relativism was designed precisely in order to explain them. It predicts variability in the semantics of knowledge attributions because it posits that knowledge attributions are sensitive to one variable standard fixed at the context of assessment. It predicts that we will reject mixed verdicts because there is only one standard fixed at the context of assessment which applies equally to all subjects under evaluation. And it predicts that we will retract earlier knowledge claims and insist (now) that they were false (then) because they are both subject to the same one standard fixed at the current context of assessment.

§ 54

Rationality and trust (Baker, "Trust and Rationality")

Judith Baker's discussion can be broken into two parts. First, she contends that a "natural and compelling picture of rationality" is inconsistent with the rationality of some important aspects of socially important attitudes of trust. Second, she criticizes several responses to her first point.

The natural and compelling picture of rationality that Baker considers is basically *evidentialism*. Evidentialism is the view that whether believing a proposition is rational for you is determined entirely by the evidence you have (§24). Belief "aims at truth," so we should accept only "those beliefs which are likely to be true," and so the rational norm of belief requires that we apportion belief according to the evidence.

Baker, Judith, "Trust and Rationality," pp. 1–13 in *Pacific Philosophical Quarterly* 68 (1987). © 1987 Pacific Philosophical Quarterly.

Now consider what this norm of rationality implies about some of our attitudes, in particular the attitudes of trust that seem appropriate to friendship. Baker sketches the following case. "Suppose I trust a friend who has been accused of [selling secrets to a foreign government], with an impressive amount of evidence brought against her." Baker has never witnessed her friend decline tempting offers to betray the government, so Baker has no direct evidence that would support an inductive argument that her friend wouldn't, or is unlikely to, betray the government. Nevertheless, Baker believes that her friend is innocent "despite the evidence." Baker doesn't come to this conclusion by "balancing present evidence against [the friend's] past record." Rather, Baker comes to this conclusion because she *trusts* her friend, and this trust "outruns the evidence" that Baker has about her friend's predispositions and character. The evidentialist conception of rationality thus rules that Baker's trusting attitude is *irrational* because it isn't properly supported by the evidence.

However, Baker contends, this verdict is hard to reconcile with how we live our lives. "We not only tolerate" this sort of trust, but "we demand it of our friends, and we think well of people in general who manifest such trust." In the course of our daily lives, it would be hard to accept that despite being irrational, such trust is nonetheless permissible, good, and perhaps even *required*.

We now move on to the second part of Baker's discussion. A natural reaction to Baker's example is to distinguish between *practical* and *epistemic* rationality. Evidentialism isn't a theory of the requirements of practical rationality. Practical rationality is sensitive to factors that will make our lives go better – matters of prudence, social harmony, morality, and the like. Epistemic or theoretical rationality is a more purely intellectual matter (though compare Fantl and McGrath's discussion in §51). In response to Baker's example and others like it, we should of course grant that it can be practically rational for belief to "outrun" the evidence and perhaps even for belief to run directly against the evidence. But it doesn't follow that it is epistemically rational to do so. We can accommodate what is clearly right in Baker's gloss on her example without accepting that

271

the trusting attitudes are *rational* in a sense that conflicts with evidentialism. Baker's response to this suggestion is to remark, "I do not think that the example sketched presents a conflict between" practical and epistemic rationality.

Baker considers several other responses to the "puzzle" of the rationality of trust. First, someone might argue that the trust in question doesn't involve belief but rather pretense or "acting-as-if" that the friend is innocent. Baker objects that this gets the requirements of friendship wrong: "what one demands from one's friend is belief, not pretense." Second, someone might argue that the trust is acceptable even if we can't establish that it is epistemically rational. Baker objects that it's not possible to accept this as "participants and agents" in our relationships. Third, someone might argue that the trust in question is irrational but an unavoidable fact of human life. Baker objects that this view "displays an alarming lack of integration" because it would involve us reflectively rejecting what we take to be true in our ordinary unreflective lives.

Fourth, someone might argue that the trust in question is irrational but this is unproblematic because we can replace it with other attitudes that aren't susceptible to the requirements of epistemic rationality. Baker's objection to this fourth response is to speculate that "the institution of morality" in human society requires that we genuinely trust one another in our relationships. For example, perhaps human children would not develop into moral agents unless the adults around them exhibited trust in their relationships. But Baker's objection seems to miss the point because nothing she says suggests the trust exhibited in these relationships must be *epistemically rational*.

§ 55

Testimony and gullibility (Fricker, "Against Gullibility")

Testimony is a vital source of knowledge for dependent social beings like us. Much of what we know comes from the good word of others. In ordinary language, "testimony" connotes a witness making statements in a formal courtroom context. But in philosophical discussions, to "give testimony" is roughly equivalent to what we ordinarily mean by "assert" or "claim" that something is true.

The importance of testimonial knowledge prompts Elizabeth Fricker to ask *what justifies us* in forming beliefs based on testimony (i.e. *testimonial beliefs*). Fricker focuses specifically on the question, what makes it true "that a hearer on a particular occasion has the epistemic right to believe what she is told – to believe a particular speaker's assertion?" Answers to this question can

Fricker, Elizabeth, "Against Gullibility," pp. 125–61 in B. K. Matilal and A. Chakrabarti (eds.) *Knowing from Words* (Dordrecht, Netherlands: Kluwer Academic Publishers, 1994). © 1994 Kluwer Academic Publishers.

Epistemology: A Guide, First Edition. John Turri.
© 2014 John Wiley & Sons, Ltd. Published 2014 by John Wiley & Sons, Ltd.

be divided into two main groups. *Anti-reductionists* claim that testimonial justification does not derive entirely from nontestimonial sources such as inductive inference based on past experience or gathering evidence about the speaker's reliability. Rather, testimonial justification is due at least partly to "a special normative principle pertaining to testimony" specifically. *Reductionists* claim that testimonial justification does derive entirely from more general, non-testimonial sources. According to reductionism, there is no special normative principle pertaining to testimony specifically.

The generic characterizations of antireductionism and reductionism don't figure essentially into Fricker's main positive view. Instead, she focuses on a particular way in which antireductionism might be understood. More specifically, she focuses on whether hearers hold a special "presumptive right" to accept testimony, a right which provides them with special "dispensation" to avoid "assessing the speaker" for trustworthiness, so long as the speaker gives them no special reason to think otherwise. Otherwise put, the question is, absent evidence to the contrary, may hearers simply assume *without assessment* that speakers are trustworthy? If hearers hold such a special right, then at least a weak version of antireductionism is true. For then many testimonial beliefs would be justified at least partly because of an epistemic principle pertaining specifically to testimony.

Fricker argues that hearers possess no such right. Such a right is tantamount to a provisional license to be *gullible*. However, according to Fricker, justified believers are not gullible believers. Gullibility doesn't satisfy the demands of justification. Fricker adopts a highly demanding view of justification: in order to be justified in a belief, a subject must "be able to defend her belief appropriately" when asked to defend it. Fricker is an *internalist* about justification. Her view resembles Laurence BonJour's (§28) and largely corresponds to what Earl Conee and Richard Feldman call *accessibilism* (§31). Fricker's view is arguably even more demanding than BonJour's because she requires that you be able to *verbally cite* the justifying factors, whereas BonJour requires only that they be accessible from your perspective.[1] According to Fricker, if you're asked why you believe P, it's inadequate to respond merely with, "Someone told me so."

Nevertheless, many people are tempted to think that we must possess such a presumptive right if we're to avoid rampant skepticism about testimonial justification. After all, it is tempting to think, we can't *always* double-check what *everyone* says. We can't *always* confirm, entirely independently of testimony, whether each speaker is trustworthy. That would be impossible to accomplish! At some point we must be allowed to simply assume, without further argument or elaboration, that others are telling us the truth.

Fricker responds to this natural thought by arguing that not only is it possible to accomplish this on any given occasion, but we typically do it automatically and routinely. Fricker's positive theory is that "a hearer should always engage in some assessment of the speaker for trustworthiness." This assessment typically takes the form of *counterfactual sensitivity* to signs that the speaker is asserting either insincerely or outside her domain of competence. To be counterfactually sensitive to signs means, roughly, that if such signs were present, you would notice them and adjust your confidence accordingly. Signs that a speaker is asserting insincerely are signs that the speaker is asserting something she doesn't actually believe. To assert outside one's domain of competence is to assert something that one might sincerely assert even if it was false. (Compare the notion of *weak safety* in §22.) In sum, testimonial justification requires "the actual engagement of a counterfactual sensitivity," which means that "if there were any signs of untrustworthiness, [the hearer] would pick them up." Fricker contends that it is "sheer common sense" that testimonial justification requires this.

---

[1] Or so it seems from what Fricker explicitly states early on in her article. Later, in Section 9, she offers a more precise statement of her view, which makes it sound more like a version of externalism (in BonJour's sense) because she seems to allow that believers may be, and in fact typically are, unaware of at least some of the factors that help justify their testimonial beliefs.

Fricker says that we routinely accomplish this, but it's natural to wonder how. We don't often find ourselves explicitly monitoring for trustworthiness or asking, "Is she being sincere?" or, "Is she asserting outside her area of competence?" Such questions are the exception, not the rule. Fricker anticipates this and accommodates it by allowing that the counterfactual sensitivity is due to monitoring that occurs "at a non-conscious level" and that much of "the informational basis" for our sensitivity is consciously "irretrievable." Nevertheless, Fricker says, the upshot of this sensitivity is available to consciousness and can be articulated, thus satisfying Fricker's demanding sense of justification. The typical hearer knows that "she can tell about that kind of thing" – that is, about whether a speaker is untrustworthy – even though "she does not know how she does it."

One is reminded of a passage in J.M. Barrie's *Peter Pan*. Wendy tells her mother, Mrs. Darling, that she (Wendy) is preoccupied by Peter Pan. Mrs. Darling recalls incidents from her own childhood and remarks that Peter "would be all grown up by now." "Oh no, he isn't grown up," Wendy assures her, "and he is just my size." J.M. Barrie then writes, "She didn't know how she knew it, she just knew it."

Fricker goes one step further in explaining our counterfactual sensitivity. She argues that it is "but one part of the broader domain of our knowledge of other minds." In order to recognize that there are other people who speak to us and thereby intend to communicate, we must apply principles of interpretation to incoming stimuli. The detection of persons and ascription of mental states to them is a theoretical enterprise. In the process of building up a theory which has as part of it the claim, "This is a person and she has just told me that P is true," we must have ascribed a comprehensive set of mental states to her. Moreover, as part of this process, we will also have decided whether she is sincere and competent with respect P. Thus, on Fricker's view, the possibility of justified testimonial beliefs derives from the very principles and processes of interpretation which enable us to identify speakers and their meaning in the first place. The relevant counterfactual sensitivity is an upshot of all that, not something additional that must be accomplished after the fact.

§ 56

Some reflections on how epistemic sources work (Burge, "Content Preservation")

Suppose that the mathematician Marjorie devises a nine-line mathematical proof with this form:

1. P. (Premise)
2. If P, then Q. (Premise)
3. Therefore, Q. (From 1 and 2)
4. Either R or S. (Premise)
5. Not-R. (Premise)
6. Therefore, S. (From 4 and 5)
7. If S and Q, then T. (Premise)
8. S and Q. (From 3 and 6)
9. Therefore, T. (From 7 and 8)

Burge, Tyler, "Content Preservation," pp. 457–88 in *The Philosophical Review*, 102, 4 (Oct. 1993). © 1993 by Cornell University Press. All rights reserved. Used by permission of the publisher.

Epistemology: A Guide, First Edition. John Turri.
© 2014 John Wiley & Sons, Ltd. Published 2014 by John Wiley & Sons, Ltd.

Although the basic propositions that featured in the argument – that is the propositions abbreviated by "P," "Q," "R," "S," and "T" – are relatively simple in their own right, the overall argument is too complex for Marjorie to hold in her mind all at once. And although each individual premise – that is, lines 1, 2, 4, 5, and 7 – is trivially obvious on its own, their conjunction isn't trivially obvious. Nor is it trivially obvious that their conjunction entails the conclusion. The only way Marjorie gets to the conclusion is by keeping track of what she has proven up till then. She keeps track of this through memory and with the visual aid of a pencil-and-paper (or a white board, or a computer screen, etc.).

Here is a relatively uncontroversial, rough working definition of a priori knowledge: a priori knowledge is knowledge justified independently of experience (cf. §43). A mathematician's knowledge of mathematical axioms and theorems are typically considered to be excellent examples of a priori knowledge. If Marjorie has a priori knowledge of each premise in the earlier argument, and if the inferences are all obviously valid, then presumably she has a priori knowledge of the conclusion too. In other words, if the inferences are obviously valid and Marjorie knows the premises a priori, then Marjorie knows the conclusion a priori too.

But the claim that Marjorie a priori knows the conclusion faces the following challenge. What about the role that *memory* and *perception* play in her reasoning? A priori knowledge is typically contrasted with *empirical* (or *a posteriori*) knowledge, of which perceptual knowledge and episodic memory of past events are prime examples. When Marjorie concludes that T is true, she relies on the lines she sees written earlier and her episodic memory of having intuited the earlier premises and derived the intermediate conclusions. Granted she knows the conclusion. But how can this knowledge be a priori? Our working definition of a priori knowledge is knowledge justified independently of experience. Marjorie's knowledge of the conclusion isn't justified independently of experience. Rather, it involves specific perceptual experiences and episodic memories.

Tyler Burge proposes a response to this challenge. Burge understands a priori knowledge similarly to our rough working definition.

He defines a priori knowledge as knowledge whose justification[1] is a priori, and he defines a priori justification as justification whose "force is in no way constituted or enhanced by reference to or reliance on the specifics of some range of sense experiences or perceptual beliefs." Nevertheless, Burge would judge that Marjorie knows a priori the conclusion T.

He reconciles this judgment with the role played by perception and memory in Marjorie's case by distinguishing different ways justification can depend on perception and memory. Writes Burge,

> An a priori justification will usually depend on sense experiences or perceptual beliefs in some way. They are typically necessary for the acquisition of understanding or belief. But such dependence is not relevant to apriority unless it is essential to justificational force.

In Marjorie's case, her justification for the conclusion is constituted by the propositions and inferences from earlier in the proof. Specific perceptions and memories enable her to access and retain the justifying propositions and inferences, but propositions about perception or memory don't form part of the justification.

The upshot: not every way of *depending on* perception or memory counts as *relying on premises about* perception or memory. On Burge's view, Marjorie knows a priori that T because she "does not justify the demonstration by appeals to" memory or perception, but rather "by appeals to the steps and the inferential transitions of the demonstration."

Let's mark Burge's purported distinction by saying that a priori justification *can merely depend*, but *cannot essentially rely*, on empirical sources. Marjorie's justification merely depends, but doesn't essentially rely, on empirical sources. So it is a priori.

With this distinction in place, it could be argued that some testimonial knowledge is a priori too. Suppose that Marjorie knows a priori that T is true, and she expresses this knowledge to us by telling us, "T is true." We accept her word and come to believe that

---

[1] Actually, he says "justification or entitlement." More on entitlement later.

T is true. Conventional wisdom is that our knowledge in this case is empirical because it depends on perceptual experience, namely, seeing and hearing her say, "T is true." But Burge bucks conventional wisdom. On his view, our testimonial knowledge in this case *merely depends* on perception but doesn't essentially rely on it. We do not reason from premises about the contents of our perceptual experience; nor do we reason from premises about the reliability of testimony in general or in Marjorie's particular case. Instead, we simply "accept the information instinctively" due to Marjorie's assertion. And since Marjorie's knowledge is a priori, the knowledge we acquire in the process is a priori too.

I'll note three other aspects of Burge's discussion. First, on Burge's view, knowledge doesn't require justification. Rather, knowledge requires justification *or* entitlement. True belief with entitlement suffices for justification. Entitlement differs importantly from justification. Justification essentially "involves reasons" that "must be available in the cognitive" perspective of the subject. Thus, along with Fricker (§55) and BonJour (§28), Burge is an *internalist* about epistemic justification. By contrast, entitlement is a positive epistemic status that the subject might not have access to or even understand. Burge is thus a radical *externalist* about entitlement. As an initial gloss on the relationship between entitlement and justification, think of justification as the result of *becoming aware of* an entitlement and its grounds.

Second, on Burge's view, testimony effectively transmits knowledge because of "the Acceptance Principle," which says, "A person is entitled to accept as true something that is presented as true and that is intelligible to him, unless there are stronger reasons not to do so." When someone asserts P, P is presented-as-true. So the "default position" is entitlement to believe speakers. We don't need reasons or justification to believe them. We rightly presuppose that they're sincere and truthful. Not only is skepticism about a speaker's sincerity and truthfulness initially unwarranted, so is "neutrality," which Burge describes as a "rationally unnatural attitude" toward others. This contrasts with Fricker's view (§55). Fricker claims that in order for us to gain knowledge by testimony, we must actively monitor the speaker for signs of insincerity or incompetence. Burge and Fricker both describe their views with the phrase "default position," but this nominal resemblance obscures potentially important differences.

Third, Burge's defense of the Acceptance Principle is complex and obscure, but its essentials are familiar from our earlier discussion of Sellars (§§8–9) and Davidson (§11). There is a necessary conceptual connection between truth, on the one hand, and belief, intelligence, agency, and language use, on the other. "A condition on an individual's having propositional attitudes," Burge tells us, is that "the content of those attitudes [be] systematically associated with veridical perceptions and true beliefs." Moreover, "the very practice of communication depends on preservation of truth." Individual minds tend toward the truth and communicative practices tend toward truth's preservation. This is the basis of our entitlements.

§ 57

Testimony and knowledge (Lackey, "Testimonial Knowledge and Transmission")

You can't get a dollar from me unless I have a dollar to begin with. That's just obvious. I might own the dollar outright or I might have it on loan, but in order for you to get it from me, I must have it. Many epistemologists have thought that testimonial knowledge works like money in this way: you can't get knowledge from my testimony unless I have the knowledge to begin with. More specifically, when I assert that Q is true, you can gain knowledge that Q based on my testimony *only if* I know that Q is true. I might have discovered for myself that Q is true or I might have learned it from someone else, but in order for you to come to know Q based on my testimony, I must know Q.

Lackey, Jennifer, "Testimonial Knowledge and Transmission," pp. 471–90 in *The Philosophical Quarterly*, 49,197 (Oct. 1999). © The Editors of *The Philosophical Quarterly*, 1999.

As appealing as that principle about testimonial knowledge might seem initially, Jennifer Lackey argues that we should abandon it. She thinks that "there are some plausible ways in which" an assertion that Q can enable hearers to come to know that Q, even though the speaker doesn't have knowledge. She supports this position by providing detailed examples.

One example features a creationist elementary school science teacher, Mrs. Smith, who lectures to her students on evolutionary theory. The school board tasks Mrs. Smith to teach her class evolutionary theory, so she extensively researches the subject and "develops a set of reliable lecture notes from which" she lectures to her students. However, Mrs. Smith is "a devout creationist" who doesn't believe a word of what she tells her students about evolution. But belief is a necessary condition on knowledge. So Mrs. Smith doesn't know that what she tells her students is true. Nevertheless, Lackey continues, if evolutionary theory is true, then "it seems reasonable to assume that Mrs. Smith's students can come to have knowledge via her testimony," despite her lack of belief and, hence, knowledge.

Why can Mrs. Smith's students gain knowledge from her in this way? Lackey's explanation is that Mrs. Smith is a reliable source of information on evolutionary theory. It seems to be Lackey's view that if a speaker's assertions reliably indicate the truth about some subject matter, and what the speaker asserts on the subject matter is true, and the audience doesn't have special reason to mistrust the speaker's reliability, then the audience can gain knowledge by accepting the speaker's testimony. Crucially, none of this requires that the speaker know or believe what she's saying. Of course, Lackey could agree that such a case is atypical, but that wouldn't spoil her point.

Another class of examples features speakers who give voice to true beliefs that would ordinarily count as knowledge, but which don't count as knowledge because their justification is *defeated*. Recall the traditional view that knowledge is justified true belief, which most theorists abandoned in light of Edmund Gettier's counterexamples (§15). Many theorists thought that the best response to Gettier's examples was to add another requirement to the traditional view – a *no defeater* requirement.[1] On this view, you know that P only if (i) P is true, (ii) you believe that P, (iii) your belief that P is justified, and (iv) your justification for believing P is undefeated. Some condition or fact F defeats your justification for believing P just in case (a) you believe P based on evidence E, (b) E justifies belief in P, but (c) the combination (E + F) *fails* to justify belief in P.

Now consider Millicent, who has excellent vision but whose physician has convincingly misled her into thinking that her vision is abnormal and unreliable. Millicent believes her physician, but she can't help forming beliefs based on how things seem to her visually. On this occasion, while Millicent is talking to her father on the phone, she sees that there is a cardinal perched on the sill of her kitchen window. This belief of hers is formed by a normal, reliable perceptual process, and she unreflectively reports it to her father. According to Lackey, Millicent doesn't know that there is a cardinal perched on the sill because the physician's testimony defeats her justification, thereby preventing her from satisfying condition (iv). However, we may suppose that Millicent hasn't told her father about the physician's testimony and that her father has every reason to believe that Millicent remains a normal, reliable perceiver. In such a case, Lackey claims, it seems that Millicent's father nevertheless can gain knowledge based on Millicent's assertion. "Thus," Lackey concludes, Millicent is "capable of giving knowledge to others which she fails to possess herself."

Why can Millicent's father know even though Millicent doesn't? Lackey explains this by noting that testimony doesn't necessarily transmit defeaters. Millicent's justification is defeated but her father's isn't. So Millicent fails to satisfy one necessary condition on knowledge, but her father satisfies it. Moreover, it seems possible that Millicent's father satisfies all the other necessary conditions for knowledge. That's why her father can know, even though she doesn't.

---

[1] For more on such views, see John Turri, "In Gettier's Wake," *Epistemology: The Key Thinkers*. Edited by Stephen Hetherington (Continuum, 2012).

In light of examples like the two we've discussed, Lackey concludes that we should abandon the initially plausible principle about testimonial knowledge which we began with. Testimony isn't a *mere* tool for transmitting prior knowledge. Instead, "testimony can itself *generate* knowledge."

Reference

John Turri, "In Gettier's Wake," in *Epistemology: The Key Thinkers*. Edited by Stephen Hetherington (Continuum, 2012).

§ 58

Memory and knowledge (Huemer, "The Problem of Memory Knowledge")

At any given time, the vast majority of our beliefs is stored in memory, and very few are the result of conscious, occurrent judgment. We see things, deduce things, get told things, and on that basis we accept them, perhaps after a bout of critical assessment and reflection. Then we retain these beliefs through memory. Often we also remember our original reasons for the beliefs, but usually we don't. Usually, we just retain the beliefs themselves. Moreover, it's natural to assume that the beliefs we retain in memory are justified, at least typically. This raises an interesting question: if we usually don't have reasons for the beliefs we retain in memory, then what justifies us in holding those memory beliefs?

Huemer, Michael, "The Problem of Memory Knowledge," pp. 346–57 in *The Philosophical Quarterly*, 80, 197 (1999). © 1999 University of Southern California and Blackwell Publishers Ltd.

Epistemology: A Guide, First Edition. John Turri.
© 2014 John Wiley & Sons, Ltd. Published 2014 by John Wiley & Sons, Ltd.

Michael Huemer confronts this question in his paper "The Problem of Memory Knowledge." Huemer's discussion divides into two parts: critical and positive. In the critical part, he critiques three possible answers that "naturally come to mind." The critique uncovers two "intuitive constraints" on an acceptable answer. In the positive part, he offers a theory that satisfies the two constraints.

Let's begin by reviewing Huemer's critique of the three "natural" answers. The first natural answer is *the inferential theory*. The inferential theory says that our memory beliefs are justified because we rehearse an argument to ourselves about memory's reliability. For example, when I seem to remember that Detroit is in Michigan, I consider that most of my past seeming memories have turned out to be correct and conclude that my seeming memory that Detroit is in Michigan is probably accurate. Huemer raises two main problems for the inferential theory. The first problem is that the argument in question is objectionably circular. It relies on memory for the crucial premise about the track record of seeming memories. The second problem is that even if we figure out how to construct such an argument without sliding into objectionable circularity, it is implausible that we actually base our memory beliefs on such an argument. "There is no evidence that I have ever employed any such argument," says Huemer, in which case skepticism about memory justification follows. The inferential theory is unacceptably costly.

The second natural answer is *the foundational theory*. The foundational theory says that memory is a foundational source of justification, in that seeming to remember something automatically gives you a reason to believe it. This approach likens memory to perception, in that seeming to perceive something also automatically gives you a reason to believe it. Huemer points out a "counterintuitive" consequence of the foundational theory: if the foundational theory is true, then a belief's justification can be increased just by passing into memory. Suppose that *based on wishful thinking* I believe that the Red Wings won the Stanley Cup in 2012. I then store this belief in memory. Weeks pass without me considering the matter again, and I forget how I initially formed the belief. Then I experience a situation that makes me consider whether the Red Wings won the Stanley

Cup in 2012. In virtue of the stored belief, it seems to me that I remember that the Red Wings did win. Importantly, I currently have no evidence that my belief was initially formed based on wishful thinking – all that is long forgotten. If the foundational theory is true, then I am justified in believing that the Red Wings won, because I seem to remember that they did win, and seeming to remember something automatically gives one a reason to believe it. Thus, the mere "passage of time" has transformed an unjustified belief into a justified one. But this is an absurd result, Huemer thinks, so he rejects the foundational theory.

The third natural answer is *the preservation theory*. The preservation theory says that memory preserves a belief's original level of justification. Memory neither increases nor decreases a belief's justification: it merely preserves. Because it doesn't allow the mere passage of time to increase a belief's justification, the preservation theory avoids Huemer's objection to the foundational theory. But Huemer raises a different problem for the preservation theory: it implies that radically deceived subjects, to whom everything seems exactly as it seems to us, are unjustified in holding almost all of their beliefs. Huemer asks us to consider his own radically deceived duplicate, "Mike2." A powerful god created Mike2 "five minutes ago in exactly the state that" Huemer himself was in five minutes ago. Crucially, this god gave Mike2 all the same seeming memories that Huemer himself has. More generally, things seem exactly the same to Mike2 as they do to Huemer himself. Intuitively, Mike2 and Huemer are equally justified in all of their memory beliefs. But if the preservation theory is true, then it's extremely difficult to accommodate this intuition. (Huemer says it "contradicts" the preservation theory, but that is not correct.) For it would just be *a monumental coincidence* that Mike2's beliefs and Huemer's beliefs differ radically in their histories but nevertheless end up with the same level of justification. We should avoid positing monumental coincidences, if possible.

In light of his critique, Huemer proposes that an acceptable theory of memory knowledge must satisfy two constraints. On the one hand, a belief's passing into memory can't increase its justification.

On the other hand, Mike2 and Huemer are equally justified in their memory beliefs. To meet these twin constraints, Huemer proposes *the dualistic theory*.

According to the dualistic theory, a memory belief's justification is a function of two factors: the quality of its source and the quality of its retention. In other words, a memory belief's justification is a function of how justified one was in acquiring it and how justified one is in retaining it. For simplicity, let's assign each of the two factors a number between 0 and 1, corresponding to the belief's justification in the relevant respect. A belief that was perfectly justified when acquired receives a score of 1 for *acquisition justification*, and a belief that was perfectly unjustified when acquired receives a score of 0. Call this the belief's *acquisition score*, or "AS" for short. A belief that was perfectly retained up till now receives a score of 1 for *retention justification*, and a belief that was awfully retained receives a score of 0. Call this the belief's *retention score*, or "RS" for short. Huemer proposes that a memory belief's *overall justification* ("OJ" for short) is the product of multiplying its two scores, AS and RS, together. A belief perfectly acquired (AS = 1) and retained (RS = 1) receives an overall score of 1, because $1 \times 1 = 1$. A belief perfectly acquired but only mediocrely retained (say, RS = 0.6) receives an overall score of 0.6, because $1 \cdot 0.6 = 0.6$. Similarly, a belief mediocrely acquired (AS = 0.6) but perfectly retained (RS = 1) receives an overall score of 0.6, because $0.6 \cdot 1 = 0.6$.

It's easy to see how the dualistic theory satisfies the first constraint, namely, that a belief's passing into memory doesn't increase its justification. It satisfies this constraint because multiplying a factor by 1 can't possibly produce a product greater than the original factor. Even perfect retention justification can't turn an unjustified belief into a justified one. More generally, even perfect retention justification can't result in a higher overall justification than the belief's acquisition score. In short, on Huemer's theory, necessarily, for any memory belief, OJ ≤ AS.

It's not as easy to see how the dualistic theory satisfies the second constraint, namely, that Mike2 and Huemer are equally justified in their memory beliefs. To satisfy this constraint, Huemer appends a "posit" to his view: "coming to believe something by seeming to remember it (in the absence of defeaters that one is aware of) is an epistemically [justified] way of acquiring the belief." If this posit is correct, then we can explain why Mike2 and Huemer are (at least roughly) equally justified in their memory beliefs. Each acquired and retained their beliefs well. That is, each received high scores for acquisition and retention, so their overall justification scores are high. Take Mike2's and Huemer's common belief that China is in Asia. Mike2 formed this belief based on the seeming memory of being taught that China is in Asia, and then he retained it in memory from there; Huemer formed this belief based on being taught that China is in Asia, and then he retained it in memory from there. Each agent acquired the belief in a justified way and then retained it equally well. Thus, their respective beliefs are similarly overall justified.

§ 59

Perception and knowledge (McDowell, "Criteria, Defeasibility, and Knowledge")

Consider the experiences that inform your everyday judgments about your immediate physical environment. According to the *dream-possibility* from §1, it is genuinely possible for those very experiences to be part of a perfectly realistic dream or hallucination, rather than accurate portrayals of the world around you. The way things look, sound, smell and feel make it appear to Descartes that he's near a fire. On the basis of these appearances, Descartes judges that he's near a fire. But these appearances are equally compatible with hallucinating or dreaming or waking, so they couldn't enable Descartes to know that he is sitting near a fire. And if these appearances couldn't enable Descartes to know that he's sitting near a fire, then it seems likely that Descartes simply can't know that he's sitting near a fire. It's a small step from here to rampant skepticism.

McDowell, John, "Criteria, Defeasibility, and Knowledge," pp. 455–79 in *Proceedings of the British Academy* 68 (1982). Annual Philosophical Lecture. © 1983 by The British Academy.

In "Criteria, Defeasibility, and Knowledge," John McDowell aims to defuse the very "tempting" skeptical reasoning from the previous paragraph. McDowell combines this anti-skeptical effort with interpretative disputes over Ludwig Wittgenstein's philosophy. The interpretative disputes fall outside our concerns here. Accordingly, I will ignore all discussion of "criteria" and Wittgenstein and instead focus exclusively on McDowell's engagement with skepticism. McDowell diagnoses a "tempting" but misguided assumption underlying skepticism. He also suggests an alternative approach to knowledge and experience, which "can cause a sea of" philosophical puzzlement "to subside." In particular, McDowell thinks his alternative will help us overcome the anxiety associated with skepticism and "traditional epistemology."

Let's first note something that McDowell and the skeptic agree on. McDowell accepts that *fallible beings*, such as we humans, can have knowledge. But he balks at the following thesis, which we may call *basis fallibilism*: the basis of knowledge needn't guarantee the truth of what is known. Otherwise put, basis fallibilism is the view that it's possible to know that Q on a basis that is consistent with the falsity of Q. Suppose it's claimed that someone knows Q on a fallible basis. "She knows it's true, although she might have been wrong, given what she has to go on." McDowell scoffs, "If that is the best one can achieve, how is there room for anything recognizable as knowledge?" Instead, McDowell seems to endorse the following position, which we might call *basis infallibilism*: the basis of knowledge must *guarantee* the truth of what is known. Otherwise put, basis infallibilism is the view that, necessarily, if you know that Q on a certain basis, then you *could not* have had that basis if Q were false (compare §§19, 48, 51).

Now consider again this part of the skeptical line of reasoning we began with: "But these appearances are equally compatible with hallucinating or dreaming or waking, so they couldn't enable Descartes to know that he is sitting near a fire." Because the appearances are consistent with Descartes's *not* sitting near a fire, the skeptic reasons, they are an insufficient basis for knowledge. Here the skeptic assumes basis infallibilism. The skeptic and McDowell agree on basis infallibilism.

Despite that point of agreement, McDowell claims that the skeptic also presupposes a "temptation that is to be resisted." The temptation is the claim that the basis of our ordinary perceptual judgments is "equally compatible with hallucinating or dreaming or waking." McDowell rejects that claim. The basis of our ordinary perceptual judgments, perceptual experience, is not "neutral" in that way. Instead, according to McDowell, perceptual experience makes certain facts manifest to us and those facts couldn't be made manifest to us in a hallucination or a dream. For example, when we perceive that our friend is happy or that we are seated near a fire, our judgment is based on *the fact that our friend is happy* or *the fact that we are seated near a fire*. Of course, if the basis of our judgments are *the very facts* that we judge to be true, then we couldn't have had that basis if our judgments were false.

Here is how McDowell formulates the temptation, where the fallible capacity in question can be either ordinary perception of our immediate physical environment or our ability to detect other people's mental states.

> Let the fallible capacity in question be a capacity to tell by experience whether such-and-such is the case. In a deceptive case, what is embraced within the scope of experience is an appearance that such-and-such is the case, falling short of the fact: a *mere* appearance. So what is experienced in a non-deceptive case is a mere appearance too. The upshot is that even in the non-deceptive cases we have to picture something that falls short of the fact ascertained, at best defeasibly [i.e. fallibly] connected with it [i.e. the fact], as interposing itself between the experiencing subject and the fact itself.

The skeptic assumes that there is some "highest common factor" between the good case (ordinary perception) and the bad case (undetected deception, such as a hallucination or dreaming). Moreover, the skeptic assumes that this highest common factor – a *mere appearance* – exhausts the basis of our judgment in both the bad case and the good case. McDowell flatly rejects these assumptions and invites us to join him in accepting the "natural" alternative picture,

293

according to which worldly facts themselves form the basis of our judgment in the good ("non-deceptive") case.

McDowell acknowledges that the skeptic's assumptions can seem tempting. But he also thinks that their allure is merely superficial. The skeptical view commits to at least two very unnatural claims. First, it accepts that perceptual appearances "intervene between the experiencing subject and the world." But the natural view is that perceptual experience is a channel through which facts directly present themselves to us. Second, it accepts that even paradigmatic perceptual judgments are *inferential*. On the skeptical view, perceptual judgments are based on the "highest common factor" of the good and bad cases, which is neutral between veridical experience and hallucination or dreaming. But the content of a perceptual judgment is *not* neutral: it pertains directly to worldly affairs around us. Getting from the neutral content to the worldly judgment would require a transition in thought, an inference. But paradigmatic perceptual judgments don't seem inferential at all. Rather, they seem noninferential. We don't move from the appearance of something neutral to a judgment about worldly affairs around us. Instead, there is a "match in content" between the appearance and the judgment. In the typical case of perceptual judgment, we simply endorse in thought what is presented to us in experience. In a word, and metaphorically, judgment echoes experience. The skeptic gives up this natural view.

Of course, it might seem to the unwitting subject of a perfectly realistic hallucination or dream that he is enjoying perceptual experience of the world around him. It might be improper to blame this victim for forming false beliefs on the basis of perfectly realistic hallucinations or dreams. But it doesn't follow that the victim has the same basis for his judgments as we do while awake. Similarly, it might seem to Jack and Jill, the unwitting victims of a fraud, that they are now legally married, having been tricked by a fraudster to pay several hundred dollars for a "marriage license" and an "official" wedding ceremony. It might be improper to blame Jack and Jill for, say, marking their tax returns as "married, filing jointly" on the basis of their "license" and ceremony. But it doesn't follow that Jack and Jill have the same legal basis as couples legitimately wed by a justice of the peace.

§ 60

Skills and knowledge (Reynolds, "Knowing How to Believe with Justification")

Many theorists think that some beliefs are justified but *not* because they're inferred from other beliefs. Rather, these beliefs are justified by their relationship to sensory experience. Call these *basic empirical beliefs*.[1] Basic empirical beliefs are *justified* and *noninferential*. For example, Ann looks at Andy standing there and believes that Andy is standing there. Suppose that Ann's belief is justified. What justifies her belief? It's natural to think that *her visual experience* justifies her belief. And what must Ann's visual experience be like in order for her to have a basic empirical belief? John McDowell proposed that her experience must be a channel through which *the fact that*

---

[1] These are obviously related to what we earlier called *foundational beliefs* (see §§3, 6–10). But I want to avoid immediately embroiling the present discussion in a broader consideration of the regress problem, so I use slightly different terminology.

Reynolds, Steven L., "Knowing How to Believe with Justification," pp. 273–92 in *Philosophical Studies* 64,3 (Dec. 1991).© 1991 by *Philosophical Studies*.

Epistemology: A Guide, First Edition. John Turri.
© 2014 John Wiley & Sons, Ltd. Published 2014 by John Wiley & Sons, Ltd.

Andy is standing there is directly present to her – an openness to the world (§59). On McDowell's view, the experience's content is the fact that Andy is standing there. Jill doesn't infer that Andy is standing there from other things she believes. Basic empirical beliefs simply endorse the fact that is directly present in experience.

Wilfrid Sellars, Laurence BonJour, Donald Davidson, and others have argued that we can't have basic empirical beliefs (§§8–11). For present purposes, let's take a suitably adapted version of BonJour's argument as our touchstone. BonJour poses a dilemma for proponents of basic empirical beliefs. In what follows, "cognitive" means "like a belief, insofar as it represents some claim as being true."

Either perceptual experience is cognitive or it isn't. Suppose experience is cognitive, as McDowell would have it. Then we can sensibly ask whether the experience accurately represents the way things are. And in order for us to justifiedly endorse the experience's content, we need some reason to believe that it's accurately representing the way things are. But then even if the belief is *justified*, it's not a basic empirical belief because it's *inferential*. The inference is based on the experience's content *plus* other beliefs about the reliability or accuracy of the experience.

Now suppose experience is not cognitive. That is, suppose it doesn't represent the world as being any way at all. Then it's pointless to ask whether the experience accurately represents the way things are, because the experience doesn't represent anything at all. By the same token, the experience couldn't give us a reason to believe anything. If it doesn't represent anything as true, then it can't give us a reason to believe that something is true. But then even if the belief is *noninferential*, it's not a basic empirical belief because it's *unjustified*.

To summarize, the dilemma goes like this:

1. Either experience is cognitive or it is not cognitive. (Premise)
2. If it is cognitive, then we can't have basic empirical beliefs, because the beliefs are inferential. (Premise)
3. If it is not cognitive, then we can't have basic empirical beliefs, because the beliefs are unjustified. (Premise)
4. So, either way, we can't have basic empirical beliefs. (From 1–3)

McDowell would reject line 2 of the dilemma. In "Knowing How to Believe with Justification," Steven Reynolds proposes a view that would allow us to reject line 3 of the dilemma.

Reynolds assumes for the sake of argument that perceptual experiences are "like itches and tickles, and unlike beliefs, in not 'saying' anything or even being *about* anything." Instead, experiences consist merely of "complex ordered masses of sensations." This entails that experiences are not cognitive. BonJour, Davidson, Sellars, and others claim that although noncognitive experience could cause belief, it couldn't possibly justify belief. An analogy can help illuminate their position. Imagine a mural with streaks of color and gobs of mud stuck to it. The streaks and gobs don't conspire to formulate a sentence. They aren't isomorphic to any object or identifiable structure. The mural has no truth-evaluable content. There's nothing it's about. It's not cognitive. Now suppose someone points to the mural and asks you, "In light of *this* [i.e. the array of streaks and gobs], what is it reasonable to conclude?" It can easily seem that the correct answer is, *Nothing*. That's how BonJour, Davidson, and Sellars think of experience understood noncognitively. A noncognitive experience can't justify belief.

But Reynolds thinks otherwise. With proper training one can learn how to respond to noncognitive items. For example, a novice piano player can be trained so that she plays a proper chord in response to the feel of the keys and position of her hand. Neither the feel of the keys nor the position of her hand is cognitive. But they can serve as the basis for her skilled artistic behavior. Moreover, this can be a fully proper basis that reflects well on her, and which she is aware of *as* her basis. In order for this to be a fully proper basis of her behavior, she does not need to *first form beliefs about* the feel of the keys or the position of her hand. Nor does she typically first form such beliefs. Rather, she simply responds to the feel and position. As another example, a person learning a language can be trained so that he utters a proper sound – "Tiger!" – in response to an environmental stimulus, namely, an approaching tiger. Neither the tiger nor its approach is cognitive. But they can serve as the basis for his skilled linguistic behavior. Moreover, this can be a fully

297

proper basis that reflects well on him, and which he is aware of as his basis.

Reynolds applies the model of skilled behavior to perception. As the examples in the previous paragraph demonstrate, skilled behavior has three important features. First, it is normative because it is evaluable according to a standard. Piano playing and language use can be correct or incorrect, and performances within these domains reflect well or ill on the performers. Second, the basis for skilled activity is subjectively accessible. Performers are typically aware of the factors that guide their skilled behavior. Third, performers don't need to first form beliefs about the factors that guide their skilled behavior. Indeed, *automatic* and *unreflective* successful performance is a hallmark of true mastery. Forming beliefs about the guiding factors typically inhibits skillful performance.

These three features of skilled performance well suit it to explain basic empirical beliefs. Noncognitive sensory experiences serve as cues or signals. We are trained to respond automatically and, often enough, unreflectively to these signals by forming appropriate beliefs. This response reflects well on us and our cognitive performance, so our beliefs are *justified*. Skilled perceptual belief is also *noninferential*, at least in paradigm cases. We don't first form beliefs about the sensations and then infer that such-and-such is true. Nor do we rehearse an argument to ourselves about prior occasions where we've had similar sensations. Moreover, the sensations are directly available within our first-person perspective and internal to the mind of the perceiver, so this model of empirical justification can respect the internalists intuitions of theorists like BonJour (§28) and Feldman and Conee (§31). In light of all this, Reynolds has clearly posed a serious challenge to line 3 of the argument against basic empirical beliefs.

Index

Epistemology: A Guide, First Edition. John Turri.
© 2014 John Wiley & Sons, Ltd. Published 2014 by John Wiley & Sons, Ltd.

Index

Index